MICK & MARIE STORY

M.G. MARZEN

Copyright @2020 by M.G. MARZEN

All rights reserved. No part of this book may be reproduced in any form or by any electronic or mechanical means, including information storage and retrieval systems, without permission in writing from the publisher, except by reviewers, who may quote brief passages in a review.

This publication contains the opinions and ideas of its author. It is intended to provide helpful and informative material on the subjects addressed in the publication. The author and publisher specifically disclaim all responsibility for any liability, loss or risk, personal or otherwise, which is incurred as a consequence, directly or indirectly, of the use and application of any of the contents of this book.

WORKBOOK PRESS LLC
187 E Warm Springs Rd,
Suite B285, Las Vegas, NV 89119, USA

Website: https://workbookpress.com/
Hotline: 1-888-818-4856
Email: admin@workbookpress.com

Ordering Information:
Quantity sales. Special discounts are available on quantity purchases by corporations, associations, and others. For details, contact the publisher at the address above.

ISBN-13:   978-1-954753-13-6 (Paperback Version)
            978-1-954753-14-3 (Digital Version)

REV. DATE: 23.10.2020

CONTENTS

Chapter 1 · 008

Chapter 2 · 023

Chapter 3 · 026

Chapter 4 · 034

Chapter 5 · 039

Chapter 6 · 046

Chapter 7 · 054

Chapter 8 · 062

Chapter 9 · 067

Chapter 10 · 084

Chapter 11 · 093

Chapter 12 · 099

Chapter 13 · 109

Chapter 14 · 114

Chapter 15 · 123

Chapter 16 · 126

Chapter 17 · 133

Chapter 18 · 141

Chapter 19 · 146

Chapter 20 · 154

Chapter 21 · 159

Chapter 22 · 162

Chapter 23	167
Chapter 24	177
Chapter 25	181
Chapter 26	184
Chapter 27	193
Chapter 28	204
Chapter 29	206
Chapter 30	210
Chapter 31	213
Chapter 32	217
Chapter 33	221
Chapter 34	223
Chapter 35	226
Chapter 36	229
Chapter 37	231
Chapter 38	235
Chapter 39	237
Chapter 40	239
Chapter 41	241
Chapter 42	252
Chapter 43	261
Chapter 44	264
Chapter 45	270

ACKNOWLEDGEMENTS

Rich Limacher (a.k.a. C. C. Writers)— editor and proofreader

Moody Blues—various poetry

CHAPTER 1

Two thousand miles and a week to the day after he started, Mickey Swift found the doorbell he was searching for. The house numbers were staring him square in the face. He no longer had to double-check her business card. He had looked at those numbers at almost every stop along the way, until they were permanently embedded in his mind. The sight of her name on the mailbox, Marie Sweet, brought a smile to his face. Then he pushed the button.

As Mick's apprehension flowed, mere seconds; seemed like hours. His mind was spinning so, he thought of the rings on her fingers, her glowing smile, her wavy blonde hair and her seductive, sparkling blue eyes. His mental picture was crystal clear but all was shattered when she opened the door.

The woman in his dreams was still in her bathrobe, her hair was slightly disarrayed, and her eyes were blood shot. Mick was somewhat surprised at her midafternoon attire.

"Surprise" was all he could think of saying.

"Well, jump my bones! You made it!" As Marie eyed him up and down, it was Mick that was surprised by her greeting. *OK*, he was thinking but he couldn't say it. His lips and mind were temporarily out-of-sync.

"My, you do have a big one," she said.

"Well I told you I was coming" was his late reply. Mick noticed her eyes were focused directly behind him, and then it registered.

"Oh yeah, how do you like it?"

"It's too big. You can't park it on the street. Pull it around to the side of the house. I'll open the back door for you."

As she watched Mick through her kitchen window pull his RV into the side drive, the word perfect came to her. *That'll work out just perfect. All the comforts of home on wheels*, she thought. *Will he go for it?* she mused. *Of course he will,* she assured herself.

She greeted him at the back door. "Come in, make yourself at home. There is beer in the fridge if you want. Help yourself. Sorry I look a fright, but you should really give a girl a call before you surprise her. You'll have to excuse me for a minute, I'm in the middle of a story and my editor has a deadline to meet, so I have to finish it."

Mick finally spit out that "OK" he meant to use earlier. He went to the fridge and retrieved a beer. He didn't feel like sitting after all that time in the captain's chair, so he took his beer and strolled out the back door to take in the sights.

There he found a red brick patio accompanied by the serenity of a miniature fountain, complete with waterfall and pond. Off to the side was a potter's wheel. An antique looking thing; with foot pedals and splattering's of earth tones. Glazing compound jars were neatly stored on shelves. The scene looked more like a giant chemistry set. Also under a protective buttress was a kiln. That would explain all the cactus and plants in the fancy pottery he saw earlier on the massive redwood shelving in the front room. Even the Keystone Cops could've figured out she had a pottery hobby.

Then he noticed the expanse of the yard—no fence, lake and mountains beyond the trees—a majestic view magnified. *Perfect spot*, he thought, *just perfect.*

While he sucked up the suds and views, Marie was in her study wailing away at her computer's keyboard. She was totally consumed by her article, so much so that she never noticed Mick when he returned. He politely stood in the open doorway for a long time,

He too was mesmerized with the way her fingers fluidly typed away at the keyboard so fast and furiously without error. He didn't want to interrupt her business anyway, so he stood there admiring her work until he heard her "sigh." That was when he realized she'd hit the Send key.

Her arms went limp and she spun around in her swivel chair.

"Oh, hi," she said and stood up in one graceful motion. "Sorry to keep you waiting, but now we can get down to business."

Before Mick could ask what business, she had him in a lip-lock. He was taken aback, but instinctively returned the passion. When they came up for air, she said, "Follow me."

She knew she had got him excited, she could feel his eagerness against her body. "I want to thank you for coming all this way to see me."

She took his hand and led him to her bedroom. On the way she explained, "sometimes I get passionately stimulated after I finish a good story, so you may as well take advantage of me."

By the time they reached her bedroom, Mick's mind was flying with excitement. He didn't expect the suddenness of her passion. His thought process was a little cloudy, but not that cloudy that he didn't realize he was about to get laid. It was just that he privately wished to romance her first, but he's been without a lover for a couple months now and he was ready to pop any moment anyway. So he quickly justified his long distant conversations over the phone, as all the romancing needed, totally disregarding the way he usually did things.

Marie's motives for wanting to make love were simple. She was extremely flattered that anyone would come so far just to see her, besides she felt that getting the sex stuff out of the way first would lead to a more honest and open relationship. Not to mention she hasn't had a lover for a couple months either. Then again, subconsciously, sometimes she felt a little insecure of herself. In the last couple of years she has been experiencing some confusion with her men friends. Just when she thought she was getting into a serious relationship, her men friends, for some unexplainable reason, just got up and left. Like vanishing off the face of the earth, no, good-bye's, no, see you later, just gone, gone as in, long gone, never to be heard from again.

The information she gathered from Mick over the phone sounded encouraging and he's such a handsome man, any woman would be proud to have him decorating her arm. But she was sensible enough to realize, good looks aren't everything. She was more than willing to give every effort to make this affair blossom, she just hoped he had the patience to let her get her work done in an unobtrusive manner. That was very important to her and she already had plans to see if Mick would meet the grade.

They were both satisfied with their first, midday, sexual foray. Marie especially, his gentleness, his kisses, the way he caressed her body, and to her delight the way he held her after he was finished. It seemed to her that he didn't want to let her go. He didn't have to say it; she felt it; a very satisfying feeling indeed. It was like having a heart to heart conversation without saying a word. Telepathic serenity inspired, she felt like penning a poem. She felt his contentment; she felt her own ecstasy.

She knew she should get up and start writing as the positive vibes flowed but she didn't want to leave the man that was causing them. So she just savored the moment and stashed the vibes in memory bank #1.

Marie had learned a mental exercise in journalist class that helped her remember vitals; details like smell, sight, sounds, colors, textures and most important feelings. Her brains (Corpus Collosum) densely packed neurons wired her left and right hemispheres and were arranged like office file cabinets. Gathered info was neatly assorted, efficiently stored in folders, faster than lightning, faster than any computer; her frontal cortex was the master CEO and Secretary, relegating facts to various lobes and her emotions that were presently vibrating hectically into the jam packed Amygdala lobe.

Mick was different, actually, they were opposite as the poles of a magnet. He was logically reasonable as reason goes; strong and sturdy as a rocket proudly positioned on a NASA launch pad but volatile as the fuel inside. Not realizing he was endowed with extra sensory perceptions, psychic sensitivity; yet didn't always understand his visions; but seemed to get by, by flying through life on his freedom wings.

Unbeknownst to them, the power that overcame their differences was the magnetism, more powerful than parallel universes, was their belief in their Constitution.

Then she said, "welcome to Lake Elsinore."

"Thank you, honestly. I've never been greeted in such a fine fashion before," he replied in an exhausted monotone.

"Would you like to rest awhile?" "Umm," he moaned.

"Well, I need a shower." She unwrapped his arm from her waist. "You rest while I get myself ready, we're going out tonight."

Mick only needed a ten-minute snooze to recharge his batteries and collect his senses. The sight of Marie with her hair wrapped up in a towel reminded him he could use a shower too. "Is there any hot water left?" He asked.

"Of course there is, silly. Towels are in the cabinet, but I only have Lady Bic razors."

"I have my gear in the RV," he said as he was hitching up his jeans. "I'll just run out to the RV and get it."

After Mick took his shower, he felt like a new man, as if washed all his road grime worries down the drain. It had built up on his trip, like the mud that cakes up on a dirt bike rider. No more, what if you wasting your time doubts. Mick felt like he was in love again, and that's the freshest feeling in the world. He was further refreshed when he spotted Marie made up. She was dazzling, like the first time they met. She didn't have to wear a dress to look exceptional. It wasn't the tight fitting outfit that showed off every curve, it wasn't her wavy hair, it wasn't her earrings or necklace, it was all those rings on her fingers, there wasn't a diamond among them. And that was the one thing Mick wanted to change.

Sure he was thinking ahead, maybe too fast, he was just thinking positively. With all those positive conversations they had on the phone, he was just thinking in fast forward. He was thinking his dreams were about to come true.

"Where are we going?" he finally inquired.

"It's fish fry night at the saloon. I thought you might like to meet some of the locals."

"Sounds good to me," he replied.

Marie led Mick to her Jeep Cherokee and they were off. He was admiring the sunset over the mountains when she pulled up to the bar. It was a quaint looking place, with hitching posts and a covered porch guarding the entrance. Very convenient for horseback riders, but the water troughs and the horses were missing. Otherwise, it resembled an old western saloon from the outside. It wasn't until they were inside that Mick noticed the etching on the full mirror behind the bar that he realized the name of the bar was the Hitching Post.

"Hi Sweetie," the bartender hollered out.

"Hi Steve. Give us a couple long necks." They sat down at the bar and Marie introduced Mick. The jukebox was already jamming with the Eagles, Desperado, when she fumbled through her purse for a couple of bucks. Money in hand she spun around and dismounted the bar stool in one motion, only pausing to ask Mick if there was something special he wanted to hear.

"Not really," he replied, "I'm sure anything you pick out will be fine with me."

She returned if on cue, Jail House Rock, started playing. "Come on Mick, let's dance."

"Huh? Nobody else is dancing," Mick meekly protested.

Marie grabbed his hand and tugged. "Aw come on, let's start the party."

Mick begrudgingly got up, he didn't want to say no, it was just that he wanted his first dance to be in a more romantic setting. The dance floor wasn't very big, but the empty peanut shells underfoot let Mick's feet glide as if he was Elvis himself.

When the song was over he made a move to head back to the bar but "Love Me Tender," came on and Marie gave Mick a halting hug. Her body swayed as she started to sing softly. She had both hands around him and her cheek buried in his chest. She could hear his heart pounding and it made her smile to herself. She felt good about herself and she felt good about having a man like Mike to hold onto. And she wasn't shy about showing her affection for him either. As soon as the song was over she gave him a passionate kiss right in the middle of the dance floor. Elvis was still working his magic after all these years, Mick thought. Even though he was already slightly embarrassed,

He became rouge dusted red when somebody shouted out, "why don't you two get a room!"

That did it, Mick tried to separate himself from Marie's grasp, his ears were full of laughter and snickering. "Let's sit down," he said, trying to avoid any confrontation. He didn't know the women who shouted the implied insult, but Marie did.

"Come on I want you to meet some friends of mine."

She held his hand and walked him over to a table of giggling girls. "Hi Sweetie," one of them said between laughs. "Bonnie, this is Mick,"

"Hi," Mick politely countered.

"And this is Joan," "Hi, hi" was exchanged.

"So Marie, where have you been hiding this hunk?"

"In my private closet, I had to keep him from your man stealing mitts."

They all started laughing again, with the exception of Mick; he looked on blankly, having missed the insiders joke. Bonnie stuck her hand out to shake, "glad to meet you Mick, they call me Bingo Bonnie around these parts."

"Welcome to Lake Elsinore Mick, Joan added. She didn't stick her hand out to shake because it would have been too awkward.

"I've already been welcomed, thank you," with the memory of that afternoon fresh on his mind, he looked at Marie and smiled.

"Bingo Bonnie huh," Mick broke the silent gaze.

"Yeah, we'll be playing down at the hall tonight. Why don't you guy's join us."

"Ah—I don't know about that. We came here for the fish fry and we didn't even eat yet." Mick was hoping Marie would back him up because he really didn't feel like playing bingo with a bunch of old ladies. She turned her attention back to Marie as Mick was doing his best to make a discouraging face without actually shaking his head no.

"Oh come on Marie, it'll be fun. We were planning on eating too, we could go after we eat. There's plenty of time." Again Mick didn't want to say no. He was more in the mood for a quiet evening alone with Marie. There was so much more he wanted to learn about her. He wasn't even close to reaching that comfort level he desired, the kind of comfort that comes with knowledge and time. Mick kind of shrugged his shoulders and opened the palm of one of his hands in a, your call Marie manner. With that, Marie sat down and said, "Mick be a dear and get our beers."

"OK."

While Mick was gone Bonnie tried to get all of her inquisitive questions in. "Come on spill the beans. Where did you find him? How long have you known him? Does he know about Paul yet?"

"None of your business, and I'll tell him about Paul when I get good and ready."

A hush fell over the table when Mick returned, but was broken by the waitress. "Y'all having fish tonight?"

"I am," Mick said. The girls chimed in, "me too."

"Four fish dinners," the waitress echoed. "Anything else?"

"Back us up with another round," Mick added.

Mick was curious enough to ask, "why do they call you Bingo Bonnie?"

"Well it was like this, my mother took me to my first bingo game down at the hall when I was just sixteen. I really didn't want to go but I was grounded at the time, well anyway, my card filled up real fast and I could have gotten bingo three different way's. So I was getting pretty excited but I knew I had to pee but I didn't want to leave. So I'm waiting for my ball to be called and then it happened. I cried, "Bingo!" Then I gave my card to my mother to take care of while I ran to the rest room. I was so excited about getting bingo I didn't realize I rushed into the men's john. So when I came out of the stall and these men were looking at me funny, when one of the guy's says, "hey lady, these aren't sinks." I was never so embarrassed in my life. But I was thrilled I got a bingo. They say you never forget your first one. I know I won't."

Mick felt like laughing, but only grinned, it was a big grin just the same. He could almost imagine being there to witness the scene.

"So anyway that's why they call me Bingo Bonnie. Besides, I still love to play every chance I get. But enough about me, where are you from Mick?"

"Indiana." Mick really didn't feel like explaining more than that, so he was glad the waitress came with the dinners.

The girls were going over old times, while nibbling at their dinners. In between wolf size bites, Mick gathered they were old friends from way back in high school. All the laughing and joking was about adolescence mistakes and misfortunes. He was politely listening in with one ear and listening to the juke box with the other. But his full attention focused back to Marie when Bonnie asked her, "have you written any good stories lately?"

"Yes, but it's kind of sad when grown men shoot caged lions and tigers for trophy's and wild meat." The tone at the table instantly became somber, like a dark cloud just hovered over their table, with a flood of rain that washed away all the gayety.

"My editor wants me to follow up on the story. It could be a big break for me, besides, now I have Mick to help me."

Help her what? Mick's mind came to a screeching halt, as if he slammed on the brakes of all other thoughts. While Mick's emptied mind filled up with the smoke and smell of burnt rubber. It wasn't that Mick wouldn't be more than happy to help her. It was because they haven't discussed anything about it yet, but he knew she was a freelance writer. More likely his thought processes stopped because he wasn't mentally prepared, because she had never asked him for help before. Then he remembered how hard she was working over her computer keys and she really didn't have time to ask him for any help plus the fact that he knew nothing about her business. Then it dawned on him, 'she gets excited over a good story.' Then that famous Mick grin crept over his face, as he gladly remembered her very words and that magical feeling he experienced that very afternoon.

As the smoke slowly emptied from that over worked mental machinery, the brake petal was released and his wheels started to turn again. Adventure came to mind and he would be glad to help her get a good story, after all it excites her. His grin was in full bloom by now.

Marie's feathers were ruffled too, as she explained to Bonnie and Joan how disgustingly terrible those men are. Bonnie herself sensed the mood swing and the passion of disgust that spewed from Marie. The slaughter of defenseless endangered animals made her sick too. Almost sorry she asked the question that allowed the gloom cloud in the room, her own quick thinking interrupted the rain with, "I've got a joke for you."

Without waiting for any response she just started, "there is this guy in a bar and he's having a hard time picking up women. He's been trying for weeks and nothing. But he sees this other guy who whispers something in the women's ears and leave with a different one every night. After a couple more weeks go by, the frustrated guy finally goes up to the guy and asks him how he does it. Simple he says, you just go up to them and whisper, 'tickle your ass with a feather.' They usually say OK, but if they get upset and ask what you say? You just reply, 'typical nasty weather.'

Thanks buddy, I'll give it a try. So the next night the guy eye's a brunette by the bar all alone. So he goes up to her and whispers in her ear, 'tickle your ass with a feather.' She immediately got upset and said, 'what did you say?' 'Typical nasty weather.' Then he goes back to his seat and has a beer. Awhile later a redhead comes in the bar. So he figures he'll try it again. So he goes down by the redhead and says, 'tickle your ass with a feather.' She really gets indignant, and says, 'what you say!' 'Typical nasty weather.'

Rejected again he goes back to his seat and has a couple of shots and beers. When a blonde walks in and sits right next to him. But by now he was pretty well soused. But he thought he would give it another try. So he leans over and slurs a whisper in her ear, 'stick a feather up your ass, it's raining outside."

Everybody at the table started to laugh again. Even Mick with a hearty laugh, squeezed out a, "that's a good one Bonnie."

Marie and Joan were besides themselves, holding their stomachs and holding back tears of laughter.

"Now I have to pee," Joan said. As if a magician waved a wand over the table all three of the women rose in unison and went to the rest room.

As the girls battered chatter about while primping over themselves, Mick paid the tab and buddied up to Steve the bartender, "nice place you have here."

"Yeah, I like it," he replied. Then in a concerned tone, that sounded more like a warning, he added, "everybody loves Sweetie around these parts friend, so you best treat her right."

Taken aback somewhat by the comment, "that's exactly what I had in mind," he replied defensively.

Timing is everything sometimes, the three blonde's paraded out as Mick took his final swig. Marie had the truest blonde tresses, wavy, over the shoulder length. Bonnie's hair had a shorter, more professional cut with light brown streaks, and Joan's was more of an auburn tint. But all of them were attired in eye boggling giftwraps. They could have passed for sisters, were as, no one could guess who was the oldest. They all looked refreshed, all strutting with a strong, yet soft and sultry sway. "Come on Mick, let's go play bingo," Marie said with confidence. She took his hand and they were off.

The bingo parlor was just like Mick had imagined it. Row after row of fold out tables adorned with chairs that had VFW tattooed on the back of each one. Yes the old ladies were there and some men. These were the guy's that looked like they were beat and battered into submission. No wonder why all the heel marks outside the entrance, one doesn't have to be a CSI detective to realized they were dragged there. They were completely disinterested at the bingo balls rolling about in the cage at the caller's table in front. Quite naturally these guys were all bellied up to the bar watching muted sports on the TV.

Some things never change, as they all turned their heads to spy at Mick and the girls buying bingo cards. And who could blame them; Mick was surprised as anyone in the room. Who would have thought that he would be escorting three beautiful women anywhere, let alone a bingo parlor.

When the next game started, Mick got into the swing of things and started marking off the numbers as they were called. He started out slow, buying only two cards, while the girls bought four apiece. He didn't really care if he won or not. More or less, figuring he only needed one card to win and trying to keep track of four cards at once seemed like work. He was more interested in just having fun, while enjoying the camaraderie.

The first four games were played without a winner at their table. Mick was thirsty for a beer and offered to buy a round for the girls. "Sure thing," Bonnie said, "I'll watch your cards for you. Mick had to wait in a small line and the bartender was somewhat, busy. On his return, he passed out the beers and sat down. Noticing his cards were almost filled, excitement festered before he took a sip. The next number was called and he marked off his number and yelled, "Bingo!" Being a man with a rich baritone voice, his bingo call reverberated like an echo. Well over and above all the chitchatter of the ladies.

He immediately brought his card up to the scorer's table where they check the winning cards. As he patiently waited for the scorer to approve his winnings, a deep scowl creased the gray haired ladies forehead. "Sir, this is not a winner," she said.

"Are you sure?" A puzzled Mick countered. "Yes I'm sure."

Mick's already thirsty throat; instantly became dessert dry. Then he had to turn around and face a thousand or so scornful, dagger eyed, ready to kill ladies. He could read all their minds, "how dare you interrupt our game,—you better leave now, before we skin you alive," looking old ladies. Mick buried his embarrassed head between his knees and made his way back through the gauntlet of the most evil stares he's ever encountered. To make matters worse, by the time he made it back to his table the girls were like slap happy giggling drunks. Tears of laughter were blinding them all.

"Thanks a lot Bonnie," Mick scolded. He should have been mad but he realized he was just initiated to bingo.

"Sorry," she chuckled between laughs. When the game resumed, they all sucked up a breath to regain their composure. When the next ball was called, Mick remarked one of the boxes the scorekeeper X out. With the very next call, Mick marked off another X out.

He looked at it an extra second, wary of making another mistake, then he hollered out, "Bingo!" then in a lower tone added, "I think."

He ignored all the stares this time and flew up to the scorer's table. "Double check it good," one disgruntled lady in the audience catcalled out. After a few moments, the scorer announced, "we have a winner, congratulations."

The trip back was definitely more enjoyable this time. Even though the evil stares persisted. "Good hit, Mick," greeted him from Marie.

"I bet you won't forget your first bingo," Bonnie said. "Oh no, I don't think so, that's a fact." Mick replied.

"I knew those numbers would eventually come up," Bonnie gleefully added.

"Well I guess I should buy another round."

"Oh yeah, that's an automatic," Joan confided.

"Well, I'll be right back then."

Mick half noticed a man standing in the back by the exit door, not because he was standing there, it was because he was dressed in a fine tailored suit. That made him a stand out, definitely out of place for a bingo parlor. While Mick was shagging beers, Bonnie noticed the man too. She immediately turned to Marie and said, "Paul's here."

Paul, reading the body language of it all, knew his message reached the right ears and casually exited.

And so it went for the rest of the night, except for Mick. He passed on playing anymore because he didn't want to win again. And he didn't want to deal with the chaos it would cause. He could vision the rowdy ladies pitching beer bottles at him if he dared win again. So he just joined the other men at the bar and relaxed. It's always easy to relax, when one quits while ahead of the game.

Periodically Mick checked with the girls, who seemed more interested in reminiscing than playing bingo. But alas, it was time to go, the last game had been called.

Marie was tired too; they said their good-bye's then Bonnie said, "see you tomorrow."

It was on the way home that Marie explained to Mick that they were going hang gliding the next afternoon. "You go hang gliding?—Where?"

"Off the mountain, silly. It's just on the other side of the lake."

"Hang gliding huh,—well I've gotta see this."

Hang gliding? Rattled around in his brain a bit. That's gotta be fun, but he decided he wasn't going to do it. He'll be the photographer, he decided.

When they got home, Marie went right to the fireplace to stoke a fire. She sandwiched some old crumpled newspaper between a couple cured split logs. Mick was admiring her handy work and form, as he settled into a comfy sofa. As Mick's mind danced like the flames he was studying, he reflected on what a wonderful day it had been, especially for not knowing what to expect. Now he wondered if he would be presumptuous to assume he would be invited again to Marie's bed, after all sleeping arrangements were never discussed. Marie had a poker in hand to encourage the flames, as the orange and yellows sparkled and warmed the room. A glissando of light reflected off Marie's pottery pieces. Mick was fascinated by the glimmer. His eyes fixated on rotund pot that flashed orange stripes over and over. It was as if they were flowing in a circular clandestine motion through a field of grass. The orange and black stripes would encircle the entire pot, only to disappear and reappear at the beginning again. As the hypnotic effect took hold of it's captive, his eyes became as heavy as the glaze he was staring at.

Marie broke the spell when she melted into the couch beside him. "Did you enjoy your day?"

"Oh yeah." He spontaneously replied. Then he kissed her forehead and pulled her closer to him. She promptly kicked off her shoes and snuggled up to Mick further. On cue, he kicked off his shoes too. He intended to ask her how he could help her, but was to comfortable and didn't want to spoil the moment. "It was a perfect day," was all he could say, before his eye's reverted back to that hypnotic pot.

The spell was cast; he was now rendered helpless. His eye's closed slowly, like a drawn curtain. Unpretentiously and carefully, he was off in a deep, deep jungle. His massive muscles flexed with every stride he took down that well-worn path. This cat had stripes and huge eyes with diamond shaped irises. He paused by a tree to sniff a tree and leave his mark. He was on the hunt, not for prey, but his mate. She was in the air; he quickened his pace. He crossed a stream that led to a watering hole. Then he leaped and bounded up some weather worn volcanic boulders. Her scent was stronger now, then, he picked up another scent. A scent that was becoming, too frequent. It was the hunter.

He crouched down low and froze, he was ready to pounce if need be. He had the height advantage and could have easily sprung down on the hunter. He could have snatched the hunter right off that elephant he was riding, driving his fangs right through the hunter's neck. That would be the best way to be done with him forever. But alas he wasn't alone, there were to many of them, and their guns. He crouched down low for a long time until the parade of elephants and hunters passed.

Then with a leap he was off to find his mate. His desire to copulate was to strong. He was willing to flirt and defy the dangers until he completed his mission. On the trail of the scent again, he quickened his pace. Alas he found her in a bed of trampled grass. She had deliberately left her scent so she could be found but she growled anyway, in a display of gratitude. He mounted her several times until exhaustion over took him. She then silently slipped away from him as he slept on the reeds.

It was almost noon when Marie gently woke Mick. One glassy eye popped open, then the other. She was sitting on the edge of the bed; her hand was on his shoulder rocking it to and fro. "Are you going to sleep all day?" She asked smiling.

"Huh? No—what time is it?"

"Time to get up," was her answer. Then she stood up and said, "you know where the shower is?" Prompting her man with the idea.

He noticed she was dressed and ready to go. But what's the hurry, he privately thought.

He was still a little groggy as he looked about and saw he was in her bedroom, but he didn't remember how he got there. Not that it mattered but he did notice, Marie was wearing a glorious smile. That perked him up enough to realize he was still lying naked in her bed. Somehow the passion of the previous night filtered back in bits and pieces. Then a smile crept across his face. He rose with all his unabashed glory swaying with his every movement, and he headed for the shower.

Scrambled eggs and toast were waiting for him, his nose led the way after he dressed. Her smile was still radiant as ever and that caused him to inquire, "what are you smiling about."

"Well I didn't think you had it in you, but you proved me wrong."

"Wrong about what?"

Now she started to blush. "You know, when I put you to bed you were sleepy and cuddly as a kitten. But you roared to life and made love to me like a tiger. Do you always growl when you're getting it on?"

"No, I don't think so." Her praise made him slightly blush, which he disguised by inhaling the eggs he had shoveled between toast. He was famished after all.

Then the back door opened, and in bopped Bonnie and Joan. "Ready?" She asked.

"Not quite," Marie responded.

"Well, shake a tail feather and get a move on. The mountain isn't going to wait all day."

"What's the hurry?" Mick inquired.

Marie informed him of the thermal currents, and how the heated air in the valley rises up the mountainsides to create the lift necessary for good long flight.

Not knowing anything about the sport, Mick just said, "oh, I'll get my camera and we'll be all set."

He knew there would be no chance in hell of him jumping off a mountain strapped to a kite. Therefore it was of the utmost importance to him, to have an excuse firmly in hand. Just in case he was prodded to fly, like he suspected he would be.

CHAPTER 2

There was a shot that reverberated throughout the cage. A close-range shot from a hunting rifle, not much of a chance to miss. It was instant bloodletting as the bullet went right through the main vein of the tigers neck.

Arrangements were already made, the head was to be mounted, the carcass skinned, and the meat butchered. The operation was well financed and run with efficiency. The Great White Hunter looked the part with short white recessed hair. His neatly trimmed white beard made his steely black eyes standout supremely.

He was the kind of man that when he removed his necktie, thought he was roughing it. There he stood in his patent leather shoes, pleated pants, and his finely polished rifle folded across his chest. He stood there and watched the lifeblood pour out of his victim.

The servants there were waiting for his signal, so that they could remove the animal from its cage and prepare it for him. The servants and maintenance personal; were paid by a company called Exotic Wildlife Sanctuary. But the reality was, while it was under the guise of a rescue facility, it was more or less a full fledge, exotic pet trade operation. They were primarily engaged in commercial activities, while passing themselves off as nonprofit organization.

Ray Smaltz is the chief veterinarian who was in charge of the day-today operations. They had to move the operation not too long ago because the State Department of Fish and Game raided their headquarters in San Diego County. With the game wardens nipping at their heels, the financiers decided to move the entire operation so they could proceed with their hunts unabated.

They chose a place up in northern California, near Eagle Lake, were they had a different operation going on. With a nonexistent sheriff department and the local politicians bought and paid for.

Cal-Con Health LTD was a highly touted enterprise and has been operating in the little resort town for over ten years now without a hitch. The boon to the local tax base was a godsend. The addition of construction and service jobs literally made Cal-Con Health superintendents in all parts of the local government. Besides the large expanse of the property already owned by the company they had plenty of room to let the Exotic Wildlife Sanctuary operate unabated.

Located well off the beaten path off the interstate highway system, nestled in a cove next to the expansive Lassen National Forest, the CalCon Health labs offered the lab technicians serenity abound. There they could concentrate on their experiments without worry, plus they had any type of animal at their disposal.

The post office and town hall shared space in one building, while the sheriff split duties with another town located 20 miles to the east. So without any spy balls around the exotic pet rescue facility was free to operate with reckless abandon.

Ray Smaltz was a tall, thin, wiry fellow with a volatile temper, but was meek as a lamb when the hunters were around. Ray knew who paid the bills, but it wasn't just the hunters Ray was afraid of. It was their bodyguards. Those suits could scare the bejesus out of anyone. There were three of them this time, standing next to their black bullet proof Humvees.

Ray knew the routine; they came for the meat. Later they would check in at the lab, spend the night at the resort and be off in the morning. Next week the cycle would be repeated with a different hunter.

All Ray had to do is supply the prey, which sometimes varied between cougars, jaguars, and lions. But it was always the meat the hunters wanted. It was Ray's job to get rid of the skins and other taxidermy trophies. Which was fine with him as he made a good living on just what the hunters threw away, not counting his take home pay. Best of all, the side money was all tax free, and all he had to do was keep the operation and camp going in boot lick clean shape. Knowing fully well that everything has a hidden tax and his was frayed nerves. He had a good thing going but he was always worried about losing it.

The other thing that petrified Ray was the fact that he didn't even know the hunters names. He just knew there were four of them, the sport hunter, the hungry hunter, the holy, and the great white hunter. They were all weird too, each one with their own special quirks, but this one the great white was the coldest of them all. It's been fifteen minutes now that Ray has been made to stand at attention, while the hunter watched the blood empty out of the one time magnificent beast. He showed no emotion at all, not a blink, not a smile or joke, just a steady cold blooded, can't wait to kill again stare, but strange as it seems, Ray could tell the hunter was enjoying every minute.

Finally he gave Ray the hand sign to remove and prepare the beast for butchering.

CHAPTER 3

Up on the mountain Marie pulled her jeep over in the parking area. Bonnie and Joan followed in their van. Marie was quite proficient in the assembly of her glider. It showed that she had done it many times before. Mick tried to help her but he just got in the way of things. So he turned his attention to the other people there. There was no line to speak of because as soon as one person ran and leaped off, another would follow in a timely manner. All floating gently in the air currents; riding the winds and eventually landing in the valley below.

"Are you sure you don't want to try it Mick? Really it's quite simple. You just move your body in the harness to steer and you'll be soaring like an Eagle in no time. There really is nothing quite like it."

"I don't think so."

"You're not afraid are you?"

"Nooo, but if the good lord wanted me to fly like an Eagle, he would have given me wings. And besides"—He paused because he didn't want to get into explaining himself.

"Besides what?"

"Besides, I don't want anything to do with harnesses and you see that thing on your head."

"My helmet?"

"Yeah."

"What about it?"

"I'm allergic to helmets."

"Oh come on, nobody can be allergic to a helmet."

Bonnie and Joan had caught up to the couple and overheard the last comment.

"That's the wildest excuse I ever heard," Bonnie said.

"Well it's true," Mick said defensively. "Try to look at it this way, what are you wearing a helmet for?"

"For safety, you never know when a gust of wind if a gust of wind kicks up. It could blow you off course and make you crash. But I've been doing this ever since I've been a kid, and I never saw anybody crash," Marie answered.

"See you said it yourself, safety and crash, why worry about such things. I just resent things that have to do with helmets because in my younger days I used to ride a motorcycle, and I enjoyed myself immensely. The wind blowing through my hair,—the sights,—and sounds and all that. Then some assholes stole my freedom by making a law requiring me to wear a helmet. I tried a helmet once, I didn't like the way it felt, it cuts off your hearing and your peripheral vision. So I sold my bike and swore to myself that I would never do anything that required me to wear a helmet again."

Mick's voice naturally rose with his aggravation. He never wanted to be put in that position in the first place, so he dealt with it the best way he could. "I can go on and on if you like."

"No—I get your point," Marie said.

"Sorry I didn't mean to bark at you, but really I was kind of wild in my youth and I probably would have jumped off the mountain without a glider back then, just for the tumble of it." Mick knew he was exaggerating a bit. But he did remember tumbling down, what seemed to be some mighty big toboggan hills with his buddies when he was a boy. Then when he got home his mother hollered at him, "what happened to your new blue jeans, they're torn and grass stained, and what hit your face?"

"I don't know, we were just playing." He felt sad that his mother had to work so hard to buy him new jeans but just the same he was glad because he knew he was loved.

All these fond memories took place in nanoseconds. Just as fast as they ran down those hills at breakneck speeds until the G forces took over and made them tumble and crash, only to laugh it off and climb back up the hill to do it over and over again.

Mick was mentally calming himself down as his memories soothed him. "So as they say, wisdom comes with age. I'm content to just take pictures of you all having fun, besides somebody has to drive the vehicles back down to the valley and pick you all up."

"Yes sir," Bonnie replied. Realizing Mick was really allergic to helmets, or what they represent to him, plus she didn't want to cause any rift between her best friend and Mick.

"OK, who wants to go first?" Joan asked partially to break up the huddle.

"You can," Marie said to get the show on the road, "I'll follow you."

"OK, let's go," Bonnie chimed in.

Mick readied his camera and put it in sports mode for the action shots. So one by one they ran off the mountain as graceful as can be. He could literally see the effects of the air currents as they actually lifted the gliders higher than there starting points.

After a while, the distance grew and Mick put on his telephoto lens. All the bright colors on the gliders made him think of butterflies, while they were fluttering around, twisting and turning in circular motions, like ballerinas in a holding pattern, Mick was snapping pictures. Sure did look like they were having fun, he thought, floating around in wide-open space. Satisfied with all the snap shots he took he hustled back to the jeep and drove back down to the valley.

Mick had just pulled up when Bonnie came down to a running stop. He thought to himself, that next time he wouldn't waste so much time taking pictures at the top, so he could hurry down and take some pictures of them landing.

So it was, but after their third flight Joan bowed out of the last flight so she could drive the van back down the mountain.

It was the last trip and Marie was about to come in for a landing when Mick noticed he wasn't the only one taking pictures. There was a man in a suit standing on a picnic table at the far end of the parking lot. Besides his attire being out of place, he appeared to be taking pictures of Marie too. Not being close enough to make out his face, still he thought he had seen him before, but he couldn't put a finger on when or where.

That thought was quickly diminished as Marie came in for a perfect landing, only yards from where Mick was standing.

"Whew, what a heavenly blast that ride was," she said upon greeting Mick. "Ready to pack it in?" Mick asked.

"Yeah I'm hungry. How about you?"

"Want to hit the hitching post again?" He asked.

"Sounds good to me, but first we have to go home and unhitch the trailer." "Are Bonnie and Joan going to meet us there?" Mick asked.

"I'm sure they will. That's were all the locals go and there isn't much else to do in this town."

They got in the jeep and headed home. On the way Mick got the opportunity he was looking for, "how am I supposed to help you with your story?"

"Oh, you don't have to do anything special. I just thought we could use your camper and take a trip up north. Think of it like a vacation. You'll see how beautiful the state of California is. We have to go to a place near Eagle Lake; it's a little past Reno. Maybe we can stop there on the way back. Basically, I have to go up there to follow up on my story. See what I can dig up, you know."

She was calmly trying to explain the situation to Mick while navigating the road.

"Competition is fierce for exclusive stories," she continued. "There are never any guarantees, it's like a crap shoot. If I score, I score, if I don't—then it will be just a nice vacation, understand?"

"Yeah sure, I'm always up for adventure. Sounds like fun anyway."

"Good, I'm glad you feel that way. I can help out with some of the expenses too. Gas gotta be a bitch for that boat.

"Don't worry about it," Mick cut her short, but she added. "No, I insist, that is what partners are for."

Mick fell quiet as he tried to decipher that magic word, partners. Then she backed up into her drive way and unhitched her trailer.

"I have to freshen up a bit before we go."

That's all she had to say to make Mick realized he had time for a beer. He raided the fridge and popped open a can. Partners, he thought, permanent partners he hoped. Now Mick realized Marie was beautiful enough to be an anchor person. He could even envision her being a TV star reporter. Her voice was smooth and professional. The how's and why's, he was lucky enough to hook up with her in the first place; he had no idea. But he was sure of one thing; he wasn't about to give up on her.

Marie was thinking along the same lines. She was hoping Mick would be her permanent partner; she was pulling for him to meet her expectations. But at the moment she had a case of helmet hair that had to be combed out. Funny thing about Mick's allergy, she didn't quite believe him. She didn't think he was afraid to go gliding either. Must be something deeper. After all he really didn't have to wear one, but it's always recommended for novices. Probably the helmet is an insult to his manhood, or something like that. Perhaps he lacked confidence, no, I don't think so he exudes dare devil, man hood. She thought she knew all about it, she was confident and insecure at the same time.

She was confident that the trip would do her and him a world of good. She would make sure he enjoyed the trip. She was insecure about getting the full story. She understood her source was reliable. But how was she supposed to accomplish her mission? What she was looking for, she knew, who, she was looking for, she didn't. All she knew was the phony animal shelter moved from San Diego County to Eagle Lake. What did she hope to accomplish? She knew that, but how to accomplish it, she didn't. She exited the powder room and located Mick in the kitchen.

"Ready to go?" She asked. "Ready as I'll ever be," he replied.

On the way to the Hitching Post Marie was curious enough to ask, "Mick, if you didn't have to wear a helmet, would you go hang gliding?"

"Yeah it looked like fun."

"That's what I thought?"

"Thought what?"

"Is it a macho thing?"

"No—not at all, it's a freedom thing. Just a little quirk is all." "You don't mind if I say I don't understand it." "No, not at all, it's just that it would take me forever to explain it all. So for the time being, why not except it. It's part of me and who I am. If you want me to explain it all, I will, but I certainly don't have time for it now."

Marie had just pulled into the parking lot of the Hitching Post. Bonnie and Joan pulled in a little earlier, and spotted them. They were waiting at the entrance doors. Mick saw them and commented, "you girls have this down to a science."

Marie chuckled a little and said, "yes; I guess we do."

They all entered together, and the table that they sat at before was empty, so that's where they parked. It was a nice place to sit, right in front of the picture window.

The waitress came over to take their drink orders and left some menu's. With drinks on the way, Mick beat Marie to the punch by offering to play the juke box. "Anything special you girls want to hear?"

"B5, K 15, and C9 came flying at him, they all had their favorites. He repeated the numbers aloud, and then again mentally while hoping to himself that he wouldn't make an error. He didn't care who the artists were, or what the songs were, he just wanted to get it right.

As soon as he was gone, Joan spoke up first, in a semi-hushed whisper, "we saw Paul in the parking lot."

Bonnie followed with, "is he going to give Mick any trouble?"

"I wish you guys would quit worrying about him. I told you it's over between us a long time ago, and nothing he does is going to change that. Besides I saw him this afternoon and would have told him off myself but I didn't want to make a scene in front of Mick. So let me handle it, OK."

"Well you're going to get your chance now, he's standing at the bar."

Steve knew what he wanted and automatically brought him a glass of milk.

Mick spent a few minutes making their selections and a few of his own. So when he returned to the table, the waitress was already taking food orders. He quickly opened the menu and chose the Bottoms Up Burger. It was a half-pound burger with Swiss cheese, grilled onions, and bacon, with all the trimmings and fries. It was a hefty meal that made him feel like he was back home.

Paul's gaze at their table was upsetting Marie, and every nerve. Finally she couldn't take it anymore. "Excuse me for a moment Mick."

Mick thought she had to go to the rest room in a hurry, her demeanor wasn't quite right. An agitated, uncomfortable demeanor that made her squirm in her chair. Bonnie and Joan were deadly quiet too. Wondering what was up his eyes followed her as she went to the bar. She was exchanging words with a man in a fine tailored suit. Then he eyed the glass of milk next to him. He was a cop, popped into his head. A milk-guzzling suit, he never met a milk- guzzling suit that didn't spell trouble. Bonnie saw that Mick was sitting on the edge of his chair and offered some good advice, "don't go over there, Mick."

He took that advice to heart but his eyes weren't removed from the scene. Although he couldn't hear what was being said he could tell the debate was becoming more heated. Then it happened, she was pointing a lecturing finger at him in a scolding manner and he slapped it away. Standing up in a flash he was on his way. He wasn't the only one to react. Steve saw the action first hand and whipped out from behind the bar in an instant. We'll never know how lucky Paul because Steve was as big as a linebacker, with a calm head. He stood between the rivals before anything else happened. He pointed his finger at Mick, and said, "you go back to your table, I'll, handle this."

Mick paused long enough for Marie to add, "sit-down Mick! I'll be right there."

And so it was, Mick turned around and Marie followed him. By the time they settled back down, the suit was gone, and his mental mumblings had just begun, "she's my girl, she's my girl." When Mick stole a glance back at the bar, all he saw was an empty glass of milk.

It didn't take long for the gaiety to return to the table, because nobody made any inquiry, of what had happened. Mick figured it was a spurned ex and that it was really none of his business.

After their dinner they had a jovial good time. Bonnie was obviously an entertainer. She could tell the funniest jokes. It was in between jokes that Mick found out she was a cruise director. A regular "love boat," as she described it.

Her and Joan were on shore leave and were due to return to Long Beach by the end of the week. The way she described the pleasure cruises, made them irresistible. Promises were made to join them on one of their cruises. And everybody was in fine spirits when they parted company into the night.

By the time Mick and Marie returned home they were giddy with exhaustion. They couldn't stop laughing between themselves. They didn't make love in the sexual form but did make love mentally. They were connected now, in various forms of undress. Snuggling each other, bodies intertwined, absorbing each other's heat. Minds melded, a bonding of moral mentality.

They were leaving tomorrow, what time, was irrelevant. It was the comfort that they felt. Vacation, adventure, work, it didn't matter to them. In either case Marie knew she could come up with some kind of story. Mick didn't care either, as long as he was with Marie.

CHAPTER 4

The yacht was chartered out of San Diego Bay by the Five Star Investment Corporation: it was a hundred and twenty footer. The associates, as they were known, were already on board. They were waiting for their boarding party, one CPA, Mr. James Kirkland and his attorney, partner, Mr. James Lee. They often kidded each other, referring to themselves as the James gang, after the notorious bank robbers, for all their success in buying out companies in financial distress. Bankrupt, or otherwise, they would divide and sell off the debunked companies assets. The only real losers being the stock-holders and workers. Who would lose their investments and retirement funds respectively. Naturally the James Gang would assist the CEO's and upper level management take out their profits first. They were known for their efficient methods of taking over companies in financial distress, and or, outright hostile takeover bids. Only the rich and corrupt, can make money from going bankrupt. That was the James Gang specialty.

It was the lure of another unsolicited takeover offer that brought the James Gang to San Diego Bay. Their expertise was legendary and were asked to participate in an informal fact finding meeting on Catalina Island. The possibilities of making more money always got their attention. The day was planned for a leisurely cruise to the island to meet the principals involved, and find out the facts of the offering.

And so it was, the James Gang introduced themselves to the waiting associates. Then they boarded the yacht. The captain was already warming up the engines. The deck hand removed the dock lines and made ready to for the cast off.

Drinks were offered but the James boy's passed, they did however partake in the fresh fruit salad. It was typical California weather, beautiful sunny day, perfect for cruising. The James boys made attempts to pry useful information through nonchalant means, but failed to stir up an informative conversation.

It was just after the yacht disappeared over the horizon that one of the associates went to the head, out of view from the guests, it was there that he opened a locked briefcase, and started to assemble two silencers on the two 38 pistols he had. Why the associates thought they needed silencers out in the middle of the Pacific Ocean is debatable. Perhaps it was their favorite mode of operation, or perhaps they didn't like excessive noise. Most likely they didn't want to alert the crew, as they were to die next.

The scheme was rather elaborate by design. The James Gang could have been eliminated in an assortment of different ways, but the Hunter wanted all evidence to vanish with the bodies. "Make no mistakes," were his orders to the associates.

With one pistol tucked in his waistband and the other tucked under his arm and sports jacket, he exited the head and hand one of the guns to his partner. Now they were in perfect position behind their guests who were leisurely sampling the fruit salad in the stateroom.

In unison weapons were drawn and fired. The bullets hit them in the back of their heads. The force sent the victims crashing into the coffee table. One fell head first into the crystal fruit dish.

The assassins moved quickly now. They found the captain on the bridge oblivious to what had happened below. He was concentrating on his duties when one of the assassins crept halfway up the ladder and leveled his gun. The captain was shot in the back, falling into the steering wheel and pulling it down with him as he fell to the deck. The yacht lurched to the starboard side forcing the assassin to lose his footing on the ladder. He dropped his gun on the deck while he grappled for the rail to right himself. His partner was behind him, pushing him up trying to help him get back on the ladder.

The deck hand was on the bow of the ship and he fell to. His face wound up pressed against the glass for the stateroom. Peering in, he was shocked at the carnage he saw inside. Not knowing what had happened; froze him for a moment. Then he realized the yacht wasn't being steered as a wave broadsided the ship, sending him sliding again. Grabbing the hand rail and pulling himself up, he looked to the bridge for the captain. It was empty, not knowing what had happened, or what to do, he carefully made his way back to the rear deck. He stopped to peer into another set of windows when another wave hit.

The two bodies that were on the coffee table were now on the floor. Half of their faces appeared to be missing. Another wave rocked the boat as he was still making his way back to the rear deck. Then he saw it, a gun with a silencer slid into view. Not knowing exactly what was going on, or what he was going to do with the gun, he had a feeling he was going to need it.

Holding onto the handrail, he made his move. He was going as fast as he could now, realizing it could be a matter of life or death. He was just about ready to bend over and pick up the gun when he was hit with pain. Nothing like he had ever felt before, a burning sensation that knocked him for a loop. He could now see that the man that shot him was from across the deck was taking aim again when another wave broadsided the yacht. With no hands on the railing because his good hand was holding his bloodied shoulder, the impetus of the wave threw him over board ahead of a passing bullet.

Out in the middle of the ocean now, bobbing with the swells he saw the gunman take aim at him yet again. He feigned going under. As the yacht separated them quickly, the salt from the seawater burned at his wound profusely. He was half hopping the yacht would turn around and finish the job, rather than linger for days out in the middle of the ocean with the slimmest of hopes for survival.

At the top of each swell in the ocean he could still see the yacht that appeared to be adrift as there was no visible wake behind the ship. He thought for a moment they were going to come back and get him. But the assassins had already laughed him off as shark bait. They were preparing plastic explosives to sink the yacht as planned. All hands and guests would be lost according to the news.

They had their escape planned to use the motorized skiff to make their getaway to Catalina Island and collect on their generous contract. Once safely on the skiff and at a safe distance from the floundering yacht, they triggered the explosion via radio frequencies. As they watched the explosion there was a time delay fuse that was also activated. That wasn't part of their plan, but alas, some of the best-laid plans, sometimes go for naught. As there were two explosions, one on the yacht, and one on the skiff. Just like the Great White Hunter wanted, all the evidence to vanish with the bodies.

The next day atop the corporate headquarters of Cal-Con Health LTD, in downtown Los Angeles, the CEO and CFO's were conferring in a meeting of the utmost importance. It came to their attention that a certain independent accountant had been meddling in their accounting practices. With the Great White Hunter standing at the podium, he reminded the other Hunters that billions of dollars were at stake and that the problem with the inquisitive accountant lay in the bottom of the Pacific.

The Hunters applauded the news. The next order of business was the lab at Eagle Lake. After the applause died down, the CEO started his rhetoric, "As you all know, our new drug Comfitine is in the late stages of development. Guaranteed more addictive than heroin, it is a super mummifying, euphoric tranquilizer. It will be available in pill or powder form, so that all the junkies who like to shoot up, will never know what hit them until it is too late. Once the drug hits the streets and all the gangbangers get hooked, it will revolutionize the way law enforcement works in this country. The gangbangers will all have to lay down their guns and work for us. Thing is, if they want the drugs, they'll have to do it, and they'll love doing it to boot. Notwithstanding, we will not seek FDA approval as it has no viable health benefits, and it will never pass their tests. However we do have another dummy drug available for certification. It's a regular animal tranquilizer that will keep our charity tax status in place. While we run our wildlife sanctuary under cover."

He paused to drink some water, then continued. "Gentlemen, we will be richer than our wildest dreams. The real money will be made on the streets, after all we are in the drug business and the kids appetites for new and more exciting drugs will never be quenched. We may even experience problems with keeping up with demand. All's we have to do is keep the stock holders in the dark a little while longer until our off book profits start rolling in. Then we have our paid stock analyzer spread a rumor and down grade our stock. When the stock drops in value, we start snapping it up. Plus our own golden parachutes and generous stock option plans, will assure us riches and power beyond our expectations."

The Hunters exploded with applause and cheers.

"Now gentlemen, as you know, according to our weekly ritual, I've had the corporate chef prepare our steak dinners. This is a fresh kill straight from the jungles of India, none other than the rarest of beasts, the Bengal Tiger."

Once again the Hunters applauded their CEO.

The Great White Hunter pushed a button on his office intercom to ring his secretary.

"Yes, Mr. DeVour."

"Tell the chef we are ready now." "Yes sir."

It was but a few minutes when the office doublewide doors opened and the head chef led an army of servers. All dressed in white, pushing sterling silver carts, smartly adorned with matching silverware and silver covered platters. Crystal goblets and relish dishes further added to the decor. Red, red wine was iced down in sterling vases, naturally it was the most expensive wine available.

The tables were set with the precision of a drill team. With the head chef looking on, as quickly as they arrived, they were gone. Only the head chef lingered, waiting for approval. Mr. DeVour finally gave him his leave on inspecting the meat.

The meat was seared over the hottest of flame for only a matter of seconds a side to lock in the blood of the rarest of beasts. It was the rarest way to cook meat if one could call it cooked at all. But it was done that way for a reason, as the Hunters were interested in keeping the blood of the beast intact. For this is where they believed the energy flowed. The fact of the matter was the Hunters were so hungry for blood they would lick their plates clean of any remnants. The ends justified the means was their mantra and the Hunters didn't care about anything else, they justified.

CHAPTER 5

Mick and Marie were getting themselves ready for the trip, and he was showing off all the room his RV had. That was until she started to load it with all of her provisions. Her laptop and computer equipment was understandable, as was a suitcase of clothes. But by the time she loaded up the third suitcase, Mick started to wonder exactly how long she thought this trip was going to take.

Then there was the hair dryer and iron, "well OK," he thought, but when she brought the ironing board, he stopped her. "Now I know that thing isn't necessary." She stopped and thought a second, and decided he was right and brought it back in the house. Then there were the pots, pans and dishes. Mick had only paper plates and plastic ware, none of which were used. He always ate out on his round about trip to Marie's house. He deliberately took the long way to soak up some of the beautiful sight this country has to offer. He hadn't even turned on the oven, or the microwave yet. Being bran new, everything was still in pristine condition. She repeatedly complimented Mick on his fine taste. She never thought a RV would have all the eminencies of home. She was in love with the fabric on the couch and the way everything matched perfectly.

She was still finding nooks and crannies to fit her stuff into. Even though she had no idea if she was going to use any of it. Like her duffel bags full of mountain climbing gear, she brought that just in case she felt like climbing. Then there were the mountain bikes she had Mick attach to her bike rack on the rear of the RV. They were going to be regular tourists, and Mick didn't mind at all. Somehow he knew his RV would come in real handy one day and he planned on enjoying this trip. Plus he couldn't think of a better way to start enjoying the rest of his life, than to start out on an adventure with Marie.

Mick got out his road atlas and started examining it, "now where is this Eagle Lake?"

"It's up passed Sacramento. We have to get on I 5 we'll pick it up on the other side of L.A. But first we have to get on 15, then 210. Don't worry, I'll show you how to get there."

He backed out of the drive way and they we're off. But they weren't alone. A black unmarked squad car followed them from a distance. The man in the car already knew where they were going, so he didn't have to follow them all the way to Eagle Lake. He wasn't even going to follow them to the interstate. He was going to head for his office in downtown L.A., and make preparations.

Marie had given the road atlas a courtesy glance, then, she set it down in the convenience compartment. It was easily accessible, being right next to the motor shroud.

She wouldn't beneeding it any time soon. She estimated it would be about a 700 mile trip and would never make it in one day. So she settled back in her chair and gave Mick a silent glance of appreciation.

He was studiously gliding his bus like RV down the highway. She analyzed the profile of his face, and felt happy. She was feeling happy about a lot of things, as her eye's outlined his wavy hair. The smooth lines from his forehead down his nose, past his lips to his chin. She suddenly felt the urge to kiss him. Kiss him anywhere. She thought of herself as a queen. She could kiss him, but didn't want to do it now but didn't want to disturb him right now. She knew she was going to disturb him good tonight. A sly grin came to her lips as she thought getting one of those bumper stickers, "if you see this house a-rockin', don't come a-knockin'." Yes, she thought she was going to disturb him good tonight. She parked the thought in memory bank #3.

It was two hours into the trip before they escaped the congestion of the greater Los Angeles area and settled into the traffic on I 5, destination Sacramento. It was already decided to find a parking place, before or aft to rest up for the night.

Meanwhile the queen was being rocked to sleep on her throne. The ride was smooth and comfortable and the eye blinds wanted to close. She would have none of it though and got up to get a soda from the fridge.

"Do you want a pop Mick?" She asked. "Yeah, sure," he replied.

"I have some work to do. I'll sit at the table, if you want anything, just holler."

"OK."

She unpacked her H.P. note-book and opened a new page. Her thoughts were high-spirited, yet inauspicious. She knew firsthand how difficult it can be for a free-lance writer. She needed her pesky info source, but wanted to rid herself of him as well. That was the bewildering part of her dilemma. Or she could work right off the news wire and be forever bored, plus she would never get her exclusive story that every writer covets.

Then there's the choice of working under the thumb of an editor, who always seem to find a way to spoil a writers fun. And then there is writing for a mainstream publication, which always involves editing by advertisers, who are more concerned with sales than the truth.

Now she's in a situation with Mick; that will allow her the freedom she needs as a person and a writer. She could see it perfectly clear, cut out the outrageous hotel bills and she could afford to go to the people wherever tragedy strikes. Be it earthquake, tornado, hurricane, or whatever. She knew she wanted, to capture the personal sides of the victim's calamity. Then, she felt, she could get the respect of her peers.

She thought hard, she thought positively, she thought within herself and found tranquility.

Thinking of success, she thought if this trip as a good omen of good things to come. Freedom, came to mind, the freedom of Eagle Lake, the freedom of gliding off a mountain came too. Her mind was light and airy now, light as a downy cloud. Gliding down a mountain or a highway, words were whirling, flying and gliding. She started typing, an ode to Freedom Wing.

Valley of Eagles on the wing Freedom they tried to sing Humming Birds were not wanted there

How can such a thing be fair How can this be

We're supposed to be free The birds had to turn around

Their ruffled feathers made no sound They took the garden path

To escape the Eagles wrath Eggs had to be laid

So in the garden they stayed In the nest a bountiful brood

The hatchlings were in a shrilling mood Soon lapping at the

flowers nectar

In Gods protected sector

As soon as she finished she sent a copy of into cyber space to her home address, and printed a copy for herself so she could read it to Mick.

She sat back down in her queen's chair. They were far enough along now that the LA radio-station they were listening too started to break off transmission; a very opportune time to kill the radio power.

"I wrote a poem. Would you like to hear it?" "Yeah, sure." She read it to him with exuberance.

"Very good," he said. "I'm no expert but I think you have talent. What does it mean?

"I don't know,—it just came to me that way. I thought I was gliding high in the sky like an Eagle one minute, then the other minute, I was content to be as small as small can be. Lapping the nectar of life from the flowers, in the most peaceful garden. It was like some kind of metamorphose on paper. Going from the strongest, to the gentlest, and enjoying being both."

"Maybe you should write some more and put them in a book."

"Oh no, I can only write them when I'm in a special mood, and I need someone special to write them too."

"Well I'm glad you think I'm someone special."

"You are, you know you are."

She stood back up and stood behind him, she leaned forward and kissed his temple.

"Are you getting hungry yet?"

"I'll pull over pretty soon."

"Do you want me to cook you something?"

"No, we're on the road, we'll eat on the road. Why make dirty dishes when it's not necessary?"

"OK, I just felt like making you something."

"Don't worry we'll be stopping before you know. Why don't you pick out some CD's to play. Elvis is in there somewhere."

"Oh, OK." That was music to her ears but she didn't play Elvis this time. She found some blues tunes and they listened to them until Mick found a winery in Modesto County. He needed a break, so in they went.

They bellied up to the tasting bar, acting a little like professional testers, they started off with the white wines first. Cleared their pallets with some rice crackers and moved on to the champagnes. Each time they sampled one they liked, Mick marked it down on the order card.

It's all a matter of personal taste, because all the wines were quality vintages. Some of the flavors were lively and some were mellow. Most of the time they agreed on which wines they liked and so it went. Those little plastic shot cups add up fast however and before they knew, they had a good buzz on going.

Mick wound up buying an assorted case of fragrant bouquet's, some Chablis, pink rose', blushes, and of course some Dom Perignon Champagne.

He could feel the wines heat in his forehead now and Marie was becoming giddy. So they decided to eat there too. All wine and no food equals no fun. Besides the restaurant had all kinds of pleasant aromas of its own. Smartly decorated with antique oak wine barrels and grape vines abound, with hanging flower baskets set to an Italian Motif.

Spicy stuffed Zucchini was ordered for an appetizer, Angel Hair

Primavera with Eggplant and Almonds for dinner. Then a hand tossed pizza to go, just in case the midnight munchies strike. Marie seemed too happy now to cook anyway. It's funny how gay a person can get at a wine sampling bar.

What wasn't so funny is the three hundred dollars Mick spent for wine and dinner. He was usually hawkish with his pennies but he cast off his ways even before he entered the winery. Nothing is free he knew, even free samples. There is always a cloud of guilt that makes a person spend more because of the hospitality.

Mick recognized these feelings before, when he used to go up to wine country back home. Going to a winery was always special to him, and he always left with that happy feeling. After all what fun would it be if after all the free samples, one didn't have the courtesy to take a few of the products home. He was sure some people would take free samples and go home without purchasing anything, but they have to be the rare birds.

Mick had carried the wine to the RV and Marie carried the pizza. He stored the wine under the sink, one of the few remaining storage spaces not taken. Marie put the pizza on the counter. Before he could ask where they were going to camp the night she was upon him. In a full passionate embrace.

While she was kissing him, she was guiding him to the rear bedroom. Once there she closed the door behind them. The curtains were already closed but it really didn't matter to them at the moment.

Mick had fallen back on the bed and kicked off his shoes. If she didn't care they were parked in the winery parking lot, he didn't either. Because the RV was so big, at least he parked it in the rear of the spacious lot. It was all over for him and he knew it. As they passionately wrestled as one, articles of clothing were discarded about, faster than a politician could shred incriminating documents.

While they were doing their thing don't you know, another couple exited the winery and the lady said to her husband, "is that mobile home rocking?"

The husband said, "yes;—I do believe it is." He looked back at his wife, smiled, and said, "let's go home and pick up where they started."

She smiled back at him, and said, "yeah, let's go."

It was a good four hours later, Mick and Marie were still in a naked state of enter twined bliss, when he heard a pounding at his door. Startled but aware mentally, he told Marie to stay put. He knew it was either a cop or an attendant. He jumped in his jeans and flung on a shirt. To the front he went to investigate the rude interruption.

It was a cop all right. The light source he followed was from a flashlight. He opened the side door. The busy bee flashlight was making its inspecting rounds with the cop's eyes right behind it.

"What are you doing here?" He barked out.

"Nothing, I was just a little road wary and stopped her for a bite to eat."

"Who's with you?" He commanded.

"Just the wife," Mick answered.

He took a step up on the step to peer in farther but Mick put his hand out to stop him, "she's indisposed at the moment, if you don't mind."

Now he pointed his flashlight directly in Mick's face, "have you been drinking?"

"No," was his reply.

"Let me see your driver's license," the cop demanded.

"What for?" Mick snapped as he was getting a little peeved at the prick.

"I'm a customer here. Can't you see that pizza on the table?"

By now Marie was dressed and came out of the bedroom. "What's the matter Mick?"

"Nothing yet."

A shakedown cops worst nightmare just appeared, a witness. The cop stepped back down on the pavement.

"I just wanted to find out if everything was alright. And just because you bought a pizza, doesn't give you the right to park here all night. You best be gone by the time I make my rounds again." The cop couldn't resist barking out his, I'm the boss bravado.

Mick just looked at him as he walked away to get in his squad and leave. "What was that all about?" Marie asked.

"He's probably looking for a tip is all. Come on honey, let's blow this pop stand."

Mick got behind the wheel and switched the engine on. Marie put the pizza in the refrigerator, and took her seat.

"Get back on I 5, we still have a way to go."

She turned the CD player back on and listened to some soft melodies by Seals and Croft. Then she got up and kissed Mick's temple again.

"I just want to thank you for a for this evening, it was delightful." She messaged his shoulders briefly and took her seat again. Somehow they both knew to hum to Hummingbird as it played. Marie thought it odd that she just wrote a poem about hummingbirds as the song played. She knew she hadn't heard the song in a long time, but still thought it was beautiful. But why was it making a resurgence in her life now? She didn't dwell on it too much, it must have been a deep pleasurable memory that brought out that poem she wrote. Just like the pleasant thoughts she was having now, she parked the day in memory bank #4.

CHAPTER 6

Up north at Eagle Lake a new day was beginning. Directly behind the massive lab facilities was a dorm and a private high school. The facility had room for a hundred kids but it was only half full. These weren't regular teenagers either. They were mostly runaways or previously homeless people who answered ads for work.

Jobs were promised to those who qualified. Roam and board was provided as part of a work while you learn program. The fact was, management preferred lost souls with no family ties. It was also desirable that they be current or former drug abusers. In a strange way Cal-Con Health had some unusual requirements for enrollment.

They had to go to school five days a week to study but the reality was they were the ones being studied. Half of them worked in the animal shelter, others did janitorial duties in the offices, and almost all did some form of landscaping.

The animal shelter was located a mile behind the school. The workers had to take a shuttle bus down a well-guarded private road to get there. The wild life preserve was surrounded by a fifteen-foot fence topped with razor sharp barb-wire. It was prison quality, used more to keep people out than the animals in. There were lots of no trespassing signs posted throughout the property, and management went all out to make sure they weren't just legal decorations.

With all of societies losers performing the menial tasks at Cal-Con Labs, it was a minor miracle that any work was accomplished, but it was. The lab was spit and polished clean daily. The fine trimmed lawns were done to meet the standard for all corporations.

The workers had to sign contracts after their initial interviews. It was during the interviews that the victims were duped and doped. They were made to feel wanted and important. A powerful mental play that takes full advantage of societies rejects. Still they were further exploited with high balls of Conicillin.

It was the new drug being manufactured at the lab, and being slipped into the applicant's sodas.

The euphoria the drug created was fast and long lasting. Virtually everyone signed on for two-year stints. There were promises of pay after they completed their contractual obligations, meanwhile they wouldn't need any money as everything would be provided for them, extras could be signed for at the commissary. It was that easy, they were members of a commune now. The perfect society, management will take care of all their needs, and they could resign for contract extensions if they want. There was only one catch; they had to take their pink vitamin pill in the morning with breakfast. It was, for their own good, they were told. And they were believed, most inductees were haplessly lethargic people until they got to that first interview. Now they all had a perky high, can't get ready fast enough to get to work, attitude. But nobody knew how long the euphoria would last, not the doctors or scientists, certainly not the workers, they didn't even know they were part of an experiment.

It was in the evening time while watching TV that some of the ex-junkies had some kind of convulsions of various degrees. All inexplicably wanted to go to breakfast but instead were subdued by the orderlies and removed from the community room, only to return in a matter of minutes, all smiles, as if nothing had ever happened. Euphoria has different effects on everyone, but the main effect was rapture. Other than that, some never could get spiritual ecstasy. These few could only get physical satisfaction but it all looked the same to the attending physicians. Damn good drug that everyone looking forward to breakfast without knowing why. Some had their suspicions of what was really going, but they just didn't give a frick. It was still every man for themselves, under the guise of utopia.

Except, for one janitor, who worked in the main office and the lab. Criminal minds never sleep, no matter what. It may be drugged into submission, it may lay dormant, and appear pacified, but sooner or later it'll rise from the dead.

As it was one Robert Dragert, a thin, frail, pathetic looking ex-junkie, had noticed while cleaning the labs manufacturing equipment, that a pink powdery residue had resembled the same color of their vitamin pills. He started out carefully gathering all the fine powder and snorting it. Voila, instant euphoria, he knew exactly what it was as his energy boost kicked in. He gathered all the powder he could and began a stash. It was a stash that was hard to keep, because into the night he would snort it all. That's when he realized; he had to get more. He consciously started to inspect all the security systems throughout as he happily did his chores. He was looking for the big score, but he didn't know where they stored all those pills they make. All he knew was that he needed more.

He looked around and saw that he was in the office, with all the people busily typing at their computers. Then he started laughing to himself. It was a chuckling snicker at first, then, it grew. Then he thought he smelled pot burning. He craned his neck to see over the cubicle dividers, to see if any smoke was rising from any of them. He saw nothing out of the ordinary, and heard only the mundane sounds of keyboard clicks and telephone chatter. Still he wondered how many of them run home and fire up a doobie. Do they smoke in their closets or party at their peril? How can they stand to sit at their desks all day typing into a monitor? They all looked like cloned robots, he thought, as he pushed his carpet sweeper down the aisle.

He started to laugh louder, as he listened to the stupid whirling rollers go back and forth, over and over the same clean carpet. He thought sooner or later he was going to wear the carpet down to its padding. He could see the ruts he making now, deeper and deeper, like a well-worn dirt path were the weeds won't even grow. Then one lady on the phone gave him a dirty look, so he covered his mouth trying to stifle himself. He didn't know why he was laughing or what had struck him so funny, and he didn't care. But he was laughing himself out of breath so he put up his carpet sweeper in the broom closet and stepped outside.

There he sat down on the ledge of a massive rose garden. Stop and smell the roses he thought. He started laughing harder than ever, as he had to hold his gut while doubling over. Gasping for breath while still laughing got him some attention from one of the other laborers.

"What's so funny?" The gardener asked.

Robert couldn't answer him at the moment, but he got up and acknowledged Tommy's presents by draping an arm over his shoulder. He leaned on him a bit as he was still sucking air desperately trying to regain his composure.

Once accomplished, Robert confided to Tom, "I'm trying to figure out how to rob the joint." Then he started to laugh again, like he was just joking, as if he was just saying 'don't take me seriously.' He sucked up his breath again. Tom just looked at him strangely, as if Robert was crazy. But somehow he believed him and started to think how and why. This is exactly how the seeds of evil are sown. What seems like harmless fun to some, are the fore bearers of coldblooded reality to others.

Tommy was twice the man Robert was, as he was never a junkie. Robert was as white as a china dish, as some of his main arteries had collapsed from his heroin abuse. His needle tracks ran over his arms all the way down between his fingers. Then when he started shooting up his legs the tracks ran all the way down to his toes.

Robert was into PCP and Quaaludes on the street. When he was in jail, he was prescribed tranquilizers to control his violent temper. His muscles got a work out in the garden and he was in tiptop shape.

Even though Robert and Tommy have seen each other many times before in the recreation and mess hall, they have never spoken to each other before. As they had to follow house rules to the strictest measure, it was also the strangest atmosphere in school were there was no fooling around in class. That carried over to no fooling around at work either. It was more like, they were a working class of zombies. Sub servant to the medical examiners. They always seemed to be wearing happy faces; pretentious happy faces at best. Somehow a few of the workers seemed to notice the sham of Shangri-La, but nobody ever complained, because they were very complacent.

School and work were their obligations under their contracts. How powerful that word that word seemed, contract, contract, it was a mental thing because none of them were old enough to sign a binding contract. That was part of the con, your contract says this, your contract says that, in reality none of them ever got a copy of their contract and nobody knew what was on those contracts but the Cal-Con Health officials.

They sure made them feel important however, with a little line like, 'you're a member of our family now, you're under contact. You'll all be professionals when you finish your training and courses.'

At times Tom would space out to, not as bad as Robert's hysterical spasm, a different kind of macrocosm. He caught himself staring at the nearby mountaintops looking for a guru. He wondered if the man in the mountain knew all the answers. So he would at times stand in his rose garden and look to the mountains for his spiritual adviser. He didn't even believe in god, actually he was looking for a way to kill his boredom advisor.

He would put his hands on top of the garden hoe, then, rest his chin on top of them. Resting and staring at the mountain tops looking for his guru. He could imagine himself conversing with the old man. 'What is the meaning of life?' He would ask him.

"Sacrifice."

"How did I get here?"

"Sacrifice."

"How do I get out of this place?"

"Sacrifice."

That was the only answer he ever gave him, and that was what he was doing, sacrificing. But that isn't what he wanted to hear because sacrifice is no fun at all. He was a changed young man now and he knew it, he didn't understand it either. Just do your time he told himself. It'll be all over before you know it. Then he could get back to being his old wild and willing self.

The way Robert said, "rob the joint," scared his mind, like a surgically implanted idea. Once inserted there was no getting rid of it. 'Rob' what? How would they get away with it? Was Robert out of his mind? There are guards all over the place. Where would they get the guns to even the score? From the guard supply room in the animal sanctuary? He made a point to find out from Robert what was so valuable to justify all the risks.

That night in the recreation room Tom cornered Robert. First he put his arm around his shoulder, then, quietly asked in his best buddy voice, "when are we going to rob the place?"

"I don't know. I don't have it planned out yet."

"I'll help you plan it. What are we going for?"

"The drugs."

"What drugs?"

"The drugs they manufacture."

"What do they make?"

"Pills—they got two pill making machines in back of the lab."

"Where are the pills?"

"I don't exactly know. They must be around here somewhere."

"I know where."

"Where?"

"In the warehouse in the animal shelter."

"How we going to get in there? They have guards everywhere."

An orderly noticed the two huddled in the corner and went over to investigate. "What are you two doing? The TV is over there."

"We ain't doing nothing," Robert nervously replied.

"Well break it up then. You know there is no talking while the TV is on. It's against the rules."

"Sorry," Tom said, and the two walked over by the group watching the tube and sat down.

Robert settled down to watch the show. It was a rerun, but he watched the stupid show anyway. All the shows were stupid to him. There wasn't anything else to do, except read his stupid school books in his stupid room. Then go to sleep and do all the stupid stuff all over again. Good thing he has his stash of smack to get him through his stupid life.

Tommy on the other hand was busy thinking of how to bust in the warehouse. He never paid that much attention to what those delivery trucks did, but to his recollection, they always stopped at the lab first, to load and unload whatever, then go to the animal shelter to deliver or pick up whatever. He knew one thing for sure; tomorrow he was going to pay special attention to everything.

CHAPTER 7

Mick never found that happy camping ground he was looking for. So he parked in the most convenient spot along with rows upon rows of semi's.

It was a truck stop with all their humble amenities. But breakfast was within walking distance. They were in one of the main hubs just outside of Sacramento. It was early and a misty dew was in the air. As stealthy as she slipped away, carefully trying not to disturb his slumber. Marie was up and refreshed, but the cool morning air crept into the spot she had vacated. Her fluttering fingers were manufacturing a wordy breeze of their own as she silently tapped on her notebook keys. It was the brief loneliness that stirred Mick. Somehow a body knows when that comforting heat is no longer within arm's reach.

It's an unexplainable personal phenomenon, were as he has experience sleeping alone and normally this wouldn't bother him at all. But when two bodies share the somnolence of the evening and then a void is created, that leaves room for the spirit of abandonment to move in. Mick just had a blast of cold quivering shivers, as if a ghost had transgressed his body and stole his soul.

He was fully awake now, in more ways than one. He could smell the coffee now, but he was going to wait for his passion pal to go back to sleep before he rose. He did somebody stretches before hitting the shower. Then it was the coffee pots turn.

"Good morning," he said, after spotting her busy ness.

"Good morning," was returned, as she paused to ponder the next line.

Mick took a sip of his coffee while looking over Marie's shoulder. "What ya writing?"

"Another poem. I took your advice,—for some reason I felt inspired."

"Good for you. What's it about?"

"Kismet."

"Kiss what?"

"Call it fate."

"Oh." He took another sip of his coffee. It was still a little hot for gulping. "Do you want go for breakfast when you're finished?"

"No, I already had some pizza. I love cold pizza in the morning. There's lots left. I put the rest in the fridge, if you want some.

It didn't take Mick but a minute to decipher that was a good idea. So he erased the smell of bacon and eggs from his mental slate and dug out the pizza. Marie had the table cordoned off with her notebook and stuff, so he set the pie on the counter by the sink and ate over that, a very convenient place for the crumbs to fall. He made quick dispatch of three pieces before he stuffed the rest back in the fridge.

With his coffee cup emptied he felt somewhat remiss with all those beer cans staring at him. So he removed one of the eye openers and popped its lid. Now that was more like it, he thought to himself. Pizza just needs a beer wash, it's a fact of life.

The pop of the top got Marie's attention. "You're having beer for breakfast?"

"Yeah, I woke up this morning and I got myself a beeeer," he mimicked a famous song by the Doors. "It'll relax me just right, we have a long way to go yet. Might as well gas up here. Are you ready to roll?"

"Whenever you are," she turned her attention back to her notebook.

Mick had gassed up and took out his road atlas to look it over. I 80 to Reno looks like the fastest way, or do you want to take the scenic route to Lake Tahoe?"

"No, go to Reno, but I don't want to stop for gambling either. We can do that on the way back. I want to get the story first."

"OK," Mick put the trans in drive and they were off. Marie put her notebook away and joined him in front.

"What's your plan when we get there?" Mick asked.

"I have a system for newsing about. You'll just have to be patient with me, because I work better alone."

Mick gave her a quizzing look that she picked up on and continued. "I mean—as far as asking inquiring questions. I get far more honest answers and such because people tend to relax and be more spontaneous, if it's just me. Like, nobody's going to be intimidated by little ol' me. You know what I mean?"

Now Mick showed no emotion at all as he drove. Marie feeling she might have slighted him somewhat, continued with her explanations.

"I know, you can be my camera man. I noticed you like to take pictures." Mick just listened and thought, 'her cameraman? Sure, why not?'

Before he could ask for details of his assignment, she went on.

"But I'd have to get the interviewee's OK first, or you could get the backdrop shots.—Er, just play it by ear for a while, until you get used to the way I do things. Like look, listen, and learn. The more we work together the easier it'll get. You'll know what I expect, and before you know it you'll be ending my sentences for me.— If you haven't noticed already, I'm a very intuitive person, and I'm not afraid to fly by the seat of my pants, so to speak. For instance, I gathered from the way you looked at the cop back at the Winery, that you have no respect for the police. Am I right?"

"Your half right," Mick answered. "Why only half right?"

"That's the difference from being a pessimist or an optimist. Is the glass half full or half empty? I know I used to be more optimistic, but life's experiences have made me harder than I want to be."

Mick was keeping his eye on the road and his voice in a matter of fact tone as he continued.

"Let me retreat to the day's when I was a kid and thought John Wayne and the Lone Ranger put all the bad cowboys out of business. Then there was Eliot Ness who put all the gangsters out of business. That was when I was an optimist, and now, almost every day, I get to read about some cop murdering or robbing somebody. They sell dope and take bribes; they commit all kinds of heinous crimes. Sooner or later it'll dawn on you that cops always have been criminals and always will be, just like the general population. Now I ask you, how can you tell which ones are crooked and who's not? They all hide behind their code blue badges. Personally, I try to avoid them like the plague. It doesn't matter if their honest or not, they're still going to relieve you of your money or rights. This is how their trained, to lie, cheat, and kill. Plus they run around in their bullet proof vest and act like gods."

THE MICK AND MARIE STORY

"That's not a very healthy way to look at thing's. You might need them someday."

"I know, but I'm used to it. I resigned myself to just deal with it like a bad poker hand. Not much I can do, but I have a couple more stories for you. You can psycho analyze me if you want." He said with a half laugh.

"I must have been about fifteen at the time, I was hitch hiking, I used to do a lot of it to save on bus fare before I got my driver's license. Well anyway I had my thumb out one day and the cops pulled up. They told me to get in the squad car. At first I thought they were going to take me to jail but they just asked me where I was going. So I told them the movies. They actually took me all the way to the theater; which wasn't exactly around the corner, my guess is that it was a five-mile hike. That'll never happen now-a-days but who knows, now when I look back at my fearless days, it doesn't take a genius to figure out they may have saved my life that day from some John Gacy type. Anyway, if the cops did something like that he could lose his job in a heartbeat beat, especially if they got in an accident, the kid gets hurt, and the parents sued the city. You bet the insurance company is going to make sure heads roll. That's why you'll never here a story like this again."

Even though Mick was talking into the windshield as he drove, he knew Marie was listening, as he would glance over once in a while to make sure he wasn't talking to himself. But she was smiling and all ears, so he continued.

"So that's when I was optimistic. So then about two years later I was driving in Wisconsin. I was going to Williams Bay on Lake Geneva. On the way I had picked up this guy who was hitch hiking, he had long hippie type hair. That was probably why this cop pulls me over. I wasn't doing anything wrong and the cop wasn't interested in giving me a ticket, but he grilled me on where I was going and I tell him. Then he tells me I can't go there and makes me turn around and go back where I come from or he was going to throw me in jail. So naturally I turn around and the cop follows me all the way to the state line, which was a good ten miles away. So I go a few miles more and let the hippie out and I turn around again. Now the hippie had explained to me that there was war-protesting going on in the city of Lake Geneva, but I wasn't going there. Mind you, I was determined to see my girlfriend on the other side of the lake, I was in love don't you know. So I figured I would just take the side roads to get to where I wanted to be. So I make it to Williams Bay but I can't find my girlfriend, Donna was her name, she was a real beauty. So don't you know I was driving around looking for her and the same State Pooper pulls me over again, and boy was he pissed. His red neck reminded me of a thermometer stuck in a pot of boiling water, with the mercury rising, until his whole face flushed as red as a stop light. I was surprised he didn't burst a blood vessel or something while he was bouncing my head off the hood of my car. He nearly choked me to death before he kicked me out of the state again. That's twice in one day and I'm only seventeen, how many guy's you know that can say that. Now, I ask you—

even though he didn't rob me of any money, what did he cheat me out of?"

"Your rights," was her reply.

"Bingo," was his.

"Now, what has more value, money or my Constitutional rights?"

"Your rights," she said again.

"Now I understand he was probably given orders to turn the hippies back at the border and he was just doing his job. And if I hadn't picked up that guy in the first place, I probably wouldn't have gone through all that. But as it was I never did see that girl again because she was up there for the summer and I wasn't about to go back up there. So I got on with my life and I should be laughing at that life experience but that's the kind of mental trauma that a person never forgets. The seeds of pessimism have been sown and that cop didn't accomplish a thing, except, force me to take notice whenever Constitutional rights are violated."

"So now, let's fast forward to a couple years ago. This is a story about my camera, the very same camera I was using the other day." He paused to take a deep breath. He knew it was the first time he was telling this one as it was the first time he told the last one. There must be something to opening up as he unconsciously felt better already. There is a certain burden and relief cycle of getting something off ones chest that has hidden healing powers, and she was glad he was opening up to her.

"I was going on a vacation and I've never been to the Mardi-Gras before, so I buy this camera and go. It's kind of a pricey thing, so naturally I thought of the possibility of getting mugged, robbed, or some kind of trouble. But no, I was taking pictures of everything in sight, just like a tourist should. I even took a picture of a sign on a house that warned about all the criminals, and to be careful. Well anyway, I spent three days at Mardi-Gras and didn't get into a bit of trouble."

"So when it was over, I left. I was going to spend the rest of my vacation on the beaches in southern Florida. I had plenty of vacation time left. So I took the coastal highway to Biloxi. They have all kinds of gambling boats down there. So I stopped to gamble a bit. I won a little and quit—my typical style. The rest of the time I was taking pictures of the banana and gambling boats, day and night shots. The motel I was staying at was in the next town over— Gulfport, it's called.

"Well anyway, they had this new pier out there and it was lit up like tunnel vision. The gulf was dark and the illumination of the lights kind of drew me in. I figured it would make some good pictures, so I walk out there and take all kinds of pictures. Zooming in and out with the lens until I get to the end. There were a couple kids out there fishing, so I took some pictures of them too. I took a couple pictures on the way back and was ready to call it a night—when all of a sudden I hear screeching tires and a big bang. No mistaking that sound, it was an auto wreck, big time.

"I had to cross the highway to get to my motel anyway. So I hurry on over there and I see a squad car slammed into a taxi. A crowd is starting to gather and emergency vehicles are flying down the highway to the scene. So I start taking pictures of the wreck. I thought maybe the newspapers might want to buy them for their morning edition. So I get pictures from all angles on every corner.

"So while I was getting my last picture these two cops come up to me and demand my film. I says, 'what for!' No wait, when they first came up they start quizzing me, like where am I from, what was I doing, and where do I work, things like that. So when they find out I'm from out of town, then they demand the film. So when I say no, they threaten to throw me in jail. They said, 'you look drunk to us, and it's illegal to take pictures of dead people,' and what else—oh yeah,—they 'needed the evidence.' Now I know they're full of shit, and I kept telling them, no.

"So then they came to grab me, and they really looked like they were going to arrest me, so I demand a receipt for the film, almost as in self-defense. So I give up the film and all they gave me was a business card with the Gulfport Police logo on it. Better than nothing and still better than going to jail for nothing. Then this guy that was standing next to me says, 'if you ain't from these parts, you gotta understand the gamblin' boats down here own the newspapers with all their ad money, and the newspapers own the police chiefs by looking the other way when they do their dirty deeds to keep their city clean,' and I concurred.

"First thing the next morning I go down to the police station to get my film back or file a complaint. So the detective I talked to promised, he'd have my film back tomorrow after he looked into it. At least I got a promise my film would be returned. I said, OK, thinking another day in Biloxi is no big deal. Then I went gambling; not much else to do down there. So I play a couple of hours, get up a couple hundred and quit. It paid for my room, plus a night out with lots of change left over.

"For some reason I get a funny feeling that I'm not going to get my film back and I decide not to check out until the film is in hand. So then I go back to the police station to see the detective, and he says, 'he didn't see the guy yet, it was his day off, and he doesn't have my film. Come back tomorrow.' Shit, I thought, they're going to come up with some kind of excuse; like, they lost it. So I go gambling again on a different boat and won. They have some nice boats down there.

"So I go back to the police station the next day and the detective gives me a different line. So anyway I go gambling again, this went on for four days but my persistence finally paid off and I got my film back. But by now my distrust of the cops took me to a 1-hour photo developer to double check. To my surprise, I actually had the pictures of the pier and the wrecked cars. So I finally blow town, and mind you, I made enough money to pay for my entire vacation, otherwise I would have really been pissed off—but I still feel cheated. Now why is that?"

"Because you were," Marie replied. "They like to protect their own. You should have told them that you worked for a newspaper and that would have never happened."

"Yeah, next time I will, because I will be. I always wanted to anyway. How much does it pay?" he asked kindly with a half laugh.

"Well, you see now why I'm a full-blown pessimist."

"Yes I do." Mick paused and continued, "Well anyway, if you have the cops violating people's rights, conservatively estimating a thousand times a day, multiply that by 30 years and you're going to have a country full of pessimistic people. Our own government and the FBI don't even trust the cops, so why should I. So now they're making the cops get videotape confessions now for all the capitol felony cases, just to prevent the cops from telling lies in court. And the only time I ever heard a politician tell the truth, was when one said, 'that the police aren't here to create disorder; the police are here to preserve disorder.' Then once his press secretary informed him he was telling the truth, he recanted his statement."

Marie started laughing and said; "Now I know you're kidding."

"No, it's true, I swear." Mick knew it was a famous political gaffe, but he couldn't resist loosening up the atmosphere with a little political spin of his own.

"Seriously though, I read this other story about this lady that called 911, she reported her astray husband was outside with a gun and threatening to kill her. She told them that she had a restraining order on him and was trying to do the right things by going through the courts. The thing was that she called them four times asking for help and the police station was only two blocks away. The dispatcher had sent over two squads but don't you know it took them twenty minutes to get there and don't you know, it was too late; she was already murdered.

"The only thing that would have saved her that day was immediate response by the police or if she had her own gun. But for some reason the city has an ordinance against owning a gun in direct violation of the Second Amendment. I don't know how they get away with that, but they do.

"So anyway the cops' excuse was that they had to do their equipment safety checks because they were just getting on duty. They actually had the balls to use safety as an excuse. There's one reason I hope I never have to call the cops for anything. Somehow it shouldn't be a surprise that politicians are using safety as an excuse to dismantle our constitution. They are well versed in this tactic.

"The mayor of this big city used safety as an excuse to pull a sneak attack on an airport. In the middle of the night he destroyed it so he could build a park. The overriding thing is that this mayor is very popular, and he would have won reelection even if he put his plan in front of the people. It puzzles me why they feel the need to practice in the arts of deception. I guess it's the nature of the beast that force politicians to become liars.

"Every election year some politician is claiming they have to raise taxes to teach the children. If they really wanted to educate the children they should teach them how to lie, cheat and steal, that way all the children will grow up qualified to be a politician. That's why I came up with a saying: 'All kids should be taught the 3 R's and how to lie, cheat, and steal, so everyone will grow up qualified to be a politician.' Pretty sick way of looking at things, don't you agree?"

"Yes I do, unfortunately it may be too close to the truth. There must be a better way. But overall I give them good marks because it could always be a lot worse."

"I agree."

"You should try to look at the bright side a little more, after all the cops do put their lives on the line every day. And I admire their courage especially after that foiled bank robbery, with those two guys in body armor began shooting them up. There is no fail proof system and it's virtually impossible to make everyone happy."

"I agree. I just wanted to relate."

Now Marie was pleased that he shared his stories with her. She stored her thoughts in memory bank #5. Communication was important to her. It brought her piece of mind, it equated to the give and take any relationship should be built with. Brick by brick, story by story, so she started to share some of her own experiences with Mick. Then she confessed some of her fears; in particular her concerns of the media giants getting new legislation passed that would virtually give them total control of the information age. It would be an exorbitant power over the news, and how it is reported, effectively putting freelance writers like herself: out of business. Then there was the most distressing fact that congressmen are plotting to systematically destroy the first amendment to the Constitution, starting with the right to burn the flag as a sign of eliminating freedom of speech.

Mick concurred with her sentiments, not that they were planning on burning the flag any time soon but would if congress passes any law that changes the Constitution. It's bad enough that they regularly pass laws that violate the Constitution for monetary or fame gains but changing the Constitution for power gains and rendering the Constitution meaningless is the most frightening aspect of it all. Especially because, that's exactly what Hitler did.

But she knew she couldn't share one story in particular, it was too early in their relationship to share that one. She more than noticed how quick Mick came to her defense in the Hitching Post and she didn't want to fuel the fire that might lead into the men acting like mountain goats butting heads. She was sure nothing positive would come from sharing that information, not yet anyway.

Other than that thought, she felt inspired, and said, "Mick, I'm going to do a little work now. Do you want a pop or anything while I'm up?"

"No—no thanks, unless you want to stop off in Reno to get married."

"No, we can't do that, let's see if we can survive this trip first, and besides, I have my heart set on getting married in Hawaii. If you don't mind?" She blushed at her confession and was glad he asked.

"I don't mind. That sounds like a wonderful idea." Mick gave her a quick smile but she wasn't looking and missed it. She was thinking, 'survive this trip, what a terrible choice of words. As fast as it came, she dismissed the thought with, 'of course we're going to survive,' she was positive of this. Soon she was typing out definite expressions on her laptop, withdrawing info from bank #5.

CHAPTER 8

There was a caravan of black Humvees leaving a stopover in Sacramento, headed to Eagle Lake. The lead vehicle contained one Hungry Hunter as he was called. Ray Smaltz had informed the hunters that he had a Cougar ready for disposal. It was Jeffery Goldstone's turn to pull the trigger.

Another suit looking for easy prey. His jet-black hair matched the sheen of the Humvees and the acid in his soul. Only one thing was important to him, his main mission as the CFO. He had to close the books or find the leaks that had attracted the corporate raiders. Then he was to keep the ritual alive, kill the beast and let the momentum carry over into their business dealings. Great fortunes were to be had and there was no turning back.

He was already proficient in murder, as it was he that set the explosives in the skiff, and it was he that hired the assassins. Of course he was just following orders from the Great White C.E.O., Mr. DeVour.

The Humvees were tooling down the highway at excessive speeds. It was outside Reno that they caught up and over took Mick's RV. He wouldn't have noticed except for the fact that they were all identical monstrous vehicles and if he had blinked he would have missed the black rockets. Little did he realize how important not blinking would be.

Mick and Marie were headed to a campground on the other side of town and as they were driving through he couldn't help but notice the three stand out Humvees parked front and center at the Resorts Lodge. It was a fancy looking lodge with chalet style. It was very inviting with an all glass entrance and elaborate decorative carvings. The modern motel spread out behind it, temporarily stole the view of the lake.

A mile further down the road, Mick found what he was looking for and pulled in. It had all the regular amenities for camping facilities with a convenience store and bait shop. He automatically envisioned himself renting a bout and throwing out a line. Then most importantly, it had a tavern for inter camper mingling, always a good spot for exchanging fish tales. Marie wanted to converse with the locals too. Nobody can compete with a local bartender when fishing for information.

So they registered and pulled into their assigned lot. The sun had just dipped behind the mountains, so there was still plenty of light in the sky. After Mick had plugged in they took a walk down by the lake to stretch their legs and enjoy the views. So hand in hand they strolled the beach. There was snow atop the distant peaks. Marie privately dreamed of climbing all the way to the top of one of those peaks one day. She always did when she examined mountains. As it was she was an accomplished climber but never had enough free time to complete a protracted excursion. But it was fun for her to just plan a route and envision the vistas.

Mick on the other hand always dreamed about building his alpine home, high on a hill with a perfect lakeside view. It was important to him to pound in every nail himself, what a wonderful accomplishment that would be, he felt. He relived that dream on many an occasion. That was when he was by a lake and at peace with himself. It was his retirement dream. He could see himself perfectly clear, sitting in his bass boat casting out his line, waiting to catch the big lunker.

With darkness slipping upon them, they made their way to the tavern. It was fashioned like an old log cabin on the outside, but rather contemporary on the inside. Naturally it had an assortment of stuffed fish posing, to catch some big lunker heads, on the wall. The bartender was a woman and the waitress doubled as the cook. It was never swamped enough to warrant more help than that.

Marie reminded Mick, "let me do the talking, OK?"

"OK." They took their places on a couple bar stools.

"What can I get you folks?" The tender asked. "A couple long necks," Marie replied.

Mick snatched up a deserted newspaper. It was the Sacramento Bee. He hadn't read a newspaper in weeks, so he gave it the once over. Marie introduced herself to Karen as a matter of formality. They exchanged all the common, 'hello, how are you' pleasantries.

"Would you folks like to order anything from the grill?"

Marie declined but Karen rattled off some specials anyway. She was doing her bit to drum up some extra business. Mick had his face buried in the paper until he heard her say "fresh rainbow trout." Then he butted in with, "that sounds good."

It sounded good to Marie too, but she had her heart set on cooking Mick a meal in the RV that evening. But she looked into Mick's hungry eyes and relented with, "OK, make it two orders."

Mick was just trying to make conversation when he said, "look at this article, some guy was rescued in the Pacific Ocean. It say's he was adrift for days off the California coast. He was found floating on debris from a boat he claimed exploded, but he couldn't explain his gunshot wound as he was delirious from loss of blood and dehydration. The FBI are investigating reports of a missing yacht from San Diego harbor."

He summarily reported what he had read, then, added, "now how can a guy get dehydrated out in the middle of the ocean is what I'd like to know."

"Let me see that," Marie requested, and read the article herself. After she finished, she commented, "see, this is the kind of story I'm after. But I would do a follow up on this guy and get as much history as I could. Then, later I'd see how he's doing after he recovers. Get a good story like this and sell it to the AP and you're in business. By the way, you can die of thirst on the ocean, cause if you drink salt water for any length of time you'll get salt poisoning, and you'll die anyway."

Their first beers went down quickly, and Marie ordered two more before quizzing Karen on the exact location of the animal shelter. 'She was planning on going there tomorrow,' she explained.

"It's on a private road directly behind the Cal-Con Health facility, but they won't let visitors in."

"Why not?"

"Because of the mental patients they are rehabilitating."

"Mental patients?"

"Excuse me, I have to serve another customer."

"What are mental patients doing at an animal preserve?" Mick asked. "Good question, I'll find out tomorrow when we go there."

The waitress delivered their trout dinners. It was at this time that Mick noticed Karen talking with another man. That wouldn't seem unusual at all except for the fact that Mick, through lip reading, thought she said, 'those people are asking questions about the animal shelter.' It didn't hurt that she was pointing in their direction ether. Then only to boost Mick's awareness, the man got up and left. That aroused his suspicions more. 'What could be so secretive about an animal shelter'?

He turned his attention back to more immediate matters, like the rainbow trout on the plate in front of him. With Karen tending the other end of the bar, Mick quietly snuck a comment to Marie, "I think you're on to something here. When she comes back this way, I'm going to throw her a curve, so just play along, I'll explain later."

Marie had no idea what he was talking about, but nodded in agreement anyway.

After a while it even became obvious to Marie that Karen was avoiding them by staying down at the other side of the bar, while they finished their meal. She had more questions she wanted to ask, but politely waited, wondering what Mick had up his sleeve. Karen finally had to come back to collect on the tab. That was when Mick inquired about fishing in the lake. These were normal questions for Mick to ask and he could tell she was giving him the runaround with her answer, "I don't know nothing about no fishing."

Mick knew better than that, unless the lake was dead or bone dry, local people always brag on how good the fishing is on their lake. He was tempted to walk out without leaving her a tip because of her attitude, but thought better of it because the trout was so good, and he didn't want to let on he was wise to her ignorance.

On the way back to the RV they stopped at the bait shop. There was a closed sign in the window but Mick peered in anyway. Through the darkness he spotted a taxidermy of a tiger posed to strike on a stand near the counter.

"Will you look at that," he exclaimed.

Marie took her turn, with her hands up to the sides of her face to shade any light deflected from the street lamps. "That's illegal," she gasped in horror.

Mick hushed her, "come on, let's get out of here."

So briskly they beat it back to their RV, and Marie sighed some relief as she sat down at the table. Her hands were trembling somewhat, not from fear but from anger.

Mick noticed it and he had the cure. He went to the case of wine stashed under the sink and blindly selected one. It didn't matter to him which one, it's all nerve tonic, as far as he was concerned. He popped the cork and grabbed some coffee cups. He sat the down between them and apologized for not having glasses. It didn't matter to her, so the apology was wasted but appreciated.

Mick half-filled her cup but that was gone by the time he filled his own. So as soon as he put the bottle down, she picked it up and gave herself a full pour.

"Not the time to be pessimistic," Mick said with a smile.

"No, this is the time to be optimistic, there's something going on here and I smell a story."

Mick had explained why he was suspicious and they discussed different scenarios and strategies. Marie thanked him for his opinions; her rage had subsided with his ever-comforting word. The wine they shared added its own comfort, and Marie was soon reflecting her own sensuous smile. Mick had read that smile before, so when the bottle was empty, it was time to fill up the bedroom.

During their love making; Marie reached physical and mental ecstasy. The excitement was everywhere. Her mind escaped her tingling toes. The wine was lapping at her shores; her feet were wading in a clear water lake. Her mind was on top of a snow-covered peak. She could see herself climbing higher and higher, leaping from peak to peak. She felt like she was capable of anything. She found herself hang gliding into the abyss of love. She was spinning, twirling into a psychedelic tiger stripped black hole. There was no turning back, not now, not ever. She didn't want to fight it either; she knew where she was going, gliding on the hypnotic airs of enchantment, right above the Garden of Eden. Before she came down to earth, she parked her feelings in memory bank # 6. Her feet lightly touched down with a perfectly graceful landing. It was there she stopped to smell the roses and she hummed her dream to sleep.

CHAPTER 9

The Hungry Hunter was up with his wakeup call. "Damn you," he cursed at the desk manager.

"Sorry sir, but I had an order to give you a wakeup call this morning."

"I know that, but damn you anyway. Can't you let a man sleep? And where the hell is my coffee?"

The manager set down the phone, he knew better than getting into it with any of the hunters. He called room service and placed an order for Mr. Jeffery Goldstone.

The Hungry Hunter finally got his lazy ass out of bed, then, took his shower. He hated his morning rituals more than anything; first the washing himself; then the shampoo, putting his contacts back in his foggy black eyes was no fun either. Then he had to do the most detestable thing. The thing was the reason why he would never shower with a woman or in a health club. He took out his instant hair can and shook it. Then he sprayed his cranium. There was this thinning spot on his head that needed daily ego attention. After that, he took out some black shoe polishing stuff and covered every spot that his poor vision saw gray. Real or imaginary, it didn't matter; he wanted his hair to look slick black and the results made him look more like a sick Elvis impersonator.

All the time he was in the bathroom he ignored the polite knocks of the room service. Fact was, the waitress was out there so long, she used her radio link to order some more coffee so it would be hot. She had dealt with the Hunters before and wouldn't be surprised if they didn't drink it at all, no matter what the temperature was.

As it was she was right, he burst out of his room and bitched about what took so long and further complained that he didn't have time for coffee now. She didn't dare say anything about it his refusal to sign for the bill or gratuity either.

He was already wired on adrenaline, he had to get his accounting books in order. He was under a lot of pressure and his position of being the Chief Financial Officer hung in the balance, the phony balance that is. He had barely made it out of accounting school and yet he graduated to CFO, because he learned all the accounting tricks to make the Empire State Building balance upside down and still make it look like a sturdy investment.

But Mr. DeVour laid down the law, 'find the leak, and find out why the corporate raiders want our business. And don't come back until you do!' So his priorities were in place. Then he was to bring back some fresh Cougar meat for the feast.

Mr. Goldstone was up to neck in cooked books when Mick and Marie rose. Marie had a chipper exuberance in her every movement. She glided through her morning routine as if she was wearing fairy wings.

Mick was a little wary from the labors of love but rested well into the night. A fresh set of batteries were awaiting him at the table. Marie had finally got her chance to cook for him and went overboard, or maybe it just looked like a smorgasbord to Mick. He hadn't remembered seeing fresh fruit cut up so neatly other than in restaurants. Then there was the pile of bacon and mound of scrambled eggs.

"What got into you?" he asked.

"You did," she replied with a smile. "Eat up, you need a good breakfast for energy," she motherly advised.

So he did. He was hungrier than he thought. When he finished he patted his stomach in appreciation. She snatched his plate as soon as he set his fork down. Dishes done, Marie was still flitting around faster than his eyeballs could appreciate her. She had energy to burn that morning, she was extremely pleased with how the trip had been going and now she was ready to get down to business.

While Mick readied himself for the day, Marie had her laptop out and was doing her thing. It was decided the night before that he would nose around the bait shop and inquire about the fishing as he went. When he was ready to leave, he double checked with her to see if she wanted to walk over with him but she declined because she was working on another poem, but asked him not to take too long because she wanted to see the animal shelter. He'd be gone only fifteen minutes, he assured her.

So he walked over to the bait shop, once inside, he froze a moment. There was something missing, and it was the stuffed tiger. He gathered himself quickly and erased the question, 'how much does this cost,' from his planned repertoire. Then he just went through the, 'how much is the license and what's biting? Do you rent motor boats?' And all that dribble.

There would be no questioning the clerk about the stuffed tiger, as there was no opening for it unless he wanted to give up his spying through the window. He acted as normal as any inquiring vacationer might be, satisfied with the information he did gather, he promised to return but not when.

She was scratching his head when he explained it all to Marie and assure each other, they weren't dreaming about what they saw. But then dismissed it as unimportant to the task at hand, now they were off to see the real deal.

Mick unplugged the RV and headed for town and it wasn't long until they spotted the Cal-Con Health facility. They both noticed the black Humvees parked front and center again.

"Boy, those guys really get around," he commented.

They followed the service road around the expanse until they came upon a dead end and no trespassing sign. They were on a two lane newly paved road but couldn't make out if there was anything beyond the rows of forest pines that enveloped the road.

"Do you think the animal shelter is at the end of the road?"

"I don't know."

"If I pull in there, I might have a hard time turning this thing around."

While they were debating about going back to town to reaffirm directions or back up and drive in reverse down the road, a security vehicle parked directly in front of them.

"You folks lost?" The security guard asked when Mick opened the door. "I don't know we're looking for the Exotic Wildlife Sanctuary."

"It's closed, can't you see the no trespassing sign?"

"Closed huh."

That's when Marie bounced out of her chair and brashly butted in.

"That's impossible, they just filed for a tax exemption status on their USU information return."

The security guard was taken aback a moment from her commanding comment, before he replied, "look lady, I'm just doing my job and I don't know nothing about no taxes. So you'll just have to turn around. This is private property and there is no trespassing."

Marie was flush with disappointment, it hit her like a tidal wave, disorientated with disparage. First it was making Mick drive her all this way for nothing. Then it was how is she going to get her story? Then: the realization that her information was wrong. Did he deliberately double cross her, no, that can't be right, she thought. Now she was cross-examining her mental, the garbage processor was running full tilt. But she was speechless as she sat back down in her chair in complete disgust.

Mick closed the door and prepared to leave. Then he noticed the emblem on the door of the security car, Cal-Con Health Security.

"That's odd," Mick said.

"What's odd?" Marie quickly quizzed.

"Corporations usually hire outside security firms for insurance purposes.

This guy works for the health joint but he's protecting the animal shelter."

"Why's that odd, we passed it on the way in."

"Oh, I don't know, skip it."

Not knowing what else to say or do, she said, "sorry I dragged you all the way out here for nothing. The story looks like a bust."

"Don't worry about it, Sweetie," Mick consoled.

"Sweetie" hung in the air like a basketball player going in for a dunk, then slam dunk swish, right through Mick's cobwebs of net.

"That's what all your friends call you, isn't it?"

"Yes, wait—stop!"

Mick had turned around and proceeded back to the main road. He stopped while wondering, 'what was up'.

She was up on her feet, she had dressed up earlier to look professional. Mick had personally never seen a blazer with so many pockets in it. She went to her briefcase and started to empty it into her pockets, note pad and pen, voice recorder and all kinds of other what knots. Her digital camera was placed inside her breast pocket; other than looking a little lumpy, she looked excited. And Mick knew that was good news for him.

"What are you up to?" He finally asked.

"I want to stop and smell the roses. I'm going to interview that gardener over there. Go drive around for ten minutes, if I'm not back, go drive around some more," and with that she was out the door but not before planting a kiss on his cheek.

Marie hastily approached the gardener before anyone could possibly stop her.

"Handsome flowers you have here." She started him out with a deliberate compliment to get on his positive side.

"Thank you," he said.

"Do you mind if I take some pictures of them?"

"No, not at all, take all the pictures you want."

She took out her camera and took a couple pictures while he looked on intently.

"What's your name?"

"Tommy."

"Hi Tommy, my name is Marie." Then she quickly struck with her first question in an unassuming manner.

"Tommy, I was looking for the Exotic Wildlife Sanctuary. Do you know where it is?"

"Sure, it's about a mile down that road."

"Is it open?"

"Yeah, but nobody goes back there except the workers, a few delivery trucks, and the Hunters."

"What do the workers do?"

"Oh, they clean the cages and anything else the boss wants."

"Who's the boss?"

"These guys." He pointed to the Cal-Con Health sign right there in the middle of his garden.

That was interesting she thought, but didn't mention her interests to Tommy. It was just the fact that the corporation wasn't listed on her fact sheet or the tax exempt statement.

"Do they own the Exotic Wildlife Sanctuary?"

"I guess so, they own a lot of stuff. If I ain't gardening here, I'm cutting grass in there."

"Hey, you, get back to work!" That bellow: was followed by three men in black suits. Nice suits don't always impress as Marie read their rude demeanor.

"You're on private property miss, unless you have an invitation, you'll have to leave."

"Well how do I get an invitation?" She snapped back.

She didn't like his bullying tone and neither did Tommy, who went back to work but was still within ear shot. He knew there was nothing he could do about it, but just the same in that short period of time that he talked with Marie, he was smitten with a crush. Nobody here had ever talked to him with a kind heart before. And he didn't like the way those men were treating the lady, and that was making him angry. So when he thought 'they'll get theirs one day, yeah, they'll get theirs,' he felt better. He actually felt some emotions, he didn't realize it with all those betablockers in his brain. But he wasn't supposed to feel any emotions. The drugs that were in his daily vitamin were to eliminate normal thoughts. The science was to eliminate the psychology of feeling and thinking in a social interacting climate. The scientists knew there were risks involved and in some cases it may be disastrous, the fact was the scientists didn't know how long they could continue the same dosage before the human anti bodies develop a protection from their poisons.

The bodyguards had her surrounded by now. It almost looked as if she was going to be gang raped, that was how intimidating they could be. But she didn't even flinch and she took a defiant posture by putting her hands on hips and added a little snarl.

"Well, how do I get an invitation?" She repeated.

"State your business, miss." The bodyguard demanded. "What's in your pockets?" Followed.

"None of your business,—I want to see the plant manager."

"You best be moving along now miss," as he took a step closer, crowding her space. She had to retreat a step only to bump into another guard.

"Get away from me," she cried out.

"No, you get away from me or I'll have you arrested for trespassing. You have no business being here." He crowded her further.

"OK, OK, I'll go," she turned quickly to leave only to bump into another bodyguard. Not only was she outnumbered, she was out gunned. She felt a very hard service underneath his suit coat. A hardened piece of steel, she used to be very familiar with all that. Didn't like it then and doesn't like the feel of it now.

"Well, get out of my way then," she barked out.

They moved slightly and gave her one direction out, and that was toward the road, she took it. Quickening her pace, not because she was scarred, but because she was pissed off. Her adrenaline was in a huff, she was muttering things under her breath that would make a madam blush. If those guys would have gotten in her way again she would have bowled them over, as her steam engine was huffing in overdrive.

She could see the RV parked across the highway. It was a city block away but she was wearing flats, so she cut right through the lawn to shorten the distance. Mick was taking all this in from the distance, he couldn't make out exactly what was going on but he could swear he saw her turn around and as she was back peddling flip some laughing men the bird.

She burst into the RV and stripped her jacket of hardware, before removing it completely. Mick could tell she was more than perturbed but had to ask, "what happened?"

"Their hiding something there, big time. I've never been treated so crudely in my entire life."

Mick was thinking of asking, 'what do we do now,' but thought better of it. He could swear there was steam still coming out of her ears. Proper thing to do was to drive away and let her cool down some. Before rationalizing their next move, he was thinking of having lunch. He had good reason for caution as he never saw Marie so agitated before. She was so restless she was actually pacing up and down the isle of the coach while Mick drove. It wasn't long before He pulled back into the campground, and Marie was finishing her umpteenth trip down the aisle.

She was racking her brain during her travels and came up with several different schemes. The task at hand shouldn't be so formidable that she couldn't overcome a few gorilla obstacles. 'If they won't let me in the front door, use the back, bingo.' Her smile came back in the flash of a camera.

She changed her slacks to jeans and blouse to T-shirt and zip up sweatshirt. Changed her flats for hiking shoes. When she reappeared, Mick asked her if she wanted to go to lunch.

"No, not now, let's go for a bike ride."

Mick saw her put her camera in her fanny pack and asked, "are we taking pictures?"

"Yes."

"Then I'll bring mine."

"Yeah, that'll work, we're just tourists."

Mick grabbed his camera case and followed Marie to the bike rack. She had quickly removed the bikes and they were ready to roll. At first Mick was a little wobbly on the wheels, so much so that Marie almost had to laugh. She courteously stopped to allow him to catch up, it never dawned on her that Mick hadn't rode a bike since he was a kid and at first it was a little awkward for him. So she explained how to shift the speeds and they were off with a,

"just follow me."

He got the hang of it soon enough and was right behind her when she wheeled into a gas station. While she was in there she bought some power bars and studied the local street map that was posted in the window. Then she inquired with the clerk on where the bike trails were and she told him that she wanted to climb the peak that was directly behind the Cal-Con Health Corp.

He told her to take the road to the Lassen Ski Resort but he added it was closed for the season. She thanked him and gave one of the power bars to Mick to snack on.

"Here, you might need this," she explained as Mick was temporarily walking off his new found, rubbery legs. They had only biked a mile so far and Marie figured they would have to bike about five more, uphill to get to where she wanted to be.

Mick was game for it, even after she explained it all to him, and she was proud of him for showing, can do courage. The road was basically flat for that first mile and Mick amazed himself with his stamina, yes, he hasn't ridden a bike for a long time and his leg muscles were burning hot, but the exercise was invigorating at the same time. After all he was following his ladylove and that kind of adrenaline never runs out. Just the same he tried to keep a positive mental outlook by thinking of the return trip. It would be all downhill, so as he was standing on the peddles doing his body waggle on the way up, his vision entailed, riding back down with his feet on the handle bars, he's leaning back lounge chair style, with a beer in hand and just coasting down the unwinding road. But you had better believe he thanked god when she finally stopped. Mick wondered to himself, 'wouldn't it have been a lot easier to have driven up here.' But not knowing what her next move was, he just resigned himself to follow along with whatever.

When he dismounted the bike he was in total disbelief of his palsy legs. He looked down at them and they were actually trembling. The heat that they created made him feel like they were melting. Now he had to hold on to the handlebars for balance. It wasn't so much that he was out of shape; it was the fact that he wasn't in shape for that particular excursion. He had used his muscles to a new extreme. But he was in awe at the view, he could see the better part of the lake now and Marie could see the better part of the Health Complex and the Exotic Wildlife Sanctuary.

"I'm going for a closer look," she said.

"All the way down there?" He asked in an exasperated tone, as he didn't feel physically able to transcend into the depth of the canyon yet.

Marie had no reservations, her athleticism and adrenaline wouldn't let her quit but she could tell Mick was spent from the ride, so she politely excused him.

"Wait right here, I'll be right back. I want to get a better look." Mick meekly protested with, "wait a minute, will ya."

"Don't worry, watch the bikes. I'll be right back."

Then she was gone as she slipped down a steep embankment. Mick watched her as she scampered away weaving in and out of the pine trees. He had found an ancient volcanic boulder to rest on but after the fifteenth minute he became unsettled about letting her go off by herself. To help ease his mind, he occupied some of his time with his camera. He captured some of the awesome natural vistas Eagle Lake had to offer.

Done with that, he noticed his legs had a new vitality; they were no longer weighted down with chains or peddles. He actually jumped up and down as if he was practicing for Marie's return. 'Where is she anyway?' Mick started to quiz himself. He jumped off the boulder and went to the spot where she left him. He was peering down, looking for her smiling face to return when he heard a gunshot. The sound echoed in his ears and widened his eyes.

With that sound came a sickness, the mind waves of total numbing sickness. While his mind wrestled with megabytes of information in nanoseconds, he realized he could keep his promise to wait for her no longer. He laid the bikes down off the edge of the road and scratched a message for her in the dirt, just in case she returned while he was gone.

He scurried down the steep decline, then, he had to dodge the pine trees as he saw Marie earlier. When he neared his objective he settled into an advantage point where he felt he could safely observe the goings on in the Exotic Wildlife Sanctuary. He took out his zoom lens and screwed it on his camera, with the lens extended he got a birds eye view of the shelter. He instinctively started to snap away at three men in dark suits. They were just hanging outside one of the many steel framed buildings, but this one in particular was by far the largest, warehouse size large.

There were numerous buildings on the site and a variety of cages and enclosures, some were empty, others were not. He made out some wolfs and coyotes, there were some bears and mountain lions, and there was someone parking one of those Humvees in the warehouse were the bodyguards huddled. Mick could not see in the tinted windows but was suspicious of the way the men were acting. Or was that just the way they ordered the worker around, and the workers seemed to be rather on the small side compared to them.

Child workers: that one kid was lugging a shovel around that was bigger than he was. Actually they looked more like teenagers in different stages of puberty. Mick had a hard time making out everything because of the distance, but there was no mistake about the kids looking lifeless as they lined up in a single file to get on some shuttle bus. As they shuffled their feet lethargically like doomed prisoners. The sight reminded him of some kind of chain gang without the chains.

It appeared to be a formidable fortress with all that barbed wire atop the chain link fence. He also noticed the automatic gates when the shuttle bus left. Probably the bus driver had a radio control opener. No matter though, he had to determine were Marie was and then call the police for help, as he knew the men he was watching were armed and dangerous. Especially the two men that just exited the warehouse with rifles in hand, only to bark out some kind of orders and then they all disappeared back into the warehouse except for the one in the safari outfit.

Marie was nowhere in sight and he didn't have a clue as to where she might be, but he felt like time was running out and he didn't have the luxury of debating with himself on what to do, but he did anyway. One gunshot? The same men she flipped the bird too. Private property? Is she in trouble? Or did she double back to the bikes? 'Where is she?' Damn it! Damn! Damn!

He became more agitated by the minute. He wasn't the only one agitated Marie was feisty as ever, especially after being sucker punched by one of the goons. Now she was being man handled and forced to sit in an office chair. She had to rub her sore jaw, partially to make sure it wasn't broken. Just her luck, she got the perfect picture of the Hunter assassinating the cougar and was going to get a couple more. The last thing she remembered was focusing on the guy in the safari suit; when, wham, lights out.

Now all the lights were on her, as if she was in an interrogation room. Prisoner of war was more like it she thought. Two of the men had hands on her shoulders holding her down, and the other two were in front of her.

"You're in big trouble," the Hungry Hunter said to her sternly.

She recognized him as the one who shot the cougar and she snapped back, "no, you're the one in trouble. Shooting endangered animals is illegal in this country."

"Wrong again, what you witnessed was euthanasia. You see that was a hybrid animal, it spent it's entire life in the circus and it was very ill. It had to be put out of its misery, but you on the other hand were trespassing on private property. Plus you ignored the warning given to you earlier. So I'm afraid you'll have to stay with us until the police arrive. Now won't you tell us your name?"

Marie was slightly dazed and confused about her predicament and hesitantly answered, "Marie Sweet."

"Now Marie, Why are you here?"

Marie was totally confused now, as she was the one who is trained to do the interviews and unprepared to answer questions, so she spit out, "I work for the Associated Press."

"So, you're a reporter then?"

"Yes I am!" She replied with a conviction and hope that reply would yield it's weight and her release.

"I see, and your companion is a reporter too?"

"She couldn't decipher how he knew about Mick but replied, "yes he is," anyway.

"Didn't my men tell you that you'd need an invitation for interviews."

"Yes they did," she humbly said. It wasn't an interview so much, as she really wanted a good story. Now she was wondering if she would get one at all, her newsy nose has been plugged. "But they didn't tell me how to get one," was her excuse.

"I see, we all have safety rules to follow you see, so I'll have to call my boss and see if I can get you an invitation. Would you like a soda or Orange Juice while we wait."

"Yes, Orange Juice would be nice."

H.H. nodded to his men and one of them left the office to run the errand. The Hunters suave attitude had disarmed Marie who actually thought the police were coming on his say so. Further the Hungry Hunter pretended to be calling his boss for an interview when the bodyguard came back and gave her the orange juice that was laced with a tasteless, odorless animal tranquilizer. Bruce the brute as he was called wasn't too good at measuring drugs and gave Marie enough to knockout a horse. It took hold of her quickly; she slightly had enough time to notice her queasy feeling. But right after the thought of being tricked came to her, she was out. The guards had to catch her before she dove into the floor and they laid here out on the long set of office furniture.

Jeffery Goldstone was explaining the situation on the phone with Mr. DeVour and they came to the conclusion, that because she had photographed him in the act of shooting the cougar, it wouldn't be enough to just destroy the film, as they will now have to shut down their Exotic Wildlife Sanctuary scheme. And there would be only one way for them to prevent her from shooting off their mouths, 'find her accomplice and drive them off a cliff.

Make it look like an accident,' was his instructions. He didn't want cops or anyone else investigating any part of their operation.

When he hung up on that conversation and explained the plan with his men, one of them suggested gang banging the bitch before dumping her body. To which HH denied his request, not that he didn't want to partake in the pleasure too, it was because he didn't want to leave any sperm evidence behind. He told his men that he would set up other kind of demeaning folly with some bimbo's back in LA. Besides they still have to capture her partner since the warehouse was not exactly set up to confine people, they bodyguards carried Marie's body to the now vacated cougar cage and threw her in.

Meanwhile Mick had made his way back to his RV on foot. He uselessly hoped she may have made her way back there for some reason. Mick's mind was racing with worry. So much so that he almost forgot to unplug the RV before pulling out. He was in a hurry to get back to the mountain bikes and see if she returned and or found his note. If not, he knew then that he would have to enter the animal compound or call the police or both.

As it was Mick was just about to pass the Cal-Con Health facility when two of the Humvees came tearing out of the private drive and headed for the campground, that was where you'll find him Ray said. He was going on his inside information. RV's are such a common sight in these parts the Hungry Hunter didn't even notice Mick as they sped past him, but Mick sure as hell noticed them. A strange feeling came over him because he would have expected them to go in the direction of the motel, unless that is, they were going to the campground looking for him.

He didn't have time to turn around and double check, so he proceeded down the road past the motel to his turn off and up the mountain road to the bikes. Even though there was no traffic because of the lodge being closed, he pulled the RV up past were the bikes were, until he found a spot that had enough room so that he felt comfortable pulling over.

Then he pulled out Marie's cell phone and dialed 911. When the operator answered, Mick said, "I'd like to report a missing person."

"We don't handle missing person reports sir. You'll have to go down to the police station and file a report in person."

"But you don't understand, she may have been kidnapped."

Mick's voice was becoming directly stressed as he recognized by her passive attitude that he wasn't going to get the results he wanted.

"Her life may be in danger, or she might already be dead!" He said with a more urgent tone.

"Calm down sir, if you'll just follow Police department procedures and come down to the police station and fill out a missing person's report, then there is a 48 hr. waiting period before we can do anything."

"Well lady, you know where you can stick your police procedures, and now I would like to report a burglary, because I'm going to break into the Exotic Wildlife Sanctuary facility. You got that?"

"Please calm down sir and come," the line went dead as one frustrated Mick didn't want to waste any more time listening to her bullshit. He noticed the afternoon light was fading when he opened the tool compartment under the RV's main body. He grabbed the tools that he thought he would need. He looked over the guardrail and this ravine looked steeper than the first one, so he walked back to where the bikes were before he descended into the forest.

It was Ray Smaltz that did the talking at the campground as he knew the owners personally. They were his partners in the disposing of the illegal taxidermy animals. When he found out Mick had just left and didn't know when he was going to return but that he was paid up for the week.

When he huddled outside with the Hunter and his bodyguards on the best way to proceed. They all had ample munitions, handguns, rifles, and tranq dart guns. So it was decided that, two of the bodyguards will lay in wait by the bait shop. The others will look for him in town. They figured he might have needed some gas or something. They all had combination walkie-talkie cell phones, so who ever saw him first was to call the others for backup and reinforcement, 'not that it would be necessary,' they all laughed. Then they went over the part of the plan to disable him, get him alone and hit him with the dart gun first or just tackle him and physically hold him until somebody incapacitates him with the dart and then they'll take them both and drive them off a cliff together, 'real accidental like, 'then they all laughed again.

Mick was a flurry of feet as he scampered downhill, sometimes he had to slide on the seat of his pants just to slow down the G-forces. The circumstances of the terrain dictated caution as he dodged tree after tree. It also carried him to the deepest part of the valley. It was right there that he saw a little clearing and the fence. Beyond the fence was his destination, the warehouse. He studied it carefully, looking for the guards but of course the Humvees were gone, they were looking for him, so the compound was clear.

That was when a sparkle caught his eye. The sun was ready to dip over the mountains and it's rays were winking at him through a natural spring. He took a closer look, the spring was coming straight up from Mother Earth. It was winking at him with blue green flashes. It was reflecting the green of the grass and the blue of the sky. The colors matched his eyes. He had worked up a mighty thirst as it was and the pure spring water was so inviting, he got down on his knees and bent over to take a drink. He thought about the last time he had tasted such a refreshing mineral water. He fell in love with his first in Hot Springs, Ark. He took another drink and one more before he stood.

The respite, revitalized his body and mind, his strength grew with it. He was now standing as tall as any man can. The mesmerizing blue green spring has done it's charge. Mick clawed his way past the last few trees. He retrieved his trusty lineman pliers and completely dismantled a complete section of fence in a matter of minutes.

It was no matter to him that he could have slipped in after the first few cuts, his animal instincts overcame him. He wanted freedom, he wanted Marie's freedom, he wanted the animals to be free too. He could see clearly now, as clear as a mountain spring. His blue green eyes focused on freedom, as he leaped to the coyote cage, they were the first he set free, then the wolves. The mountain lions were after that. These animals made a beeline for the opening in the fence and each gave the mysterious man a glance in gratitude before they dashed freely.

Then he dismantled an eagle pen, and another containing monkeys, and yet another containing Bob Cats. Finally he was at the warehouse and he didn't need a key as he gave the door a flying kick and shattered the door moldings. The sun had just set and the warehouse was dark but his eyes were focused and he could see perfectly clear, Marie was in an animal cage. That was the door he ripped right of its hinges, he was gaining strength instead of exhausting it. But he gathered Marie's body in his arms as gently as a new borne kit. He licked her face to stimulate her seemingly lifeless body. He heard her moan, so he licked her face again as he carried her out.

He carried her all the way back to the mountain spring he had found before he laid her down on the grass. He used his hands to cup some water and bring it to her lips. He heard her sigh again but she was still unconscious. Mick's sweat was wiped from his forehead and sprayed; he knew she was safe now even with the malnourished carnivores he set free in the area. Fact was; a pack of wolfs eyes glaring at the couple from the next set of trees. But Mick's scent smelled as sweet as new bloom blossoms to all the local humming birds who kindly fanned Marie's face with their wings. Then to suit, the call of the wild coyotes gave Mick their blessing to return to the warehouse and finish his freedom business. There were some cages containing black and grizzly bears left to be opened.

Mick had freedom dominating his mind and caution wasn't an option. Even if he had known that the 911 operator had reported the crank call to the sheriff who relayed his concerns to the Exotic Wildlife Sanctuary Director Ray Smaltz, the sheriff was a little too far away and was lackadaisically indisposed.

"Check your property, and give me a call back if you need me Ray."

Even though he to respond to nary a call in Eagle Lake and had no personal time to answer crank callers. Of course Ray didn't want him there anyway and had no plans on calling him back but thanked him for his concern and tip. "I'll handle it," he told the sheriff. As he made a U-turn, the Hungry Hunter paged his men in wait at the campground.

"Come on men, our guy's at the animal shelter, this is perfect, meet us there."

So it was, while Mick was cutting the Bears loose he saw the distinctive head lights of the Humvees coming up the road to the main gate. But Mick was quick this night, quicker than he's ever been in his life. He leaped up on a tractor that was normally used for landscape duties. He started the diesel engine and put it in gear, as it rolled forward he aimed it at the front gate, which was opening by radio control from the lead Humvee. The driver had it timed so that his speeding vehicle would get by the gates as soon as they were completely opened. The diesel engine on that slow moving cat was spewing a thick black cloud from its exhaust stacks combined with the dirt throw up from the tracks it resembled a tornado and all its destructive qualities.

Mick took his opportune time to leap off and hit the ground running. He raced back to the warehouse opening some parrot cages as he flew. He didn't have to look back because he heard the explosion. The Humvee had no chance to survive the impact. The driver never saw the tractor coming, so it was very elementary when their gas tank exploded on contact at the gate, they were toast.

Ray Smaltz who was riding with the Hungry Hunter and the last bodyguard barely had time to slam on the breaks and save themselves. They backed up their Humvee to a safer distance and stared blankly at the inferno blocking their path. As Mick made his way back into the warehouse, he hopped into the Humvee that was parked there, not for lack of knowledge that garage doors should be opened before exiting; he was just racing with himself and his mind. His mind was moving faster than anything he had ever experienced before. All he knew was he wanted to get back to Marie as fast as he could.

So he didn't wait for the door to open, even though he was sure he hit the radio control button. Or it was just plain to slow, it didn't matter as he squealed the tires and smashed that garage door to smithereens. But once outside, he saw the auto fire at the gate, got his bearings and turned around and headed for the hole in the fence.

He was at Marie's side in a matter of minutes. He quenched his thirst again before cupping some water and bringing it to her lips. This time her tongue licked her lips for the moisture. She was still unconscious but slowly coming around. Mick gathered her up in his arms and carried her to the Humvee. He laid her down on the back seat. He debated with himself on how to proceed, he had knocked out the headlights when he crashed through the garage door and he was enveloped in darkness. Should he take her to the hospital? But where is it? Should he attempt the dangerous climb back up to the RV? But what if he slipped and fell with her?

The moon was on the rise in the distance but would take too long to rise above him. The stars darted in and out of the passing clouds, but he felt he could see perfectly clear. Then he let out a gargantuan roar, not one of frustration but of power. He could see perfectly clear, he would follow the spring: which in turn would lead to the lake. The spring water was reflecting the slightest of starlight and he followed the trail ever so slowly. He didn't want to jostle his precious cargo.

CHAPTER 10

The Hungry Hunter and Ray Smaltz had made it by the flames which had almost burned it's self out. The wreckage had completely blocked the entrance except for a suck in gut and shimmy sideways path around the tractor. But by now the security force from Cal-Con Health Corp. had arrived on the scene, adding to the commotion.

Ray was worried about his animals. Jeffery was worried about his crook books. It dawned on him that he had left them in his Humvee where he thought they would be safe. Now as he looked through the gaping hole in the garage door, he could only imagine his life's work and his life were in the wrong hands. But it was the bodyguard that noticed the woman was freed from her cage.

Then a whole new case of, 'oh shits,' was opened. Jeffery was just realizing the enormity of the disaster and ran to the gun rack in the office and pulled a rifle out of the rack. It didn't matter that he already had weapons in the other vehicle, he needed to feel the power, he, wanted to feel the power now! Then he started to bark out the orders, "Ray, Bruce, we have to find that guy now! Clear that junk off the road! And get ready to kick some ass!"

His power trip was missing gears like a transmission without fluid. His books, his crook books, were trapped in his one-way brain like the animal he executed earlier in the day. How is he going to get them back, was his number one quest. The whole operation would go up in smoke if they land in the wrong hands. How was he going to explain it to his CEO? He's got to find the stolen auto first. There was only one road leading in and out of town, and now was the time to act. He called the sheriff to put out an APB out on his stolen Humvee, and to report the man inside murdered two of men, and is to be considered armed and dangerous. He would have preferred to cover that up too, but he didn't see any other options. Besides, the best-case scenario would to have the cops blow his brains out before he does, as he felt he might have a hard time getting away with it. He knew he needed all the help he could get, even if it took an army of men, and for that he had to call the Great White Hunter.

While trying to explain the new set of circumstances to him, he did just fine until he got to the part, 'he's got my cooked books.' Then the, 'you stupid asshole,' and every other derogatory term rang out over and over again like church bells on a Sunday morning, for sure his ears were ringing like his head was in one of them bells.

There was only one person laughing at this conversation, and that would be FBI agent Paul Dupree. He and a few other agents had set up a satellite surveillance system and were closely monitoring cell phone activities from a safe distance. It didn't matter that Paul didn't have a search warrant or court order, as cell phone conversations are free for the taker. It was he that set up Marie for this dangerous mission. He wasn't the least bit interested in the Exotic Wildlife Sanctuary facility; he wanted info on the Cal-Con Health Corp. It was a very influential person that wanted the company investigated for financial considerations. And he only knew too well that if he didn't pull Marie's strings the right way, she would have never gone along with his plan. But now she drug along that Mick fellow, he hadn't planned on any more competition. But now that an APB has been put out on an armed and dangerous car thief, he's got an automatic free shot at eliminating his rival, and a great chance to crack a financial fraud case. As it was, he would have never been able to get a search warrant without proof, and now it seemed that one Mickey Swift has what he needs, and he was going to get those books for evidence.

He had witnessed the fire by the gate alright but couldn't see how Mick had made his escape. So he packed up his night vision goggles and an assortment of other spy devices and lit out for the woods. For he was sure he couldn't travel through the thickets of the forest and get very far. But that was where he was wrong. Mick had in fact followed natures easement of the spring to the main road. The Humvee hoisted it's self-up that last embankment and he drove back up the mountain to his RV.

Mr. DeVour had been on the phone with the other Hunters in the group, the Holy and Sport Hunters. He ordered them up to Eagle Lake with their entourage of bodyguards. 'Do not fail to get those books,' were his orders. He was staying behind to take care of everyday business, 'somebody has to do it right,' was his logic. So this time there was two sets of Humvees caravanning as fast as traffic would allow.

The Holy Hunter actual name was Lawrence Marsi. He was given that moniker because he ran a bible study class for his local church. He was in fact a master in the arts of deception. He had fleeced his flock many a time in the past, and this time would be the granddaddy of them all; as he had seduced most of his congregation into investing in Cal-Con Health. Most of his flock's retirement money was sunk into his scheme. 'Ye have little faith, if you don't invest yourself whole heartily in the lord and Cal-Con health,' was one of his favorite antidote's.

The Sport Hunter was really a pedophile. His name was Richard Jollins. He was a boy scout trooper and spent most of his free time looking for boys to take advantage of. He would be the first to pat a kid on the back and say, 'attaboy, be a good sport.' But like all pedophiles, first and foremost, he was a con artist. He didn't care who or what he conned in his life, 'the ends, justify the means,' was his favorite saying.

Both of these junior CEO's dressed to their code, black suit and tie, white shirt and were the best marksmen of the group. They were armed to the teeth, so if they had to kill to get their crook books back, so be it. They had left that night for Eagle Lake, but weren't expected to arrive until early morning.

Meanwhile Ray Smaltz and Bruce the bodyguard had removed the wreckage to the side of the road, and now Ray could get his Jeep out of the compound. They had decided not to split up this time, as they figured the police would be watching the road for their missing Humvee and they would search the road that leads to the ski lodge. Being that it would be impossible to search the woods at night without dogs. But the security force from Cal-Con could maintain security at the Exotic Wildlife Sanctuary facility until the police and coroner removed the deceased.

It was when the Great White Hunter called Jeffery back and the cell phone rang in the Humvee that Mick was driving, that an automatic answering arm reached up front to answer the source. It doubly startled Mick who grabbed Marie's wrist.

"Don't," he said.

"Let go of me," she was still groggy and didn't understand what was going on.

"Help is on the way," Terrance DeVour said over the cell phone.

"Good," Jeffery replied. "We're headed up the ski lodge road to search for the vermin up there."

"Mick, is that you?" A very confused Marie asked. "Shush," he said.

"That's fine, shoot on sight, understand," Terrance DeVour ordered. "Right" Jeffery acknowledged before signing off.

"Where are we? My head hurts," she put her hands to her for head and plopped her body back down on the seat.

"Get up," Mick demanded. "We don't have time to play around." Marie just moaned, what she wanted was some more sleep. "Get up!" Mick hollered again as he pulled up ahead of the RV. He made a quick U turn and aimed the Humvee back down the road. He grabbed the three-way cell phone and put it in his shirt pocket before running around and opening the back door. She was still in a half oblivious state when Mick grabbed her ankles and slid her half way out of the seat. Her arm was caught on a valise case that was standing on the floor. Mick grabbed the obstruction and without thinking twice about it, flung it over the guardrail and down the ravine. He pulled on her arms now until she was sitting.

"Snap out of it," he cried, as he patted her cheeks.

"OK, OK, I'm up already." Somehow Marie had drifted off to a part of her life that made her think of her mother waking her up for school, but Mick had no time to dally, he picked her up and carried her to the RV. He hoped the familiar surroundings would help revive her when she woke.

But Mick didn't have time to waste as he knew they would be upon them soon. He started the RV and pulled up the road a mile. Marie was mumbling something about being in heaven, so Mick kissed her cheek and said, "don't go anywhere, I'll be right back."

He ran back to the Humvee hopping he still had time. As he didn't have much time to think of another plan he just pulled the Humvee around the next bend to a straighter part of the road when he saw the head coming around the distant bend.

He timed it right with the tractor once and all he had going for him was to try it again. He left the motor running and put the trans in drive. Then he quickly stepped out and started to run up hill as the Humvee rolled on to its intended target.

Its headlights were out, and it took on stealth qualities as it picked up speed on the downward slope. Faster and faster it quietly rolled on. Mick didn't bother to look around as he was on a different mission now.

Ray was leading the way in his Jeep and Bruce was driving the Humvee with the Hunter riding shotgun. They were driving rather slowly at a safe pace, as the mountain road can be treacherous at night. They were hunting for their man who could have been hiding anywhere and it seemed useless when all of the sudden out of nowhere, Ray spotted a big black object of death hurdling straight for him. He swerved quickly to the left hitting a boulder off the road. The Humvee had gained momentous speed on its downhill run but with no one to steer it onto its target, it fearlessly flew like a rocket and went crashing right over the cliff.

"God damn! Did you see that? Ray communicated by radio.

"We got that crazy motherfucker now," the Hunter gladly retorted.

The Humvee had taken a classic leap over the cliff and as it flew, it took the tops of several pine trees with it. The hunting crew had stopped their vehicles `and bursting branches.

They were all expecting it to explode into a fireball but all that came was a dead silence. They were all glad for that because in no shape or form did they want to take on a forest fire or the Forest Rangers.

"So now all we have to do is go down there and get my books. Then we can call the Sheriff to collect the dead motherfuckers," Jeffery said with a chuckle. It was the first time that he had something to laugh about that day. But the Hungry Hunter was looking directly at Ray when he was saying we, he meant you.

Ray just looked at him with a stupid kind of look, "can't it wait until morning, that's kind of steep and dangerous climb at night."

"No, I want my briefcase now," the Hunter demanded. "We'll wait for you here. I need my briefcase, it was in the back seat."

Against Ray's better judgment, he carefully started his decent over the side of the cliff. He was instantly enveloped into the darkness and he had no clue how he was going to make it back up without ropes. But he realistically figured once he found the briefcase, he would call on the cell phone and continue on to the animal shelter. 'The hell with him,' he thought, 'he's fuckin' nuts if he thinks I'm climbing all the way back up here,' he swore as he awkwardly descended. Fact was, he only went down a few yards, and already he didn't want to climb back up. But he had no choice, so he kept mumbling his curses under his breath as he went.

Mick had made it back to the RV and cursed too when he saw Marie was gone. But that was only momentary, as he had heard her in the bathroom. Her head was pounding and she had the sense to splash her face with water. She came out as soon as she heard him.

"Mick what happened?"

He didn't know how to answer her; he just gave her a hug and asked, "are you alright?"

"Yeah, I think so. Where are we?"

"We're together," he said, before he kissed her. "Don't ever leave me again.

I love you!" He kissed her again.

Her cheeks became flush with life, it was such a pleasant feeling, her troubling thoughts vanished. She was with her man again. She really didn't understand how it all came about because the last thing she remembered; she was interviewing someone.

"Come on, we gotta get out of here," Mick said as he turned to climb behind the wheel. She joined him in her chair. She got a better picture when Mick turned on his headlights but he quickly shut them off again. He pulled ahead slowly.

"What are you doing?" Marie asked.

"Those guy's that kidnapped you are about a mile downhill. I don't want them to see my headlights. Here," he took the cell phone out of his pocket. "When this thing rings, don't answer it, you can hear them talking on it, but you can't say nothing, it's like a three way system."

Where are we?" She asked again.

But Mick didn't have to answer, for the sign said, Lassen Ski Resort, closed for the season. Plus he had to stop, as there was a chain draped across the road.

"Damn," he said.

"What are we going to do now?"

"I don't know." He shut off the RV and got out to survey the situation.

He needed a bolt cutter and he knew it. The posts were made of steel tube and anchored with cement. Going around the posts looked impossible with his RV. But he had a hacksaw and with a little time, he was sure he could cut through the eyebolt that was welded to the post. Discounting his other options that were few, he went to his toolbox and went to work.

By that time Marie had come out to inquire what he was doing.

"Just wait a minute," he said, as his arm motored up and down like a piston in overdrive. In five minutes, Mick had that chain laying flat on the road. Then he drove over it and re hooked the chain back on the post. He had only cut out the portion of steel necessary to accomplish his objective.

Marie had watched him work mightily and started to wonder how he had gotten her out of the office she was in. There were all those men she remembered, he would have to fill her in on all the blanks.

Mick was ambling up the road again without his headlights and she was just about ready to ask, when the Hunters phone buzzed. Mick stopped, and both stared breathlessly at the phone on the engine cowling.

"There ain't no bodies down here, and there's no briefcase either."

"What do you mean there's no briefcase? The Hunter questioned.

"Must have flown out with the bodies because nobody could have survived this wreck."

"My books were in that briefcase and I need them. Do you understand?" Jeffery was furiously flustered; he would have blown his ragtop if it wasn't painted on. Bruce his bodyguard was sitting on the hood of the Humvee as useless as can be, and the Hunter would have bitched at him to, but he didn't know what to bitch about or what to do.

"We'll have to wait for day light because it's pitch black down here," Ray reported back.

"Look around some more, it's got to be there somewhere."

"It's useless, I could be standing on it and not see it. I'll meet you back at the animal shelter." Those were Ray's last words as a grizzlie's paw nearly ripped his head off with the first swipe. The phone went flying as Ray's screams were muffled from his blood and the gash in his throat. It was all over for him as the bear's canine teeth sunk into his brain. With the scent of Ray's blood in the air, the wolves and coyotes howled out their approval.

Mick had found the colossal Ski Resort Chalet, the roof looked as steep as two hands pointed skyward in prayer. There was a humungous sun deck on the underside of two chair lifts that took the skiers further up the mountain. He scoured the empty parking lot for maintenance or security vehicles, but saw none. He settled in an unobtrusive spot next to the maintenance barn in the rear of the chalet.

He was dead tired and needed to recharge his batteries but Marie would have none of that. She felt her man had saved her life and wanted desperately to thank him. So she took the initiative and grabbed a bottle of wine and some blankets.

"Come on Mick, let's sleep under the stars tonight."

"Oh no, I'm beat."

"No, no, come on now, the fresh mountain air will do you good."

She took his hand and tugged at him to follow her, he was too tired to resist. They walked out to a vast area of grass at the bottom of the ski slope. Marie laid the blanket down and Mick wasted no time lying down on it. He observed the brightness of the stars; he almost felt that if he reached up with a stretching arm he could touch Mars in the constellation Aquarius. Marie had opened the wine and brought the bottle to her lips. She needed a hit as bad as Mick did. He took the next few swallows. Then they kissed as Marie's craft hand undid his belt and zipper. The cool mountain air filled his lungs as her hand took hold of his lightning rod. Mick had just laid back down, as the heat of her lips enveloped him. His eyelids closed and his iris's rolled back to observe the stars blinking in his mind. Lightning strikes were flying through his loins, then, he saw some shooting stars that were winking at him. He's seen these stars before, they were special stars, Swift— Tuttle shooting stars. He was chasing comets in his chariot, he was full-steeds ahead, sparks were flying like fireworks. Multi colors of the rainbows glowed, and his lady in the ski was winking at him. The heat, the cold, the positive, the negative, his mountain was swollen with lava. As nature had planned there was an eruption, now every one of Mick's batteries was discharged as his tensed muscles unwound into a pool of tranquility. They both took another sip of wine and closed their eyes with heaven on their minds. She secured the sensation in memory bank #7.

The wolves and coyotes once again scented the call of the wild and howled their approval.

CHAPTER 11

Commotion a plenty at the main gate of the animal shelter, as the sheriff had emergency crews remove the bodies from the burned out shell of the Humvee and a local tow truck driver was in the process of hooking up his prize.

The sheriff was very apologetic to Mr. Goldstone, it was obvious to him that he screwed up by not answering that crank call, but naturally he never mentioned anything about that. He just kept reassuring Jeffery that they would catch the dirty dog that did this. He reassured him that an all-points bulletin was out for the stolen Humvee and Jeffery just patted the sheriff on his shoulder and said, "keep up the good work."

He knew were the Humvee was, but didn't want to mention it until he had his books in back securely in hand. So after he dismissed the sheriff, he headed for the Exotic Wildlife Sanctuary office to meet up with Ray. When he found him not to be there, he called him on the phone. When he didn't answer his call, he started cursing, as he cursed he paced. As he paced, evil thoughts popped in and out of his head.

"That fuck should have been back by now!" He screamed at his bodyguard. Bruce had his nose in a magazine and was always non responsive to the Hunters fits. Grin and bear it, is always part of a whipping posts job, but when it comes down to the dirty deeds of following orders is when he earned his money, otherwise, he was just along for the ride.

Another hour passed and still no Ray, Jeffery had paced himself out of energy and laid out on the office chair group. Not exactly his cup of tea but he wanted to find Ray and his briefcase first thing in the morning.

Tommy and Robert were making plans too. Robert was buzzed to the max and Tommy was talking about all the rumors that the workers had feed him over the last couple of days. Now this, as everybody was watching from the dorm windows as the police and emergency vehicles flashed their lights with their comings and goings. Then there were the Cal-Con Health security people, acting all confused. Confusion makes opportunity for those who make the most of it.

So Tommy figured tomorrow might be their big chance and of course, Robert agreed with him, as he didn't really care about anything anyway. That was why Tommy confided with Johnny, another big lad who was tired of cleaning shit out of cages. He wanted in on the big score too. All's they figured they would have to do is hijack a delivery truck and load it up with the goodies from the warehouse. Then they would be set for life, criminals always have a way of making crime sound good, and crime always sounds good to demented minds.

Paul Dupree had intercepted the cell phone conversations from a special satellite dish mounted atop their spy van, between Ray Smaltz and Jeffery Goldstone. That bit about the bodies flying out of the wreck, could have been the end of Marie and Mick, he thought. He also knew he had made a mistake by searching the woods with his night goggles without a compass, as he soon found himself walking in a circle. To make matters worse, the pine branches were constantly tearing at his suit, being out of his element, he bailed out of the forest on the first opportunity. But he and the Hungry Hunter planned to return in force at daybreak.

The difference being, the FBI had their maps out, their global positioning screen on, planned their search area, pinpointed their vantage points, and they had their spy van to listen into Jeffery Goldstone's cell phone activity. Plus never the one to be undermanned, Paul made a call for backup agents with a helicopter.

The other Hunters and caravan were two hours away by the time the sun rose. They didn't know they were on a collision course, but it wouldn't have mattered, they had a job to do and they were going to do it. The bodyguards were especially tired of the routine and boredom; even the slightest hint of action would let them prove their worthiness. But had they known they were about to tangle with the FBI, the bravado dogs who expand their chests while stomping on defenseless people, no doubt would have put their tail between their legs and skedaddled.

Mick and Marie were huddled in the blankets, if they were any closer they would have been inside each other. The cool mountain air has a special way of bringing two lovers together. It was Mick that moved first, a charley horse kicked in his leg, he winced in pain, and forced his leg muscle straight. Feeling a part oneness, Marie stirred too.

"What's the matter Mick?" She asked in a sleepy low tone.

"Just a muscle cramp." Mick had to massage his thigh, so Marie's pillow disappeared down to his leg.

"Well, it's time to get up anyway," Marie chirped. "Yeah, I think I'll have to walk this cramp off."

Mick got up and started hobbling around until his muscle relaxed. Marie gathered up the blankets but Mick grabbed the bottle of wine and he took a healthy good morning pull. Not only was his leg muscle cramped, every muscle in his body was stiff. It was as if his body was being held together with sticks, burning stiff sticks. The grimace on his face told Marie he was in pain, but he didn't look hurt at all. He started doing all kinds of early morning muscle stretches, as if he was a pro athlete warming up for the big game.

Marie smiled at the view when he bent over to touch his toes, then she chuckled some when he did this stretch that reminded her of a yoga class she took. None of his moves were that drastic but somehow his movements still turned her on, even the way he put the wine bottle to his lips to drink made her think of more sex. Red wine and luscious lips she was thinking of taking him again, right there and now, when "I'm hungry," popped out of his mouth.

Mick had gotten the workout of his life the day before and his body was just sending him a message, 'try to take it easy on me next time or I'll hurt you. Over and out.' He got the message all right but would be glad to do it all over again, if it got the same results.

"I'll make you something. Let's go." Marie proudly proclaimed.

So they walked back to the RV. Marie was looking for bacon and eggs but left over pizza was in the way. There was only two pieces left and Mick wolfed them down before the first egg hit the frying pan.

"Nothing like wine and pizza for breakfast," Mick cracked half-jokingly. "No, I'm making you a good breakfast," Marie countered, not knowing the pizza and wine were already gone. She was so serious about making her man a hearty breakfast and went about it with efficiency, when the cell interrupted them with, "Jeffery did you find the books yet?"

It was the Holy Hunter calling ahead to report their progress and to find out the necessity of their expedience.

"No," Jeffery replied, "The thieves went over the cliff last night with my briefcase in my Humvee. All's we gotta do is find the wreck and Ray before someone else does."

"Alright, we'll be there in a couple hours." The phone went dead. "Did you hear that?" Marie asked Mick, who was unmoved by it all. "Of course I did, I'm right here aren't I." Mick answered warily.

"Well what arethey talking about,books and briefcase?" Marie commanded.

"Oh that, the briefcase was in my way so I pitched down the ravine." He explained.

"And what about this stolen Humvee?" The questions were coming rapid fire now. But Mick was nonchalant as can be about that question too.

"Oh that, I pitched that down a different ravine."

"You what!" Marie was exasperated.

"Don't worry, they think we were in it." He explained in case she didn't understand what the Hunters said.

"We were in it?" She had a shocked look about her. "Yeah."

Marie was now into some flabbergasted state of her own, as she handed Mick his plate of bacon and eggs. She silently made herself a plate, and just because, put the empty bottle of wine to her lips for the last drop. It didn't matter if there was wine in it or not, her blanketly-blank mind needed some stimulation, more time to comprehend, or a better explanation. Her stomach growled at her and she sat down to eat, as she was real hungry too.

Her wheels were turning as she ate. She took pride in her memory for details, this time she drew blanks. She remembered going to get the story, and interviewing the men, nothing after that, then how did Mick get her out of there she wondered. Then her thoughts went to the briefcase and story. 'We got to get the briefcase back for the story,' she figured, but finally asked,

"why aren't we in the campground?"

"Ah, it's kind of a long story." That was all Mick had to say to get Marie fired up.

"Story, that's right, we came for the story. We have to get that briefcase. And what exactly did you do yesterday?" Marie wanted to hear it all.

"It was like, I didn't know what happened to you or where you were. So I ended up leaving the bikes to go look for you." He explained.

"Bikes, that's right. I was doing an interview, and those dirty bastards drugged me. My camera, what happened to my camera?" Her mind was going snap, snap, snap, whap, it hit her like a clenched fist. "I saw them shooting a caged cougar. The dirty bastards! But they're hiding something bigger than that. I'll bet that briefcase is full juicy stuff. Do you know where you threw it?"

"Yeah, but it looked kind of steep."

She gathered up the empty plates and deposited them into the sink. No time to wash them now, she was too excited about the thought of finding the briefcase. Steep was of no concern to her as she went right for her duffel bags full of mountain climbing gear. She had enough gear to climb two mountains.

"What are you going to do with all this stuff?" Mick asked. "You said the ravine was steep."

"Yeah but…"

"No buts; rappelling is the fastest way to get down, besides it's fun."

"Yeah but…"

"Mick, trust me, will ya. You do trust me, don't you?"

Mick recognized the loaded question. There impossible answer correctly.

So he kept his mouth shut, except for, "OK, let's go."

Marie didn't need all her equipment. She just took what was absolutely necessary. She hooked on her belt, grabbed a rope and pitons, and put on her helmet. When she tried to give one to Mick, he rebuffed her by putting it back in the equipment sack. He strapped on his harness and everything else went back into storage. Then he went to get the bottle of wine and a plastic bag. When Marie spotted his actions she was forced to inquire, "what are you doing with that stuff?"

"The phone is for hearing what those guys are up to and the bottle is for finishing. Then I'll have a container for the spring water."

"Spring water!?"

"Yeah-it's real good."

She didn't want to argue about how stupid that idea was. They should be focusing on the briefcase. So she just shrugged and said, "whatever."

Once they were standing over the cliff, Marie pounded a piton into the rock and fastened the rope. She gave Mick instructions covering all the how too-s, then she was over the side and in a matter of minutes she was at the bottom shouting up, "see how easy it is."

Mick did watch her and she makes everything look easy with her natural grace. Mick took a couple pulls on the wine bottle to lighten his mental load and over the side he went. He felt like a grasshopper going backwards, as he kicked away from the cliff while loosening the strain on the rope. Kick and drop, kick and drop, "nothing to it," he said when he met Marie at the bottom.

"Now, let's find that briefcase," Marie said.

Mick looked up to follow the cliff line and get his bearings. In short order the briefcase was found. No worse for wear, a couple nicks from the fall was all the damage. Mick then led the way to the spring, and on the way they shared the wine, celebrating their find.

CHAPTER 12

Only the most trusted of Ray Smaltz employees were apprised of the situation. Ray was missing. All work at the animal shelter was canceled until further notice. Early morning classes for the kids were kept on schedule, then, sent to Cal-Con Health for sanitation detail.

The older teens had figured correctly, something was up, and they were able to huddle without the guards about them. Trying to keep a secret like, 'the head vet is missing,' was impossible, even in a tight knit group. One reason was because all available men were ordered into the woods to search for Ray and the wrecked Humvee. Promotions were offered as rewards for anyone who finds them.

Secretly Jeffery Goldstone was petrified of the thought that, Ray had double crossed him and absconded with his briefcase to hold it for ransom. He knew that's what he would have done. Demented and tortured minds often find a way to do away with each other. The same was true in the Hungry Hunters case, fact was that, if he didn't recover the books pronto, it would be Mr. DeVour that would be feasting on his blood.

That was why he was leading his group of men, and Bruce his bodyguard was leading the other. They were wide spread to cover a maximum area, but no man was out of shouting distance. This tactic was sure to work so it was thought, only one thing over looked, there was nobody left to guard the warehouse.

The Hungry Hunter was just that this morning, hungry and ornery. He hadn't eaten his dinner the night before. He hadn't had any coffee or rolls that morning either. He had slept on the rock hard office chairs overnight. His fine black suit was trashed after the first mile of hiking in the woods. The pine needles had no mercy on his hair either; scabs of paint were flaking away. Now if he could only transplant his day old beard to the top of his head: that, would have made his day complete. But now that they have been traipsing through the woods for an hour now, and the sight of him could have made a zombie scream, everyone was confused when someone else did. They found the remains of Ray. Gorged of guts, the finder's fee was puke, so too were the first few who followed the scream. What was left of Ray was barely recognizable, except for his trademark safari suit.

The Hungry Hunter didn't get sick though, because now he knew he wouldn't have to pay a ransom for his briefcase and that it and the Humvee were close at hand. He looked about and saw the cliff, "leave that body be," he commanded his men, "we have to find the Humvee."

They didn't have to walk far before they found the wreckage. It had torn through the treetops and landed nose first at the bottom of a Ponderosa Pine. The twisted hunk of sheet metal looked like it had been tortured, the doors were all sprung open and the windows were popped out. Shards of glass littered the area, but there were no bodies inside, nor was there any blood. He frantically searched for his briefcase; he even ripped out the rear bench seat. He stuck his arm under each front seat, searching, searching, to no avail. His only mental relief came from the fact that, he knew Ray didn't lie to him after all, and that one doesn't have to be a rocket scientist to figure out that nobody was in the Humvee when it went over the cliff. Then he looked up and thought, 'they gotta be up there, or did they give him the slip last night.' Then a freezing chill penetrated his body like a ghost and made him shiver as he thought, 'who the fuck is that guy anyway.' 'Whoever he is, he's going to be one dead motherfucker,' he promised himself. With that thought, the shiver came back, this time it was a gut wrenching, six feet under cold malady, and if he didn't get his books back he might as well get used to the hyperbole.

Then his phone rang. The other Hunters had checked into the Eagle Lake Resort. They were aiming to get some shut eye after their long drive but called Jeffery to let him know they were in town.

"Damn it! I need you guys now," was Jeffery's frenzied opinion. "Ray is dead, and so are Randall and Curt. That crazy fuck destroyed the animal shelter last night. He totaled two of my Humvees and he's got my books!" Jeffery was all bent out of shape. Lawrence and Richard were tired. Lawrence, the Holy Hunter wanted to sleep first. Richard wouldn't let him. "Come on, let's go." He said. "A real sporty, sport hunt is on. We got to hunt this guy down. It'll be fun."

Jeffery broke in again, "I need somebody to take his crew up the ski resort road, that's where he attack us last night. I thought they drove off the cliff last night but their bodies aren't here. So they might be hiking up there and the road is the only way out. I need the other crew down here to help search the woods for them."

"Them?" Richard asked.

"Yes them, they're two snooping reporters. The guy busted his bitch out of the warehouse. Didn't Mr. DeVour tell you?"

"No, he didn't fill us in with all the details. He just said to get up here because you might need our help," Richard explained.

"You better believe I need your help. Now get your ass's down here," Jeffery demanded. "OK, we'll be right there," Richard confirmed. That was that, the Holy Hunter decided to take his crew up the ski resort road. He had no intention of marching through the woods, which was fine with Richard. He had some kind of fantasy about wild game hunting for real, for a long time. And just because he was hunting humans made no difference to him. He just wanted to kill something.

Paul Dupree and his van full of techno-wizards had gotten an earful. Paul had discovered Marie's mountain bikes earlier, and knew that was how they got up there. He was glad to hear that Marie was not in the wreck, and he was especially glad that they seem to have some books that Cal-Con Health want back desperately.

They decided to proceed up the road to the ski resort, not wanting to give up their strategic position. They calculated they could set up their headquarters at the ski lodge indiscreetly. If necessary, they could blend in as ski lodge employees.

They had to stop at the chain draped across the road. That was one obstacle they hadn't planned on. Being a super sleuth, Paul found the eyelet had been tampered with. On further inspection he concluded it had been recently cut, as file shavings glittered on the ground below.

He unhooked it and proceeded like Mick had done before him. They didn't get far when Paul spotted the rope dangling over the cliff. "Stop," he yelled. "See that?" He pointed to his discovery. "I'll get out here and have a look around." He grabbed a rifle and his binoculars, told his driver to proceed to the ski lodge and to maintain radio communications.

Then he trotted over by the rope to examine the area. Fresh tracks, one set of shoe prints larger than the other. Knowing it was them, he took out his binoculars to scan the area. Seeing no one. Plus not having the proper gear to repel down the rope but he saw a spot further down that looked like it could be navigated by foot.

He didn't think Mick or Marie would be climbing back up any time soon. Rather he figured they were headed back to the campground. He wanted the spy van to stay atop at the ski lodge to get better cell phone reception. So he reported to his staff and asked, "what time is the helicopter due to arrive?"

"Anytime, they had to stop in Susanville for refueling." His radioman reported.

"How many agents are with them?" Paul wanted to know. "Six in all."

"Direct two of them to rent cars and have the copter land at the ski lodge. On the way, be on the lookout for a RV with Indiana plates. The driver, Mickey Swift is to be arrested, he's wanted for murder. I'm going to track them on foot. I believe they may be returning to the Eagle Valley Campground, and they probably have a briefcase with incriminating evidence. I want it!"

"10-4."

Sometimes things are so obvious they are often over looked by the best of them. If the spy van would have driven around the back of the ski resort, instead of parking in front of it, they would have located an empty RV. He got his bearings from looking at the lake in the horizon. Then he jogged over to a spot where he was sure he would be able to climb down. Navigating the forest in the daylight is completely different from the night So he had no fear of getting lost this time. Over the side he went, the terrain was steep but manageable, soon he was deep into the forest below.

The Holy Hunter had parked on the ski lodge road with his crew above the cliff that the Humvee went over. While the Sport Hunter joined Jeffery below. They were arguing about wasting time looking for the briefcase there.

So they bickered about which way to proceed and settled with a guess that the briefcase may be further up. They headed in the right direction but were way to slow going on about it. Eventually they hacked and hiked another mile into the forest following the base of the cliffs and outcroppings.

Lawrence and his men had heavy eyes from the long drive and the easiest duty. They got sleepier with laziness. What started out with a couple blinks, and a decision to rest the eyes for five minutes was a fallacy. Tired eyes always lie, and his men soon joined in on the slumber.

The Hungry Hunter and the Sport Hunter traipsed through the woods until Richard spotted some eagles resting atop the branches of a dead tree. To break his boredom, he aimed at the eagle that was on the top branch. Then another eagle soaring above screeched a screech that set the birds to flight as the shot rang out. Missing his target, he quickly ejected the spent shell and started to fire wildly at the soaring glories. Cursing at his missed shots and grumbling about the brush under foot, he decided to climb back up to the road, as it wasn't that steep a climb in that area.

When Jeffery recognized what he was about to do, he called out, "don't do it."

His warning was ignored. Richard scampered up the incline with a short stair step type gait. The shots that he fired warned every hiker in the area plus the spy van parked in front of the ski lodge.

Paul Dupree would have snuck up on Marie and Mick in another minute as they were having an extra sensory experience by the spring. They both stared into the blue green sparkling spring and tasted the fruits. While their heavenly bodies were intertwined, they gazed into each other's eyes and saw heaven crystal clear. Birds were singing and there were radiant halos, feathery clouds, holy spirits, a snow-covered mountain peak, and a valley below. All these things were seen while they gazed into each other's eyes, until they heard that rudeness. That shot, that murdering rudeness of a shot. It was ear piercing, not natural at all, like an alarm clock. They gathered their things, and the briefcase. Then loping naked out in the forest, they darted between the trees like antelope. They moved so quickly not a prickly pear or pine needle could touch them. They cut their own path and Marie led the way. She had more experience and chose a roundabout uphill route. Mick had determination and he followed her scent.

Paul had to turn and face the direction the shots were fired from. He checked with, and reported to his counter parts, that shots were fired. They had nothing extra to report as far as cell phone traffic.

Paul carefully hid behind tree trunks as he inched his back. He thought he saw some movement in the distance. He darted to another tree for a better look. He saw three men looking up, no, now he saw there were four. Only one had a rifle. Why were they standing there looking up, he wondered. He ran to another tree on a more parallel route. He called his men again, "when is my back up due to arrive?"

"They'll be here soon. Keep out of sight until they do, or better yet, get out of there."

The Sport Hunter had made the climb to the top and looked down and scoffed at Jeffery. "There's nothing to the climb," he boasted.

Then he took a higher stance on an ancient volcanic bolder to get a better view. He looked around with rifle in hand. Then he pointed and screamed, "there he is."

He was pointing at Paul Dupree in the distance. Jeffery and his men readied their weapons, as Paul made a dash for the rappelling rope. There were a couple of big boulders he could take cover behind there. The Sport Hunter had the cross hairs of his rifle fixed on Paul's back and was about ready to pull the trigger when the first eagle swooped down and tore his talons into his forehead. Blood streamed from the cuts right into his eyes. He dropped his rifle and screamed. His scream was no match for the screech of the next eagle whose talons ripped into his head further. With blood gushing from his head now, he was disorientated. He turned around, he was slightly off balance and he tilted his head back to keep the blood out of his eyes, when the third eagle gouged his claw hook right into his eye sockets yanking out his life's light. Completely blind now, completely disoriented, he screamed a scream that was unrecognizable to human ears.

That was when one of the eagles feathers floated down and stuck to his bloody nose. He swiped wildly at it with his hand and his footing slipped. Down he tumbled. On the first bounce he broke his collar bone, and as he further tumble down on his trip to hell he broke a few more bones. Nobody knew for sure how many bones he broke that day but by the time he fell to the bottom near Jeffery's feet, he was still breathing. Only out of some mysterious mercy, the Sport Hunter expired.

The body guards were still staring at the lifeless body when a gunshot got their attention. Jeffery had fired off a round at Paul, that bullet went whizzing by his ear. At first he thought it was a pesky fly, then the reverb of the rifle got his full scampering attention. He ducked behind a boulder beneath the dangling rope. Protection wise they loomed large. Jeffery's bodyguards started their hooves clomping and took offensive positions behind trees. Bullets started flying in short order, Jeffery was sure he had his man pinned down and wasn't about to let him get away this time. Paul managed to scramble to one side of the boulder and popped up to fire off a couple rounds of ammo from his service revolver. That action was followed by more gunfire, the bullets were ricocheting off the rocks above Paul's head. He scrambled over to the other side of the boulder and squeezed off a few shots from his rifle. He saw the Hunter hiding behind a tree, he saw three other men in similar positions. But as soon as Paul ducked behind the boulder they advanced further into a more aggressive position.

Paul got on his radio and called his men for help, he was having a panic attack. "Mayday, mayday, officer under fire." He wasn't used to being shot at and he didn't like it one bit. He was a director, not a field hand, he wasn't supposed to be shot at. Beads of sweat gathered on his brow. 'Where's the helicopter,' he cursed. That wasn't the first time he's said that. He was an information officer waiting to bail out of Vietnam. He was on the top of the embassy building cursing, 'where's the helicopter.' He was scared for his life; the only reason he was there in the first place was because he learned the language in school. He was only supposed to do interrogations and that was all. His congressman father promised him when he accepted the position. Besides, it'll make me look good, his father said. But with bullets flying he wanted out. Then as now, he wanted out. His hands were shaking and didn't know if he could hit any target. He called on his radio again for backup.

The FBI helicopter had just flown over the chalet and landed next to the van. Four swat team members bailed out of the copter in a trot. They were all decked out in helmets and flak jackets. They piled into the van, which transported them to a favorable position above the cliff. When Paul knew they were in position he gave the order "shoot to kill."

Paul was hunkered down behind the boulders and the FBI swat team picked out their targets. Four shots to the head rang out almost simultaneously and the Hungry Hunter and his men were dead. The echoes in a ravine travel differently when trees absorb the sound. The shots that were fired from above traveled unobtrusively into the ears of the kids. Tommy, Robert, and Johnny had commandeered the shuttle bus unnoticed. They were in the warehouse loading it with boxes of Comfitine Vitamin pills. There were so many boxes it would have taken five semi-trucks to remove them all. But they were happy loading up what they could. It was Tommy however that had the foresight to raid the office too. He saw rifles on a rack. He grabbed them first. While he was stealing munitions he also saw a fanny pack and a camera on the desk. They looked familiar to him, and he took them too. But the shots stirred them to leave early, "let's get while the getting is good," Tommy said.

They were all giddy, laughing as they worked. But they weren't out of the woods yet. Tommy hadn't had much experience driving a bus, but he managed to zigzag his way down the road. Then when he passed the dorm he waved at the captive kids who gathered at the windows. They let out a cheer and that got the attention of the orderlies who witnessed the shuttle bus disappear past the Cal-Con Health building. Robert and Johnny had opened a case of pills. They tried to figure out how much money they would make by selling them. 48 bottles, times 100 pills, times 500 cases, times a dollar a pill, they laughed as they guessed. "What good is school anyway," Robert questioned with a smirk. Then Johnny laughed some more. Then they opened one of the bottles and took some pills for themselves as Tommy drove.

The orderlies were on the phone to Cal-Con Health security reporting the missing shuttle bus. The security guard at the front desk was the only one on duty and couldn't do anything about it but call his supervisor. He in turn reported it to the sheriff's office and then reported the situation to the Great White Hunter. The other men that were in on the search for the briefcase gave up and retreated back to the animal shelter. They had heard the gunshots too and assumed the hunt was over.

The Holy Hunter was awaken by his cell phone. Mr. DeVour wanted to know what was going on. He said, 'he didn't know but would find out.'

"You had better," he was warned.

Two of the FBI agents took advantage of the rappelling rope and joined their boss below. The other agents stayed up top on the cliff and kept their weapons fixed on the victims, while the other agents proceeded cautiously to examine the remains.

The Holy Hunter had turned around and driven back to Cal-Con Health with his caravan of Humvees. There were two other teams of agents in their rent a cars following in close pursuit. The helicopter had taken off to join the agents at the Health center. The roadside agents were picked up by the spy van after it was confirmed that all the targets in the valley were dead. Then everyone was to meet as backup on the front lawn of Cal-Con Health Corporation.

The Holy Hunter was throwing a hissy fit after his arrest. "I'll have your badges," he swore at the agents. He was arrested for weapons violations and he was handcuffed, along with his men. They offered no resistance but were still considered suspects in the attempted murder of a Federal Agent.

"Your fucking nuts," Lawrence Marsi cursed when he found out the charges.

"Don't you know who I am?" He continued.

The arresting agent responded with, "no, I don't. And at the moment, don't care. I'm following orders and proper procedures. When this whole thing gets straightened out, then you can have your say meanwhile I suggest you close your flap trap, because you have the right to remain silent, anything you say can and will be used against you in a court of law."

Usually the Miranda warning will shut a suspect up, but not Lawrence; he always had pride in the fact that he could bullshit anyone out of everything.

"I'm going to sue the fuckin' shit out of you guys, and I want you off my property."

"So you own this corporation?" The agent asked.

"Yeah, I'm one of the CEO's, I'm Lawrence Marsi." His voice toned down some, now that he had the agent's undivided attention.

"Then Larry do you have a firearms owners identification card?" The agent caught him off guard already.

"Ah, no."

"Then who's guns are these?" The agent asked.

"Ah, maybe I should wait for my attorney," he said meekly.

The agent came right back with, "there was an APB put out on a black Humvee and you have two of them. Are they yours?"

"No, you blooming idiot! They belong to the company." He snapped back, and his real colors showed up in a hurry as the Holy Hunter was all kinds of flustered. Tthe fact that the FBI agent was making him look like a fool in front of his own company didn't help, plus the indignity of being in handcuffs was pissing him off to the max.

Then finally a supervisor exited the building and came over to inquire as to why his boss was arrested. The Holy Hunter was just put into the back of one of the rental cars until further support arrived.

"There must be some kind of mistake. I called the sheriff to report a stolen bus." The supervisor offered as explanation. The arresting agent responded with, "we're taking all necessary precautions to ensure our safety. Do you know anything about the men that were shooting at our agent?"

"No! Absolutely not, nobody from our company would do that." The supervisor retorted emphatically.

That was when Paul broke in on the radio. "We need to call in the coroner and our forensic evidence technicians. I'm coming in, over and out."

While the FBI were in a buzz of radio conferences Mick and Marie had saw their helicopter take off. They had made their roundabout way back to the RV and while descending the ski resort road, he noticed they had company as the chain had been disconnected from its post. They only stopped to fasten their bikes back on the RV. Marie had opened the briefcase and was studying the ledgers. She couldn't make heads or tails out of it, but it fascinated her just the same.

Mick had turned on route 44, a scenic route, not because it was the shortest route and not because it was scenic, he let his instincts be his guide. Some how he felt that no matter which way he turned, trouble was going to follow him. Least he knew, that he was following trouble, as that was the same course the kids took in their stolen bus.

CHAPTER 13

Tommy had gotten the hang of driving the bus. Robert and Johnny didn't care as they had opened a case of vitamins and sampled the goodies. They were useless as useless is, their heads were undulating with wobbly thoughts, and with the occasional bump in the road, they looked exactly like bobble head dolls.

Tommy had warned them not to take the pills but they argued,—'one won't hurt.' But they didn't stop at one, even though the first pill had taken full effect. Besides they felt the need to experiment so they could tell the customers what kind of high to expect.

Now Tommy was a little smarted than his partners as he had palmed his pills at breakfast time and he had weaned himself from the effects days before. He already went through a bout with the sweats and convulsions that came with the drug withdrawal. The only way he made it through was by focusing on his roses. He loved his flowers. So, he relented to their request, because they were arguing about where to go. Johnny wanted to go home to Phoenix. Robert just wanted to get high so he sided with Johnny. Portland was home to Tommy and since he was driving that's where they were going. Plus he knew the streets and the people that could off the drugs for him.

Further on down the road he wasn't a bit surprised that Robert woke up with stomach pains. He was crying like a baby. 'I'm hungry, oh—my stomach, I'm hungry, let's stop and get something to eat.' But Tommy had already stopped, he pulled off the scenic route at Crater Lake.

"You hungry Robert?" Tommy politely asked. "Yeah, I said," he snapped back.

"Have a vitamin until I find us so food."

"Good idea," he took two and got his buzz going again. These pills made him feel all warm and oozy. The stomach pains that made him feel like a voodoo doll were gone. Those weren't just pin pricks his stomach felt, the acid was eating away at its lining. Heartburn was nothing compared to the size of this ulcer. And now he was snoring again.

It sounded like profanity to Tommy. He got off the bus to check out the view of the lake. The snoring reminded him of his drunken father. His father would come home after a drunken stint and smack him around for the fun of it. He used the excuse, 'you're eating me out of house and home!' He also blamed him for his financial problems. It was never his own fault for losing his money gambling and drinking. It was always Tommy's fault no matter what. Sometimes he used to get beat for practice or so it seemed, because the old man couldn't think of a reason. That was until that one fateful day he was snoring in his recliner. This day his snoring was annoyingly loud. Tommy had been going through some growing spurts as most twelve year old's do. But this time the snoring was ringing in Tommy's stereophonic mind and he had a baseball bat in his hands. He imagined his father's head to be a cartoon alarm clock, just like the ones on TV. So he started to smash it. One strike, two strikes, three strikes, you're dead out.

He was glad that insentient, foul, rumble of a fart going backwards was finally silent. And he was glad to go to the juvenile detention center anything would be better than taking more beatings at home, going from one jail to another would be a relief, he thought.

What he didn't know was, one of the many side effects of the drug Comfitine was that with the normal breathing muscles relaxed, the soft palate vibrated when sleeping. But Tommy had his own room at the CalCon Health dorm as everyone else. So he didn't have to put up with anyone's personal noise. Now he has two useless companions and he wasn't going to put up with that useless racket.

He was the only sober one, and consciously pulled over in an isolated area, trying to be careful not to draw attention to himself or the shuttle bus. Then as looking over the cliffs at Crater Lake, he knew what he had to do.

Back at the bus he shook and woke up Robert, telling him it was time to eat. Robert's stomach had calmed down and he was no longer hungry. He was so used to taking orders, his conditioning led him to follow Tommy. He looked zombie like as Tommy led him to a cliff above the lake. His eyes were glazed over and he walked with a drunken wobble.

"Where are we?" Was the last thing he whined before Tommy led him right over to the edge of the cliff and gave him a little shove. He didn't even have the reflexes to scream as he fell. Tommy counted three bounces before he hit the water. As Tommy watched, he thought, one more "snort-bag" to dump and then he would have peace and quiet. And so it was that Johnny, in his myopic state, walked off the cliff in the very same fashion.

Lemmings, Tommy thought. They walked off the cliff just like lemmings. That thought made him laugh: but he didn't laugh long or hang around to gloat. He got behind the wheel and drove.

He hit the next town, Old Station, and had to pull over for gas. That was one problem he hadn't counted on. Plus he didn't have a dime to his name. He parked in the drivers rest lot. Panhandle the gas money, popped into his head first. Then he looked around for things to sell. He inventoried camera, fanny pack and an assortment of guns. Those he didn't want to sell.

He started to search through the fanny pack and spied a wallet. Upon opening, he found the bills, lots of them, 'eureka,' he thought. Now he had enough money for gas to get to Portland. Then he spotted Marie's driver's license. His heart fluttered for his rose lady. He just promised himself that he would return her property when her saw her riding in an RV, that pulled up to the pumps. He put the money and driver's license in his pocket but grabbed the camera and ran over to her by the gas pumps.

"Marie, Marie," he hollered out.

Somewhat startled, Marie turned around to look.

"Tommy?" She questioned her memory and spoke with surprise to see the gardener.

"I have your camera."

"You do?"

"See," he held it out for her to see.

"Were did you get it?" She asked inquisitively. "From the warehouse office."

Mick just looked on as he was busy getting a fill up.

"Why thank you Tommy," Marie said. "Would you like to join us for supper?"

"Sure would," he fired back. He was hungry after all but he would have accepted the invitation even if he wasn't, just to be with Marie.

Marie introduced Tommy to Mick and said, "Tommy returned my camera, wasn't that nice of him.—By the way—I asked him to join us for supper. You don't mind do you?"

"No, not at all, he deserves an award to." Mick reached in his pocket and gave Tommy a twenty. Marie gave Mick a 'that's not enough look,' that, he read and peeled off another twenty.

"Here ya go," Mick passed him the money. "Good deeds should be rewarded," he added. Marie sighed at the cheapster, she figured that, he didn't realize the pictures were worth more than the camera. She didn't want to make a big issue of it either, she would borrow a hundred from Mick and slip it to Tommy latter.

Marie walked Tommy over to the dinner as Mick parked the RV appropriately. She wanted to ask Tommy questions about the operation at Cal-Con Health and the Exotic Wildlife Sanctuary facility.

They all settled in a corner booth and ordered cheeseburgers with fries, before Marie started her interview. She started out with caring questions like, "where are you headed?" "Where are your folks?" "Do you have a place to stay?" Now that Tommy was relaxed, she was ready to hit him more intrusive questions about the business.

Tommy was a natural player, he learned the sucker sap look in reform school and mastered it on the streets. But he tried to tell Marie the truth, his responses were more like automatic half-truths. When he said, "Portland," that was true. When he said, "their dead," that was half true. His father was for sure, but he conveniently left out the part why. His mother might as well be dead for all he knew, as she walked out on them and the marriage a long time ago. He was sure he could stay at his older sisters house as they always got along, but then again he would have to find her. Most likely though, he figured to live on the streets until he got his thing going. He kindly left that plan out of his answers too.

After supper Marie started to ask about the animal shelter. Those answers he gave complete and was happy to do so. They made Marie smile and he was smitten in love with it. Mick he ignored completely as he was just an old fart as far as he was concerned. Besides he sat there like a boring old wart and Tommy bet his mind that he snores at night.

When she finished with the interview, Marie asked Tommy if he needed a ride, which he declined, saying, "he was going to take the bus."

Then she gave him her telephone number, made him promise to call her when he got to his sisters. She explained that she might need more information from him as she was mad at Cal-Con Health, and it sounded like they were breaking child labor laws. There for it was in his best interest to call her for if he is due any money's for his work, she would help get it for him.

"That sounds good to me," he said, but didn't mean it. He knew he would have enough money from the stolen drugs. All's he had to do was get to Portland, but what he really wanted was Marie.

When all was said and done, arrangements were made and she slipped him an extra hundred dollars. She made him promise to call her one more time and with that, Tommy left.

CHAPTER 14

To say the least, the Great White Hunter wasn't a happy CEO. Two of his fellow hunters were dead. The FBI were swarming his Exotic Wildlife Sanctuary facility and interrogating his employees at Cal-Con Health. What he wanted to know was what the FBI agents were doing in the forest in the first place. The fact was, his men were looking for a car thief that destroyed their property. Try to protect your property and get murdered, unbelievable, he thought.

In his shrewd calculating manner, he told Lawrence to cooperate fully with the investigation. But reminded the Holy Hunter not to let them search the property or contents without a search warrant. In other words, get rid of them as fast and as politely as you can. Blame them for the fiasco and if they as any inappropriate questions, kindly refer them to the corporate attorney.

After conferring with the corporate attorney about his own business, the sly Great White Hunter called his stockbroker and started to unload his formidable holdings. He had a feeling the gig was up, otherwise the FBI would have never been in the forest. He wasn't about to risk his personal fortune on a lost cause.

Figuring on the worst case scenario, the FBI were in possession of the books, best case, they were lost. Second worst, the reporters had them, and the FBI were going to get them next. Recovering them intact before they become news, improbable but not impossible. Racking ones brain with thoughts of doom does take a mental toll. He slapped his forehead with the palm of his hand, wondering how all his fine laid plans could disappear overnight. 'Fuckin' idiot's,' he blamed his own men. His brain rattle enough, he took out his frustration on his desk. Only stopping, when his hand pained him.

He did put out a finder's fee for the briefcase with the taxidermist who worked for Ray. Plus he was now in possession of the names of the reporters who registered at the campground, Mickey Swift and Marie Sweet. 'One nosey bitch and a bum leave eight of my best people dead, who the fuck are those motherfuckers anyway,' he was so pissed off at the revelation he slammed his fist into the desk one more time. Crack, aaahh, he cried, the pain raced through his brain. He had broken a bone for his pinky finger.

Pain or not, he started to count the men that were still alive and that he could trust. The Holy Hunter and his bodyguards, he wanted to stay at Cal-Con Health until the investigation wound down. Then he was going on an extended vacation, mainly to avoid any prosecution, civil or criminal, then to close down the phony off shore companies. When the employees and investors find out their stock is worthless, there may be additional hell to pay and he didn't want to be around for that either. Figuring the Holy Hunter is very good at that kind of bullshit, because he's the most diplomatic, he would leave him behind to handle that shit. Then he was going to leave behind two of his best bodyguards to hunt down the reporters, regardless if he gets his accounting ledgers back or not. Those two have hell to pay, as the Great White Hunter promised himself a long time ago, anyone who gets in his way is going to be eliminated, one way or another. He was in a sorry mental state of bankruptcy and he felt, the two people who desecrated his plans, would have to die for their crimes.

The FBI had concluded their interrogation of Lawrence Marsi and his bodyguards. They were cut loose, as there was no evidence to hold them. The forensic team had problems of their own. They spent the entire day going over the crime scenes and they weren't even close to completing their tasks. They did find various finger and foot prints that that belonged to the victims and various foot and finger prints that were unidentified. The strangest thing of all though were all the tiger tracks, they were everywhere. So when the lead technician reported to Paul his findings, he was put in a state of questioning shock.

"Are you sure?"

"Yes I'm sure, there's a trail of them starting at the cliff, over to the hole in the fence. They go to every animal cage, through the warehouse, back from the main gate and into the forest where they disappear. Then there's the Humvee tracks that lead back to the main road."

"That's impossible," Paul retorted.

Defending his findings, the forensic lab tech said, "no it's not, because those are the facts."

Paul was dumbfounded. "I saw the guy."

"What guy?" The lab tech questioned.

"Mickey Swift! He came up here with Marie. Paul exclaimed. "And where is this guy now?—What did you see him do?"

"I don't know but I'll find him."

To date, this exercise in spying hasn't worked out like Paul had imagined. First, the love of his life, picks up a phony phone sweet talking jock, silver tongue con artist, is more like it, Paul thought. All that rubbish about marriage and adopting children, raising a family, rubbish.

He laughed at that conversation the first time he heard it. He didn't think she was seriously considering such a ridiculous endeavor, especially with a stranger, some hick from Indiana. Ha, he laughed.

Fact was, Paul had Marie's phone bugged to keep track of her. Special equipment planted to oversee her every coming and going. Perks of his job, Paul rationalized. Then he picks the perfect scam to get her into CalCon Health. If he could only talk her into trading sex for information, then he would have it made, he thought. He would be assured of being director of the southwest territories and maybe director of the entire bureau. Then they would be happy, he thought. Then they would be the perfect couple.

He decided, to put the pressure on the phony phone con artist. He was sure he could get rid of him once he proves, that being with Marie would be fruitless and death defying.

Right now his main concern was gathering evidence against CalCon Health. If he's not careful about the way he gathers information, his unethical methods maybe exposed and lead to an acquittal. But he has a perfect batting average so far. Besides, his political clout complimented his prosecutions, and that was why he rose through the ranks with promotions so fast.

Now he's saddled with an attempted murder case with four deceased persons of little consequence. What he wanted was a financial wrong doing case. Now management is well aware that the FBI will be going over their business dealing with a fine toothcomb and they will not have the surprise advantage anymore. Financial crimes by CEO's being the toughest to prove without substantial evidence, at any rate, he knows he's got to get the accountants ledgers. From deciphering intercepted cell phone communications, he was sure Marie had them. And as soon as he gets them from her he can wrap things up on this end and he knew exactly where she was going.

Paul was wrong about that too. Mick and Marie had pulled into the city of Redding. Marie wanted to call her editor and fax him some vital material to back up her story. She was real excited that her editor was absolutely ecstatic with her story. But he made her go back for the follow up. He commended her for digging up the story about an American Corporation violating child labor laws and killing endangered species for sport. But he had a news flash that there was a firefight with FBI agents there and at least four people were killed. He explained that he was going to send a camera crew there and he wanted her to meet them there.

"This could be your big chance at the big time," he promised her. And he assured her he would inform the California department of child and family services about the child abuse.

And so it was, she finished faxing herself a copy of her story for her records and a list of all the off shore companies in the ledgers. She found that part of the ledgers most intriguing. Some of the counties listed she's never heard of and they seem to have done the most business with CalCon Health. That could be worth looking into further.

Mick saw her bat her longing lashes at him, and he knew he was turning around to get the complete story. At this point they were telepathically in sync, Marie had noticed to as Mick turned around and headed back without out instructions or complaint. Naturally she felt bad about wasting time but she was glad her man understood how important the story was to her and their future.

"My editor is sending me a camera crew, they're going to meet us there." She offered as explanation, even though none was necessary.

"I'll get to report my story on TV.—And there's more, we missed the firefight between the FBI agents and the Hunters. Four of the Hunters are dead, is my understanding. Dead people make bigger headlines than child or animal abuse. That's the pecking order of the news business."

"Then let's get the complete story. For sure you'll be the prettiest anchor woman on TV," Mick said.

Marie blushed some and said, "thanks."

By the time they got there, media crews were swarming the street in a frenzy. Nobody was allowed on the property as the Cal-Con Heath security force blocked off the road. The FBI had the crime scene at Exotic Wildlife Sanctuary blocked off with police line tape.

Marie's camera crew flew up from LA in a helicopter and landed in a field directly across from the lab. The road was lined with trucks, cars and vans from competing media stations. It was very chaotic at the entrance road, as camera crews were vying for the best positions. Poised to pounce on anyone with information, dare they try to leave without giving up some tidbits.

Mick stood in the background as Marie gathered her crew for an intro report. She posed with the Cal-Con Health building strategically focused in the background. Once finished she went to Mick and explained, "I'm going for some aerial shots. Might as well take advantage of the helicopter since it's already here."

She gave him a quick kiss and said, "I'll be right back."

When they were all aboard and the whirly birds rotors started, Mick saw Marie wave and smile, he waved back but couldn't smile. Something bit at his heart, a gnawing bite. The copter was airborne now and Marie's face was out of site.

Then the thought, 'what if the helicopter crashes,' crept into mind, along with the nausea in his stomach. Why did he feel so ill all of the sudden, he wondered. He held his gut and stumbled like a drunk to the RV. He planned on laying down for a minute. When he got there he saw the bottle of wine with the spring water. He took a sip to settle his queasy stomach. Then he took two gulps two satisfy his thirst. Then he went to lay down on their bed. A power nap was all he wanted. Then when Marie returned to him, he would be ready for her, he thought. Actually Marie was the only one who could make him feel better. He rolled over into the fetal position and slept.

But that's when he saw himself running the bases on a baseball diamond. He had just hit the baseball and his team was cheering him on to run. All his childhood friends were there. The ball was still in the air as he rounded first, and the fielders were chasing after it. And so he ran, by the time he stepped on second he noticed a shoelace on his PF Fliers had come undone and the leftfielder had retrieved the baseball.

"Run Mickey run," was what he heard and that's what he did. By the time he reached third base his other shoelace came loose but he tagged the base and headed for home. The left fielder had thrown the ball to the shortstop, the relay man.

The race for home was on. "Run Mickey, run!" The shortstop had thrown the ball to the catcher. But Mickey was almost home when one of his gym shoes came completely off, then the other fell off too. There was this big kid in a catcher's mask blocking the plate and he was ready to catch the ball and did. The throw was high and Mickey slid under him, kicking up a cloud of dust in the process.

The umpire stood there and looked for what seemed to be an eternity. "Safe!" He called out. "Safe at home." Mickey's home run had broken a tied game.

"We won, we won!" His teammates now cheered. Mickey was so proud that he helped his team win. One of his teammates picked up his shoes and handed them over. Mickey stood there at the plate dusting off his pants, as his other teammates circled around him cheering, "speech, speech!" Mick was so happy he didn't want the moment to end. "Speech, speech," came the request again, but in his moment of excitement and glory all he could think of to say was some quotes he learned at school. "There's nothing to fear but fear itself," a giant cheer rose from everyone, even the players from the loosing team chimed in. "Hooray, hooray." So then Mickey repeated another quote, "ask not what your country can do for you, ask what you can do for your country." They even cheered louder this time and clapped too.

Mickey wished his father could see him in all his glory. He had passed on naturally the previous year. That is why Mickey started to think about the fathers of the country when he said, "most of all I would like to thank the fathers of our country, they guaranteed me the right to speak freely here today, and I would like to thank them for giving me my other rights too. For without them I would not have been able to hit this home run today. And remember you don't know what you have until it's gone."

The crowd was in an uproar with cheers and applause, while some adults were dumbfounded by the profound comments coming from a child.

Mickey put his shoes back on and laced them good and tight. He kept on smiling until the last of the cheers died out. His pals took turns patting him on the back as everyone prepared to go home. Mickey put his baseball mitt in the basket on his bike. Now he remembered his mother had asked him to buy some milk on his way home. Jumping on his bike, chest full of pride from hitting the game winning home run, he peddled like the wind, faster and faster he went. He couldn't wait to get home to tell his mother all about the homer. He looked down at his shoes to make sure his laces didn't come undone, he didn't want them to get caught in the chain, and he didn't want anything else to trip him up.

So at the store he bought the gallon of milk and headed for home. But on the way he heard a distress cry from a cat. He stopped his bike and looked in a box on the side of the road. That was when he witnessed kits being born.

He was mesmerized by the whole affair. One by one they were being born, as the mother cat cried out in glory or hunger. Mickey didn't know which, or what to do. Then he thought about cats liking milk, he found an old hub cap on the side of the road and filled it with milk. He gave it to the mother cat and she lapped at the milk and meowed her thanks.

Then he got back on his bike and peddled down the road until he heard some yelps. It sounded like a dog was hurt. He got off his bike to investigate and found a mommy dog in her den. She had some brand-new pups too. They were all yelping as if they were hungry. So he figured, if cats like milk so will dogs. Beside a pile of dirt was a bottom of an old clay flower pot. He dumped out the dirt—keeping back some to plug the drain hole—and then filled it with milk. He watched the mother dog lick the milk up and she barked out her thanks.

Then he got back on his bike started to head home, but looking into the basket he noticed that all the milk was gone. Not wanting to disappoint his mother and not wanting for her to be mad at him, he decided to ride out to the forest preserve and fill the jug with mineral water. Everyone loves mineral water he reasoned. So away he went, he peddled his bike as fast as he could. When he got there he filled up the gallon milk jug and headed home.

The sun had set by this time and his mother was terribly upset. She thought something happened to her son. She was frantic with worry. She even called the police. "My son is missing," she told them, "he should have been home hours ago."

"Sorry ma'am, there's nothing we can do now," the police told her. "Give us a call tomorrow if he doesn't show up. Then you can fill out a missing person's report."

She took a seat on the front stoop and cried her eyes out with worry.

She looked up and down the street, waiting, crying, praying; then Mickey finally turned the corner racing like a bolt of lightning. His mother was so thrilled to see him again, she gave him the biggest hug he ever had. She didn't even bother to scold him, and when she found out what he did with the milk, she smother hugged him again.

"Mick, Mick wake up, Marie was now besides the bed hugging him. "I did it! I did it! I got my first TV spot. I'll be prime time. Oh, I'm so excited. Thank you, thank you." She was piling kisses on him when she noticed all the dirt on his face and pants. Then she realized why one of the bikes was off the rack and leaning against the RV. She assumed he was bike riding while she was touring in the helicopter.

"I think you need a shower," she said as she playfully undid his jeans.

Mick got the hint in a flash and was in the washroom faster than lightning. He was refreshed alright, and he had energy to burn. Marie had barely put out fresh sheets before they were wrapped up in them.

"I missed you," he said as he kissed her.

She felt his strength heather up inside. "I guess you did," she gladly replied. "I love you," he said.

"I love you too," she returned.

His body stirred time and again. Marie gladly welcomed him. Never before has she experienced something so healthy and natural. She had numerous urges to fulfill and they were all met. She had orgasms that were fantastic, and now she was feeling a little guilty about enjoying them so. Finally she had to beg Mick to stop, he was turning her into putty and her mind was spinning faster than a pottery wheel.

Besides that, they were still parked on the side of the road and there was an incessant amount of distracting noise. All the sirens and horns blaring, she hoped to pick up where they left off that night. In a remote spot, more romantic perhaps, with candle light, wine and song, "save some for later," she meekly suggested; as she parked the memory in bank #8.

She hurriedly dressed, as the outside noise became more obtrusive. Not that there was more or less before, in fact she was just enjoying herself so, she was more oblivious to it during their passion. Her stations helicopter had already taken off and she was mindful of the long trip home. She was also aware that her job wasn't finished there, what happens to the children concerns her. And she had planned on following up on that story. On her way outside to return the bike to the rack she saw a gallon jug sitting on the counter. The label said milk, but it looked like water. She stared at it a little closer because she thought she saw something in it, blue green crystals to be exact.

"Mick," she hollered out. "Yeah," he answered.

"Where did you get the water?"

"What water?"

"The water in this gallon milk jug."

"Oh,—I don't know."

"Well it looks like that spring water.

Mick took a long look himself and said, "your right it does." Not knowing how to explain the oddity, he confessed, he got it. But he didn't remember doing so, but then again he did remember something; a surreal dream, and it was a pleasant one at that.

CHAPTER 15

Tommy had made it to Portland alright. He hit the old haunts first. He was looking for his old buddies under the viaducts near the downtown exits. 'Those were the days,' he thought. Rooting through the trash bins, looking for perfectly good food that was thrown out on a daily basis. On a good night they would get pizza, on a bad night they would phone in fake orders until the pizza joint pitched out their extras.

But his old buddies were gone. He found out his old partners were in the juvenile detention center on drug, or misdemeanor theft charges. Or they were just gone, like he was, and nobody knows where they went. Just the same, the new group of kids took over his old territory. They were a likable group and Tommy made friends with them fast.

Same old stories though, parents kicked them out for one reason or another. Or the parents were drunks and abusive, some were just plain runaways. The gothic look was in and parents just hated their makeup and piercing jewelry. 'To hell with them,' the kids said to a man.

Tommy was wise to all the old hustles and slackers. He had money making propositions for them all, but he was very selective on who he was going to let work for him. He let them all try the pills he was pushing and he was an instant hit. Some described the high as being better than ecstasy. At five dollars a pill he would front the chosen ones enough to get started. Tommy was boss, they all agreed. The city was divided into districts, 'very professional,' Tommy thought. They would split the profits but Tommy knew that if he had ten guy working the park and the gin joints they weren't even old enough to go in, he would make out like a champ.

After one night he had more than enough money to get a motel room. After the second night he rented a storage locker. That is where he off loaded his goods. Then he dumped the shuttle bus in a parking lot at the airport. He figured it would sit there for a month before the cops ever get wise to its presence. Meanwhile he bought himself a 4x4 pickup. That would allow him to do some gardening by day and drug dealing at night.

There was one thing that haunted him though, and that was Marie's face. He saw her on TV, the late night news. He went out and bought a picture frame and inserted her driver's license in it and placed it on the nightstand next to his bed. He saw her report on the Exotic Wildlife Sanctuary and the dead Hunters. But he didn't understand all that bit about the FBI acting in self- defense. He was just glad there was no mention of him or the stolen dope. One thing he did realize was that if he needed more dope, it might be a lot harder to get next time. But as soon as he got enough people hooked, he was going to double the price on what he had.

That was the least of his concerns. He was also thinking, he might not need any more dope if he could have a girl like Marie. Her smile was in his dreams, her smile was like the flowers he tended, beautiful. The only drawback was that guy she was with, "that cheap old fart," he thought. One thing he knew for sure, "that guy snores."

Paperwork, paperwork, paperwork in triplicate: that was Paul Dupree's job now. Then there were the inquiries, internal briefings, and the hush, hush of the political spin. Justifiable homicide, self-defense, why the Hunters were firing at a federal agent who identified himself as such, is unknown.

The audio tape recordings of the cell phone conversations were labeled classified information. None of it was made public nor was the reason why the FBI was there. Freedom of information papers were filed, that was a confidential investigation so none were answered.

Internally there were questions about the accountant's ledgers and briefcase, because of the audio tapes. Teams of agents combed the woods, and both crash sites, nothing. They don't like to come up empty. So Paul convinced them they were irrelevant to the case at hand, if they ever existed at all.

Paul still wanted the books though and he called Marie, first to congratulate her on her story, then to inquire about the lost briefcase. She politely denied knowing anything about a lost briefcase. He thought she was lying to him, but wasn't exactly sure. On the grand scale of things, it didn't matter, the financial investigation of Cal-Con Health were proceeding on schedule. Further if he did receive stolen material, there might be more questions than he care to answer. But there were more questions he wanted to ask, like how did he do it? How did he get away without leaving any evidence? And who the fuck is Mickey Swift?

He should be in jail already with a murder or manslaughter charge wringing his neck. Why couldn't forensics find evidence of him being there is what Paul couldn't figure out. He desperately wanted him out of the picture with Marie so he already had put out tracers on him but came up empty, nothing, blank, nada. He was bound to dig up some dirt on him sooner or later. So he used his political contacts to press for an IRS audit. That threat has worked before and is likely to work again.

Truth be told, Paul was in agony, he couldn't stand for Marie to be with another man. "When will she see the light?" he often asked himself. "I'm the only man for her" was a phrase that stuck in his head like an old scratched album. Only this needle would skip mercilessly: titch, I'm the only one for her, titch, I'm the only one for her, titch, I'm the only one for her—titch, titch, titch. His mind was mumbling thoughts again, "she's my girl, she's my girl".

At times he thought he was going to explode. Then he would calm himself down with some deep breaths and stick his nose back into his work. Working long hours with lots of paperwork used to do the trick for him. But that was when Marie was his. They used to have so much fun together, dine dance and romance. 'Doesn't she realize I can make or break her, we can be king and queen, media darlings,' he thought. Now it didn't seem to matter what piece of paper he was looking at, be it a wanted poster or crime report, now the same thing would pop up like unwanted computer ads, 'who the fuck is that guy,' titch, titch.

CHAPTER 16

The Holy Hunter couldn't have gotten back to the LA offices quick enough. Not only did he have to use every ounce of his wits to stand up to the FBI, then he had to pacify all the questions by his lab scientists and managers.

The Great White Hunter had flooded the stock market when he put up his ten million shares for sale. The brokers took notice as the value dropped. The brokerage houses followed suit, dumping their holdings. Then the story hit the news wires about the gun battle with FBI agents, and the stock prices sunk like rock on water. The Holy Hunter was holding that rock as he returned to his offices only to find Terrance DeVour had left, urgent overseas business was his excuse.

'Keep the ship afloat,' were the words on his personal message board, 'will call in a day or two,' was the final insult. 'That fuck bailed out on me,' Lawrence thought correctly. He had the stock market report on the office TV and it didn't look good. He had lost a fortune in a matter of days. 'What was he going to do now,' was the question he was asking himself. 'Hide in the office,' was the only immediate answer he thought of. He already told his secretary to hold all calls, especially from church groups and investors. He didn't want to talk to anyone except Terrance DeVour.

That's not the way it works though, there were lenders and mortgage holders to deal with. There were bankruptcy rumors. The SEC was starting its own investigation, and then there was the rest of the board members.

"Our accountant has met a tragic end. We need time to straighten things out," was his lame excuse. All the while he was preparing to sell off his stock holdings too. Even though the stock value dropped 95% in two days, 6 million of one is better than 6 million of none. He knew bankruptcy loomed too. He prepared a letter of resignation to present to the remainder of the board of directors. Not only did he want to sell his stock, he wanted a buyout package and his golden parachute.

In Sacramento the office for abused children had taken the remnants of their laborers and placed them in detention centers. Back in Eagle Lake, the scientists and lab technicians were complaining about their worthless 401K plans, and the towns people that relied on Cal-Con Health were reeling with worry about their main benefactor. Homes quickly went up for sale with no buyers. While the Great White Hunter was doing some prostitute in Calcutta. Silently he was laughing all the way to some Swiss bank.

There were many troubles brewing for Cal-Con Health and for every investor that sunk their life savings in the belief that they were going to discover the miracle pill that would solve every ones problems. The witches brew was boiling in the mind of the Holy Hunter. Slowly the steam whirled around in the empty chambers. He didn't even notice his trigger finger slowly and repeatedly pulling on the imaginary gun. He was thinking of more dastardly deeds, too many to count, too many to remember.

"It's a small world after all," he sang to himself. Then he'd change the verse to: "It's a small world, poisoned all." His reflex finger was pulling faster now. "It's a small world, exploded all."

The phone would ring and ring, but he was too busy, he was blankly looking out his office window, his finger twitching away. Outside he saw the hordes of reporters waiting to pounce on him with questions. That imaginary gun he was firing never runs out of bullets. That's why he saw himself surrounded by dead bodies. He had mowed down all the reporters with his machine finger. But he knew he was going to escape out the back door, he had to save his ammo, his poison, his explosives. He inhaled deeply, he could taste the aroma of gunpowder on his tongue, tch, tch.

Mick and Marie were peacefully enjoying one another's company at home. Her editor called and said she was a big hit and was preparing to make her an offer to do TV specials and various investigative reports. Things were looking rosy for Marie's career.

She had requested to go to Sacramento to interview the children from Cal- Con Health, but her request was denied. Their wards of the state now, it's a dead issue at this point, the editor had explained to her. Besides, there under age and not considered credible witnesses. Plus nobody really cares and whatever the outcome, it won't sell. She was kind of upset with the frivolous responses, but she was used to rejections and was tired of them as well.

Relax, she was told, take a couple days off and enjoy. He'll be getting back to her, he promised. So it was, the best way for Marie to relax was on her pottery wheel. She loves to while away time creating pottery. In solitude she could put her mind in a special place. Escape the rush, rush of daily life, forget money woes, writing deadlines, and boyfriend blues.

This time was different, as Mick was reading the newspaper at the kitchen table drinking his coffee. She looked at her man through the sliding glass patio door, 'what a lovely man,' she thought. As she looked at him, the sunlight reflected off the glass and penetrated her soul with a new wave of feelings.

It was more than that though, now she wanted to look at his proposals with a more serious light. She felt an unfamiliar combination of happiness and loneliness, a longing for more, the need to listen to the patter of little feet and the need to teach. She put her hand to her warmed heart and felt it palpitate.

Turning away she asked herself, 'what she was doing outside?' Oh yes, she momentarily experienced a lapse of direction. She then went to get a wedge of clay and tools out of the storage cabinet. She felt the need to create something this day.

With the garden hose she wet the clay and the sponges in her bucket. To remove air bubbles or soft lumps, she kneaded the clay. In automatic mode now, her skillful hands molded and folded the clay until she had a cone.

Carefully centering the cone on her pottery wheel, then she started to manicure it into shape. Taking care with every step, she dropped and opened up the hole. A cool slurry of clay oozed between her hands and fingers that gave her mother earth pleasure. After cleaning the bottom and skillfully centering the rim, she started to raise the wall. Then removing the excess clay and putting it into the recycle bucket.

Mick had taken a seat by the water fountain and had been watching her silently but studiously, for some time now.

"Oh, hi," Marie said upon discovering him. "You're quite the pro," Mick complimented. 'I've just started," she said.

She went about her business building the rim. Then she brought out her tools and sculpted some, giving the work a unique texture. Done with that she used a fine wire to cut the vase off the wheel and carefully slid the pot onto a prep board.

"Are you finished?" Mick asked.

"Oh no, I have to let it leather up so I can trim it. Then the kiln and glaze."

"Oh."

"Do you want to make one?"

"Oh no, I couldn't."

"Yes you can, come on. I have some extra clay right here. You can make a small one. I'll show you how."

"Oh, OK." Mick acted reluctant. But he really wanted to try it, so he was persuaded rather easily.

Marie gathered up some clay from the recycle bin and started to show Mick how to make it homogenous and knead it into a wedge for coning.

"This stuff is slick," Mick said upon discovering how working with clay feels. They were both dressed in jeans and T-shirts. Marie's clothes were already spattered with earth tones. Her hands were wet with slurry and arms covered with drying clay. Mick was getting the hang of working the wedge, pressing his palms into the clay and making the proper folds. He was also enjoying the experience, as he was, all smiles.

After he coned the shape, he plopped it down on the wheel. Marie helped him center it. Then she showed him how to drop the hole and made him do the rest.

"Now raise the wall," she said.

Marie was comfortable with Mick and this meant dressing down to earth too. So comfortable in fact, that she was braless this day. Mick had noticed before, but not like he was noticing now. She had to bend over to show him how to raise the wall. She took his hands in hers and taught him how to press the sidewalls. Mick's concentration had forsaken him for the sight. His foot slipped off the control pedal.

"No, keep the wheel going at a steady pace," Marie reminded him. "Not too fast and not to slow." The electric motor that drove the pottery wheel had a pedal that controlled the speed of the spinning table. But Mick had a hard time controlling his eyes along with everything else with Marie's beauties dangling in front of his face. It wasn't that he hadn't seen them before, it was something about the way they gently swayed with her every move.

His eyes weren't the only thing he had a hard time controlling. His tool was painfully hard as it expanded against his jeans. Unwillingly his foot pressed harder on the pedal sending slurry spattering in every direction. Now part of the sidewall had collapsed and the clay would have to be reworked.

Marie was about ready to scold him for not being careful but noticed his bulge instead. She reached for the garden hose and sprayed him with water playfully.

"Hey," Mick cried out in protest.

"Cool off big guy," she said with a laughing smile.

Mick had to stand up now and was dripping with water and laughter. He put his earthen hands out to cup Marie's face, and he kissed her. He left his hand prints on her cheeks, and no amount of water was going to wash away his desire for her. After the kiss he removed his T-shirt in one fell swoop exposing his chest.

Marie's hands still full of clay, began to glide them over his chest, then she returned his kiss with passion. She ran her slick fingers all over his muscular back. The slick slurry made them both feel sensual. Marie stepped back for a moment to remove her top. Then Mick artistically arranged for her breasts to be glowing in earth tones as she arched her back in an inviting posture. He grabbed some extra clay and played like he could permanently cast those pointy nipples.

Marie undid his belt buckle and dropped his jeans. She wanted his manhood to spring freely. 'What's slurry good for the goose is slurry good for the gander,' Marie thought. He completed the thought by kicking off his sandals and stepping out of his jeans.

"Hmm," Marie started eyeing him with an artist's flair. Mick's perfectly sculpted body gave her an idea. She grabbed some extra clay and started to form a mold around his erection. The both of them were laughing and tried their best not to crack up completely.

"You look like a roman statue," Marie said. Then she twisted and removed his mold.

"What are you going to do with that?" He had to ask. "You'll see, when I finish."

She set the mold aside and grabbed the hose to wash him off a little but Mick had other ideas. Soon their slick bodies were interlocked in slippery motions, and they were rolling in the grass besides the water fountain. Chests gliding over each other, souls penetrated in passion. Twisting, turning gyrations, sweat and earth intertwined with the sun's rays beaming down melding natures beauty.

Mick and Marie were in the mind's eye, Garden of Eden. She inhaled the scents of earth and flowers; looking up seeing iridescent blue green throat feathers of hummingbirds shimmering in the light of the sun. She felt the breeze of their wings hum. Butterflies fluttered the passion in her groin. Thinking she was in heaven she looked at her man and realized paradise was with him.

When Mick retreated from her she laid listless basking in the sun, the once moist clay dried quickly into a cake. She felt revitalized, like new skin was growing under the clay flakes. He was lying right beside her enjoying the same hearth felt pleasures.

He was spent from all his exertion, he was breathing deeply to regain his strength. He enjoyed the feeling of clay drying on his skin too. But it was Marie who made him feel like he was the Michelangelo's David, nature's purest form of art on a pedestal, proudly displayed, for eternity. Peaceful bliss they shared that day as they lay naked basking in the sun until the screech of an eagle stirred them as the animal circled high above.

Marie stood first, "come on Mick we had better go in." She grabbed the garden hose and washed the dried clay away, Mick stood there smiling while marveling at her gorgeousness. When it was his turn she playfully turned the nozzle to full blast.

"Hey," he protested.

So they shared another laugh and she notched the nozzle back to a reasonable force. Then she maneuvered the nozzle in an up and down motion like she was washing a car, while he spun around.

"We still need a shower, before you join me though, I'd appreciate it if you would spray the patio down for me." She handed him the hose and gathered their clothes.

"Aren't you going to finish your creation," he called out to her.

"Later," she said, but immediately filed today's love theme in memory bank

\# 9. Tossing the soiled laundry in a hamper, she continued on in a glowing, naked, exuberance to her laptop. A poem was about to be born.

Beside the love and exhilaration they shared, the two of them had already created a living work of art that day.

CHAPTER 17

In Portland, things were going good. Tommy had his system down lower than a base drum. Cash, he was running out of places to stash it. Moneyed now, he had more friends than he could count. He was indifference to most, except a couple kids named Squirrel and Chucky. Squirrel was a skinny little kid with buckteeth, hence his nickname. He was caught in an alley once and beat up by some older teens for the fun of it. Now he runs everywhere.

Squirrel hangs with Chucky, who's large for his age, partially for protection and camaraderie. They were best buddies before they hooked up with Tommy.

The three of them would be walking down the street and bling, bling Squirrel would run up to the corner, look both ways in his jittery way, and run back to report the coast was clear. At first Tommy thought he was looking for the cops. But in fact, he was looking for the bullies that beat him up. That was a dirty fighting gang of mean kids. Squirrel wanted no part of them day or night, body guard buddies or not. The Black Knights gang wasn't to be messed with. They had guns and knives, and didn't want any other gangs on their turf.

Tommy wasn't afraid of anything like that though. He had his own guns. He did enjoy Squirrel's and Chuck's company, they treated him like a king. Squirrel was especially helpful, he knew more things about the neighborhood people than anybody and was an eager informant.

One thing Tommy liked about Portland was the abundance of flowers, roses especially. Portland's climate does wonders for the native flora. With daily sprinkles, one never had to worry about watering the roses. Dust for bugs, fertilize periodically and pick the weeds, mostly pick the weeds. Then sit back and enjoy the aroma and beauty.

He had hooked up with a garden center that he used to work for. Earning extra money pushing broom was a thrill for him before. Learning the business as he went. Was his bonus. This time was different. He no longer did the work for just the money. He did it for solitude, him and his roses.

Once Squirrel and Chucky found out what Tommy did during the day, they constantly bugged him asking if they could help. He always said he didn't need any until one day he had a big work order and to get them off his back, he relented. He had away about him that made the job sound easy. Squirrel was to mow the lawn and spread the fertilizer. Chucky was to help him lay down a brick walkway.

On the way to the job site, which was in northwest Portland, they stopped off for coffee and donuts. The kids were excited about going to their first real job and were light hearted and happy. All were laughing and joking about how fast they were going to knock out the job and then go to the waterslide amusement park.

Pulling up to a nineteenth century home, Squirrels eyes bugged out at the enormity of the lawn. Chucky did likewise when he saw the size of the pathway. Mansions have fountains, and the pathway encircled a weather machine sculpture. The task at hand required removing flagstones. If one measured them by how far Chuck's jaw dropped opened, you could see they were some rather large flagstones.

The first thing they yanked off the pickup truck was the lawnmower. It was a newer model with drive wheels. Tommy primed and started it, then gave Squirrel instructions on how to use the levers. The grass was long and heavy with dew, he got about five feet before it stalled the first time. Tommy made him restart it and threw in a few tips like, 'don't try to go to fast.'

He and Chucky grabbed some shovels and the wheel barrel. Both attacked their chores whole heartily. Squirrel struggled mightily with the grass. He swore it was made out of Brillo pads. Chucky thought he used to have big muscles until he started wrestling with flagstones. Now that he was a real life Fred Flintstone, he found out there was nothing to yabba dub a du about operating a wheel barrel full of rocks was either.

All in all they were half finished by noon. Squirrel complained that his arms were ready to fall off and Chucky said his back was killing him. Tommy laughed at them and teasingly called them pussies, but let them take a break. They laid flat out on their backs under the shade of a tree while he ran to the store for cold pops and snacks.

In the heat of the afternoon they convened with their chores and the devil. Cursing at themselves, mostly for begging to get this gig and their blisters secondly because they hurt. Tommy had worked at a steady pace and was actually enjoying himself. Of course he was in better shape and used to the strenuous labor. His friends were steely in their desire to do well, so they carried on despite the pain.

At day's end they were too exhausted to go to any amusement park. Tommy had split the pay evenly with them. They had already graduated from sleeping under the viaduct to sharing a room with a real bathtub and they planned to use it.

On the ride home, they did chide Tommy about working so hard when he could make a living selling drugs. They were satisfied with their pay, but they were looking at the blisters on their hands when they bowed out of future ventures.

Tommy just laughed while lecturing them, "hard work makes the man." Then he added a half confession, "I used to know some guy's that died because they did drugs."

Then he laughed in a spooky kind of way. Squirrel and Chucky silently looked bewildered at each other, like they didn't understand where he was coming from. He dropped them off at their motel room and told them to meet him at the pizza parlor latter. He was buying.

Tommy needed a bath too. That had become his routine now, especially before a night of hawking drugs. When he got to his room, he went right over to the framed driver's license and gave Marie a kiss before he readied himself. The nightstand was beginning to take on a form of its own. There were scented candles and small vases with roses arranged in an adoring manner. The fact of the matter was, the picture on the driver's license was dwarfed by the shrine. He had plans for getting a larger picture but at the moment he didn't have the time or the wherewithal.

Tommy was already seated in the corner booth when Squirrel and Chucky arrived. Squirrel wasn't his normal jittery self and Chucky lumbered along slower than usual. Both had glazed over eyes and weakly plopped themselves down in the booth. They had taken Comfitine to relieve the pain in their sore muscles.

Tommy admonished them immediately for using his product. That was kind of hypocritical because he had let them experiment with it before. Never the less, he didn't want them coming to meetings high.

"Didn't you guy's learn anything today?" He asked with a disappointed tone.

"Yeah, your trying to kill us," Chucky mumbled with an attitude. That comment was uncalled for but he was not his usual self. He was exhausted and cranky because of it.

"We just took one, to take the edge off," Squirrel explained. "You kicked our asses today,—every bone in our bodies ache," he further justified.

"That's cause you guy's ain't in shape. I need guys who are straight. You can't be in this business without your wits about you," Tommy scolded.

He was pissed off at his guy's but not that mad to get up and leave. Besides he had already ordered pizza, one for them and one to go for the homeless kids outside. Now that he could afford to buy pizza he was all for treating the kids that are now wearing the same shoes he used to.

Being looked up to like a father figure was a good feeling but the reality was like swallowing a double edge sword. Buying pizza for the homeless kids was a very good deed, but the ways and means of selling drugs to make it possible left a bad after taste. His sword-swallowing act was mentally alive and well, so much so at times he swore he could taste his own blood rushing down his slit throat.

Kids looked up to him because he had money and dope, but he didn't want the kids to be users and losers. He just wanted them to sell it to the disco drunks and party freaks. Junkies are going to be junkies no matter what, he figured and to justify what he was doing he had to lecture. Get his point across without sounding like a despised Sunday School Preacher was the tricky part. Somehow he was going to make them understand.

Tommy didn't understand the same thing preachers don't understand, some people welcome ruin. No matter what is done and said, no matter how hard the preacher tries some people are going to develop a mode of self-destruction that is impossible to stop. Double edge trick rules and laws will never stop people that need freedom to explore. They have to find out for themselves and condemnation for their actions only make matters worse.

Squirrel's eyes were bigger than his stomach. He thought he was so hungry that he was going to eat the whole thing by himself. He only had two pieces and was stuffed. Chucky was twice his size and had three pieces and was full. Not a normal thing for growing teens like Tommy had no trouble scarfing down the remainder.

While he was eating though, he went on and on with his lectures. The kids nodded their heads in agreement at everything he said. Then it happened, Squirrel and Chucky started to nod off. They couldn't help it, the combination drug, food, boring talk and the lack of activity made their eyes heavy. Lack of oxygen in their blood made them look like zombies stuffed in church pews rather than teenagers living it up inside a pizza parlor.

Then one of them made a snorting noise. Tommy suspected it came from Chucky but it didn't matter. He slammed his hand down on the table with enough force to make them snap to. All the other patrons gave a glance over their way too, only to hear one more overt tongue lashing. "You dudes haven't heard a word I said have you?"

"Yeah, yeah—we heard you." They replied in unison. "We're just tired from working all day," Squirrel added. "Yeah, I think we better go home and crash," Chucky said. "What about our customers?" Tommy asked.

"They can wait," Squirrel said.

"No they can't. Never make customers wait," Tommy barked. "Give us a break will ya," Chucky said.

"Oh, you guys want a break? Then go home. I'll take care of business." Then to throw in a dig, he said, "I don't know why I thought you guys could handle this job in the first place." He grabbed the extra pizza and threw a twenty on the tab tray and walked off in a huff.

Squirrel and Chucky looked at each other and realized they had better follow him to apologize or they might lose their jobs. So they did. They walked like a couple of drunken sailors but they didn't have to stagger far. Tommy was out by the dumpster talking to some kids.

He was lecturing a new audience on the values of hard work, while they devoured the pizza. Squirrel and Chucky joined the group. The little walk they took did them a lot of good. It got their blood circulating again and fresh air in their lungs swept away their drowsiness. None-the-less, they were standing there shifting their weight from one foot to another trying to maintain their balance. They really weren't listening to what Tommy was saying either, their mental buzz had its grips and they felt no pain.

The kids realized Tommy was a righteous dude but he was also boring. Soon after the pizza was gone they all took off. That being done, Squirrel and Chucky said they were sorry and promised to never let it happen again. Being buddies again, Tommy excused them and told them to go home and sleep it off. He'll make the deliveries that night. It was really a matter of driving around to the local parks, collect what he's owed and dish out some more goodies. So it was, Tommy bade them farewell, see you tomorrow and all that. Jumped in his pickup and took off.

Squirrel and Chucky started their trek to the motel. It was only a two block walk but half way they had to pass under the viaduct they used to call home. There they used to use cardboard for mattresses and old clothes for blankets. Huddled between the steel beams atop the embankment they were protected from the elements and felt safe.

This night however, lurking between the pillars they walked upon four guys wearing black leather jackets with matching berets, they were the Black Knights. Squirrel was not his usual wile self and they were quickly surrounded. The area was not part of the Knights turf, never the less surprise was their tactic and revenge was their motive.

Heroin was the Black Knights business and usually didn't mess with the small stuff. But one of their members heard raves about this new designer drug on the street and copped a buzz. While he was under the influence of Comfitine he decided to get higher and shot up with some heroin too. The mixture was instantly fatal. Figuring the designer drug was behind the rash of OD deaths that was killing their best customers. The hookers and pimps were dropping in epidemic proportions and the word on the street was they were pushing dirty heroin. Now their only customers were the diehard junkies, the kind that never cared if they lived or died in the first place.

While pressing for the source of this designer drug, Squirrels name came up and now he was going down.

"Squirrelly," the leader of the pack said. "Fancy meeting you here." They pretended their meeting was coincidental. They had in fact been stalking the underpass for days now. "You got drugs for sale?—Well do you?" The pack leader was pressing.

Squirrel, didn't like the name Squirrelly, it carries rude connotations. He didn't like the guys laughing behind him either. He looked for a place to run but the prospects of getting away at this time looked dim.

"No, we don't have any drugs," he said.

He felt a shove from behind and stumbled forward into a waiting grasp.

Now, he was being held by an arm around his neck in a choke hold.

"Hey, leave him alone!" Chucky said, before being sucker-punched from behind. Before he could react to that, he was struck with a lead pipe. The blow to his head sent him stumbling sideways. Off balance, he crashed head first into the concrete embankment. He was unconscious now, as the two Black Knights rifled through his pockets.

Squirrel was helpless to protest as he was trying to gasp for air. Then he was punched in the gut, knocking all the air in his lungs out.

"Look at all the money this kid has," one of the robber's hollered out.

Upon further search they found some foil packets with pills in the elastic of his socks.

"Hey, look here. I thought you guys said you didn't have any drugs," the other robber said. Then he stood and showed Squirrel what he had in his hand.

"I'm only going to ask you one more time, where are the drugs?" The leader demanded.

Squirrel couldn't have answered if he wanted to; he was still in a chokehold and ready to pass out. His feet were off the ground and he was hanging on to an arm for dear life.

"I think this kid is dead," the robber who was still standing over Chucky said.

The leader wasted no time taking out and flashing his switchblade. Then he rammed it into Squirrel's chest. He was let go and dumped right on top of Chucky. Immediately the Black Knights took off running.

The police didn't find them until the next morning, after a unanimous tipster called 911. An ambulance was called for Chucky. He still had a pulse. The coroner was called for Squirrel, he expired during the night from a punctured lung and the loss of blood. The crime scene was sealed off for investigators. People had gathered to witness the action. But the crime scene had already been contaminated. Sometime during the early morning hours Chucky had unconsciously pushed Squirrel off himself. The sticky blood that had drained from Squirrel's lifeless body soaked his clothes and an irritating hard object was poking his arm.

His stupefied mind didn't allow him to realize what had happened to Squirrel. He didn't even realize he was living in a nightmare. That nightmare was just about to begin because the cops wanted to know why he killed

Squirrel. They figured it was over a drug dispute. The detectives have lots of experience in like situations, where one guy is so drugged up he kills his partner without realizing what he did or why, and then passes out.

First the police had to find out who the kids were and all they had to go on was a motel key they found in the victims pants pocket. The newspapers and camera crews were all over the scene making the cops jobs even more complicated. Dead homeless kids were always a pain for police to identify, especially if there were no personal IDs on them, which was true in this case.

The other methods of discovery were to look through files of pictures of reported missing children, if they were reported, and the final option being asking for public help.

While overlooking the crime scene, a detective muttered to the coroner, "They never had a chance to live."

The coroner had seen this too many times and he recognized the distraught face on the detective. Then he said, "Yeah, no matter how hard you train for the inevitable, each case makes the soul more callous. What a waste in a world full of it."

CHAPTER 18

Transportation of a stolen vehicle across state lines is a federal crime. The Portland police had located a stolen shuttle bus in the remote parking lot of the airport and the report lay's on Paul Dupree's desk. Among the files, there is another report from the California authorities stating there are children missing from the Cal-Con Health files. One Thomas Riggins, one Robert Dragert and one Jonathan Gates were reported missing with the bus.

Tactically using the Amber Alert System brought immediate results in finding two teens fitting the descriptions posted. They have yet to be positively identified, as they are deceased. Battered and or beaten, they were found by local authorities in various degrees of decomposition floating in Crater Lake. Autopsy reports were in progress.

Because the shuttle bus was discovered in the Portland area, Paul deduced that the survivor's name was Thomas Riggins, as that Portland was his last known legal address. Paul already had his hands full trying to the financial reports he needs from Cal-Con Health So he assigned an underling agent to investigate the tie ins regarding the kids and stolen bus.

Forensic science takes its own time and Paul was going to have to wait until all cases ran their respective courses. Meanwhile he was looking for ways to unload his workload, he had some spying to do; Marie spying to be exact, tch, tch, tch. Marie is mine, Marie is mine, is mine; he couldn't stand for her to be with another man.

Options were few for the Holy Hunter. Investors were calling for his head along with Terrance DeVour. However the Great White Hunter was conveniently out of the country and he had to handle all the complaints. He sat in his office chair staring out the window pondering his next move. With 90% of the labor force laid off, the Eagle Lake Lab was all but shuttered.

He still had to run the Health Insurance Division and his personal cash flow was at an all-time low. But he still had an ace up his sleeve with all the Comfitine pills warehoused at the now defunct Exotic Wildlife Sanctuary.

A clandestine operation was already underway. Arrangements were made with a top L.A. street gang to distribute a new designer drug named EPC. Some of the pills have already been moved to a warehouse and were now available for black market operations.

The pills were never thoroughly tested and it wasn't even a consideration to get FDA approval. What the four Hunters had planned was now going to be a one-man enrichment plan from here on out. It mattered little to him if the FBI were watching his every move or not. He had it figured out that if he got popped, he would become a government informant and rat out his onetime partner Terrance DeVour.

Not that he was going to be handling the day to day operations of the pill distribution network, his underlings were more than qualified to handle the dirty work, as they were hired right out of the penitentiary. Fact was, the first shipments of EPC were already scheduled for delivery.

The Great White Hunter had been sending memos in regards to the phony off shore companies he diligently closed, but for every one he closed, he opened up another. The design was to further complicate the money trail. He had stopped over in Greece for a shopping spree. He was in the market for a new yacht. They were treated royally by the ship builders and have been on several cruises in the Mediterranean Sea.

Having navigated a deal with a broker from Athens he chose a multimillion dollar craft that had all the amenities one could expect. It was going to be his floating office building and palatial residence. He had to wait for some special remodeling he wanted done. So how to occupy his free time was no problem, he had hunting on his mind.

The Great White Hunter had never been on an African Safari before, and that was going to be corrected. He had the thirst for blood again, it was his lust, part of his soul. Even while he was cruising with the entire Mediterranean in front of him he couldn't see the beauty in front of him. He only saw himself and a beast in front of his rifle-scope. Imagination caressed his nostrils, as the aroma of the sea was replaced by the smoke of a spent shell. The great beast was felled. His slaves rushed to drain the beast's blood for him. A silver chalice was filled and he drank the warm liquid while his servants bowed before him, the new king.

Satisfaction for him was down the Nile on the Serengeti Plains. In due course, arrangements were already made for the Great White Hunter to go on safari. But for now it was one more night in port, then they would take a chartered flight to Africa.

Tommy heard the news on the street before he ran out and bought a newspaper. Reading the newspaper was always a special event for him as he rarely does it. The circumstances in this case demanded it of him. He couldn't believe Chucky stabbed Squirrel like the police claim. Especially when the word on the street was, the Black Knights were seen hanging in the area.

The Portland Police were aware of that rumor too, but lacking eyewitnesses they were satisfied with what the evidence told them. One Charles Fogerty was being treated for a concussion and as soon as the doctors release him, murder charges will be filed and he will be tried as an adult.

The news hung heavy, like a tarp under a foot of snow, on Tommy. He was buried under the quilt of guilt. His bed was no sanctuary either. He laid there staring at the ceiling fan and his mind twirled full speed. Eyes closed or open, it mattered little. His visions were hemorrhaging psychedelics. A collage of faces, some were old, some were new, but they were all staring at him as they spun. Some were pointing fingers, some were laughing, other's frowned. No one cried, not even Tommy, he was tough, he was hardened by work, by life.

He saw blood and gore before, guns, knives, baseball bats and clubs. Those weren't the visions that made him sweat though. He saw his mother and father. She was complaining at him, his father was beating him and he was trying to avoid them both. Something came over Tommy; he crushed the roses in Marie's shrine in his bare hands. Thorns pierced his skin but he felt no pain. Perspiration dripped from his body like a rain cloud. His anxiety was intense, his muscles unusually tight. The visions kept coming; they were attacking in unrelenting intervals. He gasped for air while he trembled with chills. He was fatigued and desperate. Hour upon hour of restlessness caused him to search for a respite. He took a pill of Comfitine. The pill took hold fast, his weary eyes folded in exhaustion.

Complacency woke with Tommy as he readied himself for work. He beat a happy trail to the garden center, it was as if the previous torturous night never happened. But another unwanted hangover awaited him. The police were anxious to talk to him. The medical examiner's report was interesting enough to warrant further investigation. Both of the boy's blood tests revealed they were loaded with an unidentified barbiturate.

A different observation revealed blistered hands. So when Chucky was interrogated the night before when he regained consciousness, he revealed the source and their names, but nothing more. Except to say, he never killed anyone and that they were accosted by the Black Knights gang, but remembers little of it.

Armed with more information and a possible witness the police had to play out the hand. With their quarry cornered in the middle of the garden center they pounced with precise questions.

Cool, calm, Comfitined, and confronted, the detectives questions didn't faze Tommy. All his emotions were spent the other night and drained with the morning bath water. Now a river of Comfitine flowed in his veins and a steely reserve in his mind.

"Do you know Brian Post, also known as the Squirrel?" "Do you know Charles Fogerty?"

"Did they ever work for you?"

"How did their hands get all blistered?"

"Where were you Wednesday night?"

"Where did Brian and Charles get their drugs?"

"Do you know who the Black Knights are?"

He took his time deciphering and answering their questions, his thinking was running under a caution flag. But he answered all their questions like a master craftsman.

The cops were hoping Tommy would lie about one or more of the questions they already knew the answers too, so they could give him the third degree. Liars are easy to trip up and the police are very good at doing just that. The only question they didn't know the answer to was the one about the drugs. What kind were they or if they were illegal. They could have been chugging cough syrup or huffing glue for all they knew. But they always throw in the drug and alcohol questions for good measure, regardless if they went unanswered or lied too.

So then the police remixed and shuffled the same ol' questions to see if they could confuse him, they didn't succeed. Actually whenever they tried to twist a question, Tommy would straighten it out and answer the same way he did the first time. On and on they tried to trip him up with the owner looking on in the distance. Didn't matter to Tommy, he was holding a pat hand.

Finally the police tired, exasperated at the lack of success they warned Tommy not to leave town because they may have more questions for him later. 'Leave town,' was now planted in his brain and it sounded like a good idea. Problem was he still had a storage locker full of pills. To complicate or simplify matters was debatable as his boss fired him immediately after the police left. "Can't have the police scaring away my customers" was his rube. Didn't want any negative publicity brought on by employees was the reality.

Tommy took it in stride and bid his farewell. The reality was he was burning up inside with ideas. He had a different kind of logic, Marie logic and he was going to make his dreams come true, Marie true.

CHAPTER 19

"Let's go mountain climbing," Marie said.

They had finished breakfast and she had a case of cabin fever. Not exactly that, but she did have so extra energy to burn, waiting around for her editor to call with her next assignment was exasperating, she needed some action.

"You're not talking about Mt. Everest, are you?" Mick chided.

"No silly, there's plenty around here. I have a favorite spot right down Route 74."

"And what do we do when we get to the top of this mountain? Look down at the valley from where we came?"

She gave him a quizzing look as he answered his own stupid question.

"We could get a good close-up view of the valley, if we just stay at the bottom and save ourselves a lot of work," Mick teased on.

"Very funny."

Mick was wearing a wry smile that Marie had come to recognize. She used to have a hard time of telling if he was telling the truth, playing around, or if he was a bit neurotic. Now she sees right through him and his dry logic humor.

"Come on," she said. "It'll be good exercise."

Mick surrendered without a whimper, he knew he would follow her anywhere and Marie knew it too. So they loaded up the RV with her gear and headed on down the road. It was on the way when Mick confided in her that he didn't have any experience mountain climbing. She assured him that it's an easy climb and it's good to build stamina. For her, this exercise is fun, pure and simple. "Bring your camera with. I want to show you something," she said.

"Sure thing," Mick replied in agreement.

Soon enough they pulled into a parking area in the Blue Jay State Park and Marie shut off her cell phone. Then she removed the rings that adorned her fingers, one finger at a time in a ritualistic manner. She had a serious look about her, as if she was going through a mental transformation like an athlete readying oneself for the big score. Then she got the gear that they would be using together, while Mick filled his canteen with the spring water from Eagle Lake.

The beginning of the trail was well worn by other adventurers and it spidered off in a web of directions as they hiked. Mick started to wonder what he had got himself into as leg muscles started to heat up, in particular the front of his thighs. Then he thought of all the gear he was hauling made him feel like a pack mule and what was he going to do with an Ace Hardware store on top of a mountain.

Marie was already strapped into a harness and sounded a bit like a reindeer as the hooks and gadgets clinked together as she trudged ahead. The climb was getting steeper now and the boulders getting bigger. Erosion had erased any resemblance of a path and Mick was starting to look for an elevator button on the rock wall or a cave to crawl into. He hopelessly figured there must be an easier way to get to the top and he was looking for just that. At least his mental conniving kept the muscle pain away.

Marie merrily pressed on jingling as she went. Sure she would pause to see how Mick was doing and no matter how many times he mentally complained, he never spoke of, or let any discomfort show. Except she was curious as to why, twice now she saw him poke his finger at the side of boulders, as if there was some kind of button there.

They were better than half way up the mountain when they came upon a sheer cliff wall. It may have the Matterhorn for all Mick knew, he was no Spiderman and he wasn't even going to attempt to climb that thing. He put his mental foot down and took off his backpack, it landed with a thump at his feet. Then he parked his butt on a rock at the cliffs site staging area.

"See, I told you it was an easy climb," Marie was proud of her man and her smile confirmed it. He took a well-deserved drink of spring water from the canteen and passed it to Marie before he said, "no way are you going to get me on the side of that cliff!"

Not only did the cliff go straight up 100 feet, but there was also an overhang at the top. Indeed it did look impossible to climb to the untrained eye. Weather-eroded nooks and crannies made it a challenging, but far from impossible, climb. Any experienced mountaineer would see the cliff as a welcome mat. The cliff didn't even daunt Marie as she has danced on this cliff before, and that was her plan today.

"You don't have to. Sit here and take your pictures."

Indeed it was a very picturesque site. The sun glistened against the fortress; the shades and crevices gave it a personality, a formidable one. The wind and rain streaked the giant with facial features over the centuries and it called out to all mountaineers, 'climb me, climb me'.

Marie sat next to Mick while she rummaged through the backpack. They had been wearing regular hiking shoes, but now she pulled out a pair of tennis shoes. It was a special shoe with a sticky black sole and is popular among cliff climbers. She only packed the one pair and had no intention of letting Mick climb the cliff with her even if he wanted too.

She put on her climbing helmet. Then she pulled out an eccentric and wedged the opposing cams into a crevice. She hooked up the rope and carabiner attachments to her harness. She powdered her hands with chalk and slowly started her climb, stopping only to hammer in pitons and attaching more carabiners. Slacking out more rope, she climbed onward.

Mick looked on in awe of her bravery as she methodically crept away and up the cliff. He was so mesmerized by the whole affair, he almost forgot he was supposed to take pictures. He took out his telescopic lens for close ups. Soon enough she would be too far to get facial expressions and he didn't want all of the pictures looking like a flyspeck on a humungous wall.

Marie was in her element now and was about ready to start her cliff dance. She climbed out far enough and taunt her rope. She had transverse the cliff to the exact spot to optimize her swing, then she let go. Mick wasn't ready for this daring foolishness and almost dropped his camera, saved for the strap.

But she was pumping her legs as if she running sideways on the cliff. At the end of her swing she turned around and started running the other way. Like a pendulum on a grandfather clock she ticked to and fro. Mick quickly got over the shock of it as she looked to be enjoying herself. Defying gravity, her head was full of exhilaration. Although tethered by rope and harness, to her it was a freedom like no other except hang gliding.

As she swung, the colors of the cliff wall flew by as fast as an ever changing kaleidoscope. When gravity slowed her swing she invaded a ballerina's dream world. She kicked away from the cliff and did some pirouette somersaults that were as graceful as any trapeze artist.

Mick had long regained his composure and set his shutter speed for sport action. Marie's dance reminded him of a butterfly dancing from flower to flower with graceful fluttering wings. She continued on in her own little word with different acrobatics until she tired. Mick had taken a full roll of admiring film and was most proud of his ballerina subject and her obvious agility.

The cliff was a popular spot for admirers who look up from the park below. On this day there were two extra. Two men in black suits were aiming binoculars upon the cliff above, they the bodyguards the Great White Hunter left behind on assassination detail. 'Make it look like an accident,' were their orders. There was a price to be paid for exposing CalCon Health and the great Terrance DeVour wanted to collect the dues.

Making fatal accidents happen is an art to these guys, often it takes great patience. The creative challenges are great and so are the rewards. In the information department, they had gathered all that was necessary to do the job. The opportunity would be next.

They weren't the only snoops in town, as that very minute Paul Dupree was copying the files he sought. 'Liar,' he thought. As he ran copy after copy off Marie's multi-function fax machine, he examined the ledgers entries with a curious eye. He couldn't make heads or tails out of their entries.

He had no problem getting into Marie's home office, he's been there many times before. May as well had his own key the way he so slickly picked the back door lock. He also knew Marie wasn't at all precarious with her files. The cabinet wasn't locked and her faxes with regards to CalCon Health were front and center. 'She's too trusting,' he thought. 'That Mick is going to rob her,' he assured himself. 'Besides Marie belongs to me, Marie belongs to me,' tch, tch, tch.

Having a folder full of ammo, it was time for Paul to skedaddle. He knew he still had plenty of time but he liked to practice his stealth, so he went into her bedroom and opened her dresser drawer and spied a silk panty, he brought it up to his nose and inhaled. A scent got his attention and his heart rate immediately increased. He smiled as he smelled, a sense of relief and satisfaction came over him and he stuffed the panties inside his suit pocket. He wanted to get back to headquarters to let his financial forensic team examine the bookkeepers ledgers. He was excited because he knew he was one step closer to indictment, and as soon as he was finished with this case, he would be one step closer to getting Marie back.

Marie had climbed back to Mick at the staging area and they had a tender hugging moment before he asked, "are you crazy?" He didn't really think that, he was just overly concerned.

Marie smiled and said, "no, it's really quite safe. Besides I was having a celestial experience. There's nothing quite like it you know."

"I don't think I'll ever find out either, momma didn't raise no—no mountain goat. Why you couldn't even get one of those out there!" Mick's natural protective concern for her was jamming his thought process and Marie glistened at his flattering apprehension.

They hugged and kissed before carefully repacking their gear for the decent. Pausing to look around the valley below Marie said, "isn't it beautiful?"

To which Mick quipped, "yeah, let's go back down for a closer look see."

Marie had an exuberant feeling like she just went through a hundred aerobic classes and not a muscle was sore. Stretched like a spindly yoga expert yes, but not sore. Her heart was light and fluttery too. One of these days she would climb to the top of that mountain but not today. She wanted to keep that challenge in front of her. It wasn't an overwhelming desire to conquer this mountain or any other for that matter, as long as she kept attainable goals in front of her and in focus.

Mick on the other hand was glad to be going downhill. It's always easier but that doesn't make the trek any less harried. He took up his usual position and followed Marie's lead. Behind his superficial façade, he was glad to be on the mountain with Marie, it had been a very edifying experience. There is a point to accomplishing something that may seem stupid to some, yet moves another's soul transmontane. Inner peace of attainment is a quiet glory that lasts as long as the blood flows and the heart pumps.

Marie knows it too, and it wasn't the view of the valley that she wanted to show Mick. It was the inside of his soul, a place one forgets to look for peace, but it's always there. So many obstacles of daily life can blind a person to the importance of it; like a mountain can hide a setting sun, like a moon can eclipse the light of day.

Mick had a new energy now and it wasn't because it's easier going downhill, it was more like a religious experience that secretly transpired him. He was still following Marie like a magnet clings to steel, it was easy, it was natural, and it was peaceful.

Upon reaching the RV, they stored their gear and quenched their thirst with spring water. There was a quiet solace about them now, souls satisfied with their industrious day. Now it was time to feed their bodies, the Hitching post was suggested and agreed upon.

Taking their seats, Mick pulled out of the parking lot and headed down the winding road. Marie put a smooth jazz CD in the player and both were enjoying the mellow sounds. As the park road winded through the forest both unwound and sank comfortably into the captain's chairs. The ride was uneventful until they came upon a slight downhill grade before the stop sign entering route 74. It was there that Mick's brake petal inexplicably lost pressure.

"Hold on!" He hollered. That got Marie's utmost attention. "What's wrong?" She fired back.

"The breaks are out!" Mick explained with urgency.

Then he shifted the transmission into low gear and it took hold to slow the RV some, but it wasn't nearly good enough. Mick put his foot on the emergency brake petal, nothing. That didn't do the job either, too late, to fast the intersection was upon them.

"Hold on!" He hollered again as he hoped a quick prayer that there wouldn't be any oncoming traffic in the intersection. He only had time for one quick maneuver, a dangerous one. First he swung left and then back to the right, the coach swayed with the turns. Then at the optimum angle he took a hard left that tipped the coach upon two wheels. Fortunately the RV was bottom heavy with tools and gear or they would have rolled over. Even more haply, the highway was void of oncoming traffic.

The RV swung and swerved until Mick regained some semblance of control, but an oncoming truck was barreling down upon them. He was on the horn cord full blast and his rear wheels were smoking burned rubber. As things were happening as fast as life flashes before one eyes, he passed the

RV in a blink, missing only by inches.

Fractions of seconds one way or another would have left the RV looking like a sardine can. Mick had enough time to gulp at their luck while Marie unclenched her grip from the chair arms and said, "whew! That was close."

Even traveling at 10 MPH can be disastrous and they were approaching another downhill grade. So he deliberately pulled over in the emergency lane as there was a curve ahead with a guardrail. He deliberately scrapped against it, aluminum against steel, sent a horrid, ear piercing screech, throughout the RV. The RV shuddered as it scrapped and the steering wheel was hard to control but it was working. Mick kept forcing the RV into the railing until it ground to a halt.

"What happened?" Marie asked.

"I don't know." Mick shut off the engine. "I lost the breaks. Damn!" He slammed his off the steering wheel. "Are you all right?"

"Yeah. What now?"

"Call a tow truck, will ya?"

Marie was dialing in an instant. Mick got up and gave a superficial effort to open the door, which was pinned against the guardrail. He went to the window and slid it open. Meanwhile a good Samaritan who witnessed the action from a safe distance pulled in front of them to offer assistance. Mick climbed out the window and Marie followed.

"The tow truck is coming," she told him after her feet hit terra firma. "Good," he replied as the Samaritans approached.

"Is every one alright?" They inquired. "Yes, we're fine thank you," Mick said. "What happened?" One inquired further.

Mick delayed his answer as he looked past the couple at a black Humvee with tinted windows slowly cruised by at a gawker's speed. Momentary thinking, 'curious on lookers,' vanished in a flash and replaced with, 'I've seen that car before.'

His speech was hesitant but his mind was quick. "Ah... I lost my breaks somehow."

"Do you folks need a ride somewhere?"

"Ah... no, I don't think so. Marie, how long for the tow?"

"He said he'd be here in a half hour."

"We'll wait this out then, but thanks for the offer."

"All right, good luck."

The couple turned and started to walk away. "Thanks for stopping," Marie shouted after them. "Yeah, thanks again," Mick joined in.

"No problem, glad to see every ones alright," they said as they got in their car.

Then Mick turned to Marie and asked, "how many black Humvees do you think are in this state?"

"I wouldn't know. Why do you ask?"

Not wanting to start a worry bird nest, Mick just said, "oh, nothing."

Then he walked to the front of the RV to pop the hood for inspection. But before he flipped the guard rail he caught himself when he realized he would have to climb back in through the window to release the hood latch under the dash first, and while he was at it, better turn on the emergency flashers too.

It was easy getting back in as he used the railing for a step ladder and before he came back out again he reloaded his camera with film figuring he might as well take some pictures of the damage for the insurance company and his claim. He thought there was several thousand dollars in damages and his RV would be out of commission for a while.

Marie was on her cell phone when the tow truck driver pulled up. He had an assignment for her, a follow up. One of the kids from Eagle Lake committed suicide while under government care in Sacramento. There have been other reports of rebellious behavior and he wanted her to get the story straight. Political careers were in the balance, 'find the neglect,' were her orders.

Mick was explaining the situation to the tow truck guy as he was hooking up the RV. He wanted to make sure he got a full explanation regarding the break failure and not just a bill. Before they all piled in the truck's cab, Marie told Mick she had an assignment in Sacramento.

"Good," he said. "We'll have to work around the RV. It'll be out of service for a while." "

That's OK, we can use my jeep and live out of a motel for a week or so." That being agreed upon, they had the tow truck driver drop them off at the house.

CHAPTER 20

While in port on the island of Santorini, a picture post card part of Greece, blue sea and white buildings were nestled among the greenery. Along the narrow lanes lined with fabulous jewelry shops and restaurants, Terrance DeVour was introduced to a gem dealer by his ship builder, who turned him on to a business venture.

The intriguing part was the opportunity to get back into the black market. The diamond business was well regulated, but notwithstanding the challenge of short circuiting the system, the proposal was exactly what he was looking for. He knew all too well how to corrupt officials; it was just a matter of how much.

While they were talking it was explained to him about the rebel problems in Africa and the labor strikes in the granite pits. The thing was that every time suppliers cut off shipments of Qat the laborers would strike as the workers considered the leafy narcotic more important than money. Qat was harvested daily in the high altitudes of Awade in Ethiopia and flown in to distributors. Natives chew the leaves into a slimy lump that bulges the cheek, similar to chewing tobacco it's never swallowed. It stimulates the mental activity while the chewer falls into an introspective stupor. It also acts like an amphetamine and diminishes hunger. That's why the ritual is done in the early evening.

That bit of information really got the Great White Hunters mind doing cartwheels. Qat sounded like a mild form of Comfitine. If he could get regular shipments and introduce his drugs here he would be king of the granite pits. Then he wouldn't have to worry about the FDA or the FBI anymore and could set up a new drug lab in Nigeria.

Back in Athens, Terrance DeVour scheduled a meeting with the French Banque Africane in the capital city of Abuja, Nigeria. One more bank account and company, needed to be opened. There was a tremendous opportunity to be had running a granite quarry as a front for his precious stone export business. Diamonds and Africa were synonymous as safari.

Feeling his Exotic Wildlife Sanctuary caused the downfall of his Cal-Con Health Insurance business, he knew he had to get it right this time. While his penchant for the kill grew, so what better business could he get into that would allow him to have an entire game reserve as his personal hunting grounds plus a diamond and Comfitine black market to boot.

Abuja was ideal because of its central location, easy accessibility and salubrious climate. He didn't plan on living there but did want to build an office complex and a lab. The university there would be a source of employable managers and the Nigerians still sell their children to the labor traffickers providing cheap child labor.

Their chartered jet landed and his entourage was whisked away in a waiting stretch limo. His meeting with the bankers went quickly as they were eager to please. They wanted private capital to promote economic development. The president of Nigeria was especially glad to have American businessmen in his country because he knows the full weight of the mightiest army in the world follows them. That reason alone is enough to keep all the different rebel factions at bay.

After all the business dealings were settled it was safari time. They went back to the airport for a flight to Bwanda, lion and uncut diamond country. The Great White Hunter was out of his element now. His hunting guide made him remove his suit for attire more appropriate. At first he felt like he was naked without his "power suit," and the khaki outfit felt too baggie. The one thing he refused to wear was the safari helmet. He didn't want anything covering his glowing white hair.

They set out for the plains in their all-terrain Land Rovers. Gone were the days of standard-bearers, but the crew did comprise a varied, talented group. All drivers were professional hunters, trackers, and skinners.

Terrance DeVour had procured a special hunting license issued by the Nature Conservation Union. There would be no poaching this day, but he would be allowed to keep the meat and hide from one kill. For now that was the best he could do being non-indigenous.

When the Europeans first began to settle in Africa in the late 19th century, the colonists shot game for meat and hides principally for survival. There seemed to be an unlimited supply of game but as the hunting increased and the wildlife decimated, hunting became a regulated sport.

The Great White Hunter was a different kind of animal as he cared little for regulation or sport. Ritual and blood was his motivation, all related to the way he consumes business dealings. Go for the kill, the throat, the blood of his competitors.

Safari's used to take weeks of preparation, no more as he and his body guards got in specialized Land Rovers. In short order the company was out of the city and off the main road rushing between thickets and clusters of trees headed for the rolling plains. They cut through a confluence of streams and dodged around the clumps of trees that lined them. Scattering various species of screeching birds as they went. Scores of antelope, gazelle's, and Briza Oryx were on the hoof because of the invasion.

They were now tearing through Acacias shrubs and other thorny varieties of weeds and Savanna type grasses. Giraffe were spotted off in the distance but they were headed to a watering hole that the lions used as a base for their survival.

They have only been traveling two hours or so and Terrance DeVour was sick of the bumpy ride as well as his bodyguards. Not wishing to expose their soft underbellies non dared complain. They just silently wished for the good old days and the immediacy of shooting caged beasts. The sun beating down on the Great White Hunter made him conspire thought in that exact direction, but not today, he was going to tough this one out for bragging rights.

The full effect of the blazing sun didn't take it's full effect until the safari guide stopped the Land Rover on the top of a hill. The breeze of the open vehicle had dissipated the heat somewhat as they traveled but now all were perspiring as there was no breeze at all. Vastness lay before them. Terrance DeVour couldn't enjoy the beauty of it. His eyes were peeled on a pride of lions. On the other side of the watering hole they were lounging in the shade of a lone tree.

The lions all focused on the intruders. Other than their heads they didn't move, their bellies were laden with Zebra meat. They had seen men and vehicles before on photo op safaris and were not terribly disturbed by man's presence. Just the same the male begrudgingly took his superior pose, shaking his magnificent mane in his natural, how dare you disturb my nap posture.

The safari crew exited their Land Rovers. Some were glad to stretch their legs, Terrance went right for the gun rack and ammo. He hurriedly grabbed the biggest rifle with the best scope. The rifle and cartridge he choose, was big enough to bring down an elephant.

"You're a hundred yards out," the guide said.

"I know, I know," Terrance coarsely confirmed.

"Aim for the heart between the shoulder blades and squeeze the trigger slowly for."

"Keep your yap shut will ya! I'm trying to aim here." The Great White Hunter detested the guides coddling instructions. He put his eye on the scope and focused. There was a deadly quiet for a moment, even the birds held their chirps until the big bang. The rifle recoiled into Terrance's shoulder. His groan was muffled by a lions roar.

Animals scattered for miles around as the shot sound echoed the chaos. The lionesses were well into a trot and the king of beasts hobbled after them. The smell of blood was in the air and a burning pain in his hindquarter. The bullet had hit above the joint on his hind leg. The bullet had ricocheted off bone and ripped a hunk of muscle out the rear, leaving the lion crippled. In the greater cycle of African life crippled was as good as dead.

The lion followed his lionesses with an awkward hopping limp while the hunting party threw congratulations at the Great White Hunter. He accepted the accolades with pride. "Nice shot, nice shot," his bodyguards exclaimed but the guide knew better. They had to track the animal now and fast before the lion found sanctuary.

He interrupted the hunter's cheer with orders to get back in their vehicles and follow him. They all recognized the urgency in his tone and obliged.

The lion was staggering toward some high grass where he could lick his wound. The lion's instincts smelled doom, he carried on regardless. Reaching the safety of the tall grass was in sight. There the lion could better defend himself. His front legs churned forward and his one good hind leg kicked after.

These were familiar grasses the lion was headed for, he was born not too far from there and his pride hunted from the very same. He staggered onwards for sanctuary when another gunshot rang out. The guide had fired this time and the king of beasts was dead. Felled on the age of amber waves.

"That was my kill," bemoaned Terrance DeVour.

"You can have the credit and everything that goes with it, but I couldn't take a chance of this one getting into the bush. The terrain is unsuitable for the vehicles," he explained.

"Oh," Terrance said pacified. But he still didn't like being told what to do by a mere contracted servant. The lionesses were hunkered down nearby and deaths blood filled their nostrils. Their own fears and survival instincts made them more dangerous than normal. They were more than capable of protecting themselves if the hunters dared tread into the tall grasses. They wouldn't get the chance. The skinners had hoisted the carcass into the flat bed of a refrigerated equipped Land Rover.

The bloodletting started immediately. Terrance DeVour didn't have his silver chalice like he wanted but dipped a ladle into the collecting pan and drank from it. At one time that was a native ritual, Africans did it with goats and other kills for nutritional and religious purposes. Now the ritual is mostly passé except for the most rural villages.

The hunting guide felt disgusted by the sight but kept quiet as he needed the money his services provided. With the kill in hand they headed back to Bwanda were the meat could be properly butchered. While that was being done, the impatient Great White Hunter scored his first diamond deal. This was all prearranged by the president of Nigeria, money works wonders. The prize in the package of uncut diamonds was a rare cut and polished Blue Nile diamond, the rarest of gems.

The uncut stones were properly registered and readied for export while the Blue Nile diamond was secretly cemented to the inside of the lions skull. Terrance DeVour worked rather quickly as he had a suitcase full of diamonds before the lions skin was properly dried. Feeling tired from his busy day, and with the evening upon him like a dark cloud, he decided to lay overnight in the fanciest hotel in Bwanda. Fancy as it maybe, it was still a slum unit according to his standards.

It was just like him to change his intentions on the spot. He sent one of his bodyguards with the diamonds back to the chartered jet on the tarmac to relieve the pilot and crew who were on standby. He knew his yacht was still in dry dock being refurbished and it wouldn't benefit him to hurry. Besides he really didn't like sleeping on airplanes and it was going to be a long flight back to Athens.

CHAPTER 21

Tommy had traded his 4x4 pickup for a cargo van. He had to empty his storage locker; he didn't dare leave his dope behind to be found by some storage locker people or the cops. Besides, being fired and all, he would need the dope money more than ever until he gets enough to set up his own gardening business. Perhaps, he figured, that the rose business might be better in southern California, as it isn't a native plant and needs a lot of water and tender loving care for cultivation. One thing he was certain about, he was no longer welcome in Portland and he had to bring Marie some roses.

He headed southwest out of town on rt.18 to Rose Lodge, one of the places on the map that he always wanted to visit. After spending the night he took the coastal highway 101 on his way to his destination. It would have been a faster trip if he took Interstate 5, but he hated traffic and all the hustle bustle of speeding trucks. Rudeness of traffic going nowhere fast, never having time to stop and smell the roses was another thing he hated, actually it drove him mad. At least 101 offered gazes of the Pacific, green lush forests, and an aroma of nature he could taste with his nose. Also the landscape offered plenty of places to camp on his long journey, he reasoned.

Options were planned. He had buried his drug cache under a homemade bed of plywood and sleeping bags. If it rained he could sleep in the van, or weather permitting, he could sleep under the stars. Stocking up on Coleman cooking and other camping accessories offered him many choices of roughing it.

He was going about things famously until that first night. Camping out at Rocky Creek Wayside, he fired up his propane grill and cooked himself some hot dogs and beans. All went well, but when he tried to outside on a grassy knoll next to the beach a fog rolled in that made him shiver. Being half asleep he looked out over the fog riding the ocean waves. He heard the rolling waves break at the shoreline but thought he heard Squirrel and

Chucky calling to him. "Come heeeer, come heeeer, sploosh, sploosh." He wiped the sleep from his eyes and saw them in the fog floating atop the waves. They had a transparent glassy look about them.

That sent him scrambling back inside the cargo van where he broke out in a panting sweat, but that wasn't the worst of it. Now curled and cowered in his bed shaking with what he thought was a fever, the ocean waves made noises that permeated the thin skin of the van. Between the sweats and chills his teeth chattered from Comfitine withdrawals. He felt like driving away but when he tried to stand his foggy brain syndrome saw the boys at his windshield clawing to get in. They were all squiggly and distorted but were calling for him to come out and play, he locked the doors and clutched a bottle of Comfitine pills, then dug out his pistol and rifle from hiding. He wanted peace and quiet along with security.

"Get away from me, you snore," he cried over and over.

He fidgeted with the child proof cap in his shacking hands until he got a pill.

"You can't have any! Now go away!" he hollered at the windshield, until the narcotic took hold. He was just about ready to blow holes in his window when he just collapsed back on his bed.

Mick and Marie were in Sacramento busy interviewing authorities in regards to the children but Marie was still denied access to them. As wards of the state the government authorities were giving the children medication but the antidepressant drugs weren't working.

Adverse reactions: due to unexplainable chemical imbalances; were being recorded by doctors, and so far tests were inconclusive. But the public will never find out about them because of privacy laws and authorities are always reluctant to admit their failures.

The facts about the suicide were also hidden from the press and Marie was being stonewalled. Not even the Freedom of Information Act could help her get at the truth. Frustrated with the bureaucracy, Marie crumpled up her written notes and threw them into a garbage can. Only after a moment did she dig them back out and uncrumple the paper. On second thought she realized her work was just beginning.

They did find out however, that two caseworkers were fired for dereliction of duty even though there was nothing they could have done to prevent the tragedy. From the management's point of view, the firings were a matter of discourse, 'better you than me.' Public outcry always needs a scapegoat, before political fallout.

"I have an idea," Marie said with and instant burst of energy. "Let's go interview the terminated employees. They might have a different spin on the story."

"Whatever you want," Mick replied.

"If it wasn't for the publicized lawsuit filed on behalf of the terminated employee's, Marie might not have been able to locate them so readily. She had to get her questions pre-approved by their attorney and he would have to be present during the interview. The lawyer's willingness to cooperate was encouraged by a desire to garner public sympathy and enhance his reputation. Marie found the employee's to be forthright. She learned exactly how unruly the children were. Antidepressant medication was doubled in all but a few cases with little effect. The children literally had to be loaded up with barbiturates to end their upheaval. The odd thing was, Marie was told, the kids resented being rescued from CalCon and all of them wanted to be returned. The medical staff theorized the kids were bored, coming from a social labor intense environment, to an isolated, regimented military style school put the kids in a state of social shock.

The witnesses further explained that no one was really surprised that one of the boys committed suicide. Unfortunate as it was, it was completely unpreventable. Nobody can prevent such things, they rationalized. How does one stop a person who is bent on eliminating one's life, they quizzed.

Armed with a good deal more information, Marie thanked everyone for being cooperative. As soon as she typed out the story on her laptop, she called her editor. And after talking to him, Marie gave Mick that look again, the way she slightly cocks her head and opens her eyes full with her pupils staring ever so large. He knew they weren't going home yet, and then she asked, "can we go back to Eagle Lake and have a look around to see if there's anything else we can dig up?" Mick didn't even bother with the why's and what-for's. He matter-of-factly just replied, "Yeah, let's go fishing."

CHAPTER 22

Terrence DeVour personally called the Holy Hunter at Cal-Con Health's Corporate Headquarters. He had a new agenda, he wanted to replace the local African narcotic Qat with Comfitine. His workers in the granite pits would never know or care about Qat after they were hooked.

Smoothing things out with Lawrence Marsi was no problem, as long as there was lots of money to be had. They were both playing off each other, neither one trusting the other. Lawrence was promised shares in the new venture and wouldn't have to put up any capital. The new company wouldn't be carried on Cal-Con's books, so any impending bankruptcy or indictments would have no bearing on the granite business.

The Great White Hunter conveniently left out the bit about the diamond and gem business, and the Holy Hunter failed to mention the deal he had going with the local L.A. street gangs. They were already snapping up his inventory of Comfitine.

The deal Terrance DeVour put forth, meant starting production back up at Eagle Lake. For that he would need production workers and an influx of capitol, which he was promised. Illegal aliens came to mind. They could be given room and board in the old kids dorm. The Feds were busy looking for accounting infractions and weren't the least bit curious as to what Cal-Con was producing. As far as they were concerned, it was all a write-off for research and development—which of course made Terrance's proposal plausible. Plans were set in motion that very day.

The FBI were in motion too, slow motion. The complexities of all the off shore companies Cal-Con Health owned had the financial forensic team compressed between bookends. Irregularities galore, questionable transactions were the main menu. But nothing positively illegal could be proven, yet. Indictments were going to be slow to follow unless something more damning than bankruptcy was found, and it was Paul Dupree's job to find it.

Further on down the road, Tommy had survived his scare and felt a lot better after he landed in Venice Beach. The old hippie and muscle beach gathering spot for L.A.'s freest vertebrae. He took special pleasure watching the bikini clad bosom species sway while zigging and zagging down the parkway, dodging the pedestrians while zooming past the gift and souvenir shops on their roller blades. He was rebuffed trying to converse with them however and found they were very rude. He was also oblivious to his own odor and unkempt appearance. They were not like Marie at all, he thought. His Marie was kind and beautiful like a rose.

Beach combers were easy to find, a virtual cabaret of personalities in all kinds of shapes and sizes. The ones with the boom-boxes offended Tommy's sensibilities the most. Always acting cool and aloof while rudely cramming their rap music down his ears, it sounded like they were snoring. They were drowning out natures music of playing children caroling in the surf. Sometimes he felt like going to get his guns and put them boom boxes out of their misery. Then he'd calm down while listening to the children splashing and laughing. They only added to the euphonic harmony of swishing waves. He thought back to the times he used to participate with his buddies in high tide folly. For him the good old days were a mere five years ago.

He almost forgot his mission as his thoughts hypnotized his mind. Then he spotted what he was looking for. A young scruffy teen, much like he used to be was competing with the sea gulls and flies for food in garbage cans. He introduced himself and offered to buy him a burger from a vendor. He wound up buying him two, Boogie was famished.

At first Tommy felt Boogie out with small talk to find out if he was a druggie. 'No,' he was homeless and broke without a job.

"How'd you get your nickname?" Tommy asked.

"From my parents.—I used to dance around a lot when I was a kid."

"Then what happened?"

"They got divorced Texas style."

"How's that?" Tommy wanted to know.

"Mom shot my dad for cheatin' on her. Then they put me in a home. I hated it an took off. So here I am."

Tommy told him he could make a lot of money and give him a job if he promised to not take drugs. He said, "yeah—sure." Then came the job offer and the explanation that started with, "all's you gotta do is."— Boogie didn't have much else to do so naturally he accepted Tommy's offer.

Tommy went into his lecturing mode, "you see, drug users are like worms. When it rains they come to the surface so they don't drown, but when their out on the pavement they're as good as dead. If they don't wind up being bird food or bait, they shrivel up from dehydration as soon as the sun comes out.

—Yeah drug users are a lot like worms, never satisfied with their lives. They crawl out of their holes for drugs and keep on doing it until their dead meat. In other words if the cops don't get em the drugs will, you just can't use drugs a deal. Get my drift?"

"Yeah, I get ya." Boogie replied.

"Once your customers get hooked on this stuff they'll be crawling out of the woodwork to get more, an we'll be the ones in the money." The sorry thing is Tommy couldn't take his own advice anymore. His own addiction had a firm hold over him and he was only fooling himself when he promised he'd quit like he did before as soon as his nightmares stopped. He was taking two pills a day now, one to get him through the day and the other to get to sleep at night.

"What kind of drugs you pushing?" Boogie asked.

"It's like a dreamland vitamin,—like ecstasy only better, more powerful, it makes you all warm and cozy on the inside. Comfitine is on the label, it's an antidepressant."

Tommy liked Boogie, they hit it off like a two man band. That's one of the reasons he cautioned him about using drugs. He didn't want him to wind up like Squirrel and Chucky. He fronted Boogie a 30 pill container and told him to get at least five dollars a pill and they would meet up tomorrow to square up. With the arrangements settled Tommy stopped at a flower shop to buy a bouquet of roses before he headed out to Lake Elsinore.

The ride went by full of anticipation quickly. He imagined Marie's smile and greeting him with open arms after he gives her a bouquet of roses. Then they would be happy. He would be her gardener and grow her all the roses she wanted. While his fantasy crush reflected positive thoughts, there was one negative that kept blurring the picture.

He dismissed that thought several times already, but somehow the vision crept back, only to be banished again. He was sure she got rid of that cheapskate, and he was already gone because he snores.

It didn't take him long to find Marie's house after he pulled into the town's main gas station for fuel and directions. He was impressed by her spacious ranch house on all that property but just as he thought not a single rose bush was planted. Tommy knocked and knocked at her door and was sourly disappointed when he realized she wasn't at home.

At first he paced restlessly on the walkway while conversing with the bouquet. Mostly he kept repeating the same gibberish, "it's supper time,—she should be home cooking dinner." Then his pacing quickened with adrenaline, "where could she be?" He worried. He couldn't understand why Marie wasn't home.

This time while pacing past a window he saw his reflection, but he didn't see himself, he saw his father. "He's snoring," he hollered at the window. After blinking and rubbing his eyes his vision changed, now he saw Mick and he was the reason Marie wasn't home. "He's snoring! He's snoring!" He hollered again.

Not being able to stand his own reflection and imagination he picked up a stone from the walkway boarder and threw it through the window. Instant gratification settled over him as his reflection disappeared with the smash. 'Now she'll need me more than ever,' he thought. 'She'll need me to fix her window,' he reasoned.

Then he returned to her front door and fastened the bouquet of roses to the handle. Getting in his cargo van his hands suddenly started trembling furiously, so much so he had a hard time getting the keys in the ignition as they fell to the floor. He didn't understand why he broke Marie's window and he didn't understand why she wasn't home. He pounded on the steering wheel as he screamed, "why isn't she home!"

Perspiration formed on his forehead as a chill shook his body, he couldn't handle the discomfort anymore. Grabbing his pill bottle and fumbling to get one out, then swallowing his piece of mind. He felt flush and calm instantly but promised himself that was the last pill he was going to take without realizing the power of the medication and the grip it had over his young body. He didn't drive far before the sight of hang gliders caught his eye. He pulled his cargo van into a forest preserve parking lot to watch them. 'Kites,' he thought, 'soaring kites.' His mind had calmed down to the point of a hypnotic trance. His eyes fixated and drifted with the kites while remembering when he was younger. A more peaceful time when he had a big ball of twine wrapped around a broken tree branch. He and his boyhood chums would spend the whole day flying kites, as long as the wind held out or as long as their kites didn't snag a tree.

He didn't feel like driving back to Venice Beach anyway. Knowing he wasn't supposed to hook back up with Boogie until tomorrow, he decided to stay the night in the park. He was sitting on a picnic bench gazing skyward at a kaleidoscope of colors, pretty fancy colors. Flying roses with extended petals, with a bumblebee, front and center feeding on the pollen. Rose petal kites floating on a breeze, he laid down on top of the bench and folded his arms under his head to get a better view. As he relaxed there was an awakening inside, and a smile bloomed like an opening rose bud. It was the first time he's smiled in years. He was in a heavenly valley seeing incredible things.

But alas, now the sky was empty, and it saddened him to see the last hang glider land. But he decided he would like to fly in a kite too, decisions like that make him happy, he closed his eyes to envision his first flight.

There he was he saw, he was completely naked, rising above everything. Out of his mere mortal body, he was wearing orange, black, and yellow stripes, and flew like a bumblebee. Buzz, buzz he went along looking for his rose. Buzz, buzz he found his Marie, the prettiest rose of them all. She was not like other rose's, she spread her pedals and flew with him, as he suckled at her pollen. Buzz, buzz, buzz, the flight of the bumblebees sung, unencumbered by such physical limitations as gravity or misery. They were in love, Tommy's smile was back full bloom.

Then the warmth of the sun that was shining his face set behind the mountain changing his mind set. He sat up on the picnic table to watch the oranges and yellows dip behind the black mountains. He was hungry, so he made camp and cooked himself some hot dogs and beans. He planned on sleeping in the van right where he was parked tonight. Squirrel and Chucky's ghosts will never find him here, he thought. They're not real, must have been my imagination, a flash back must have got the best of him. He reasoned.

CHAPTER 23

Mick and Marie were back in Eagle Lake. The street was devoid of traffic, but there were some cars parked at the resort. Pulling in the lot, he parked front and center, in one of the very spots he had saw the black Humvees occupy. They went in. Not sure if they wanted to spend the night there, they went straight to the bar.

Mick was going to let Marie do all the inquiring, both were curious about the state of affairs at Cal-Con Health. They knew two of the company officials meet their demise at the hands of the FBI. That fiasco was written off as a case of mistaken identity. How unfortunate for the Hunted Hunters.

Mick opened up with ordering two beers and asking, "how's the fishing?"

"Terrible, I haven't heard of anyone catching a fish in a year." The bartender answered before fetching the beers. Mick privately thought, 'that was odd, two local bartenders claiming the fishing was bad. They really should learn to bullshit the tourists better, for business sakes.'

When the bartender came back with the beers, Marie stood up and reached over the bar with hand extended to introduce themselves. That maneuver exposed her glorious cleavage to the bartender, now she had his undivided attention before she asked question one. Right after she completed the introduction she casually mentioned, "looks like a slow night."

"Yeah," he said. "It doesn't get much slower than this."

The bartender was wearing a white shirt and a black bow tie with an apron tied around his waist. The bar and resort was delicately decorated to cater to the upscale society.

"It was a lot busier a couple weeks ago when all those press people were here," he volunteered, and that was enough opening for Marie to start probing away.

"Why were the press here?" She quizzed, pretending not to know.

"Some big shots over at Cal-Con got in a gun battle with the FBI—they lost," he informed her. "Matter of fact, they used to come in here. Ignorant people they were. Poor tippers, too."

Mick looked on passively at a sports program on the TV, acting disinterested, but had an ear dialed in on the conversation. He was again impressed on how efficiently Marie gathered the information she wanted.

The bartender was no contest to her and he was more than happy to chat. He liked her charming smile and voice. He particularly liked the way she tossed her golden tresses back and put the beer bottle to her succulent lips. Besides he had no other customers to entertain and in between the stories he was telling about Cal-Con and what happened to the employees; he was secretly dreaming of bedding Marie. But whenever he would ask a personal question directed at, 'what are you doing later?' Marie would right the ship and get the bartender to answer more questions about Cal-Con Health and the employees.

'What a skill Marie has,' Mick was thinking as he ordered another round.

Marie had the bartender drooling information. Some of the most interesting to her were the facts that 90% of the town's people were laid off or displaced elsewhere in the organization. Illegal aliens with green cards were bussed up, "from god knows where," as he put it. They live in the back where the child laborers used too, was his understanding. But he couldn't say for sure because of all the security they have there.

He also mentioned that the government pulled the license from the Pet Rescue Facility and that part of the operation was closed down. But trucks still pull in and out, so they're doing some kind of business.

Then he went on to talk about the most amazing thing. "There's this new mystery floating around about the taxidermist. Seems he went hunting with his dogs to get the grizzly that killed his friend and he never came back, but his dogs, they were black labs, now they're gray. The wife said they came home that day with tail between their legs and hid under the porch and won't come out, and they haven't been the same since.

"That started a rumor about the ghosts of the tiger man. Some say's it's just a grizzly, some say's it's a tiger loose on the loose, and some say's it's a man. No matter now though," he continued, "it's becoming folk lore and legend, cause a group of men with more dogs went in on a search and they started by the tore out section of fence were all the animals escaped from. The dogs would act crazy on the spot, then take their handlers off in different directions, mostly circles, until they all meet back up at the bottom of a cliff. Then the dogs would be acting crazy again because they couldn't climb it because it was too steep, too steep for any grizzly or tiger to climb too. Not deterred, some of the men doubled back and climbed to the top, via another route, were they found evidence of a mountain climber's rappelling gear. A piton was pounded in the rock above the cliff but the rope was gone.

"Anyway," he continued, "the only tracks they found were from the grizzly, wolves, and coyote's, and they all dead ended at the cliff. But there are all these wolf calls and coyote cries at night, they have a supernatural eerie shrill, so we know there out in the forest. It's just that they can't find them, that's why their saying the woods are haunted, and that's how legends are born."

"Very entertaining story," Marie complimented with a generous smile. Mick finally broke in with, "I'm hungry."

"Me too," Marie replied, because she was finished with her interview.

Mick left a generous tip to the bartender, generous by his standards anyway, because he knew the information Marie retrieved from him was important to her. They decided to spend the night and registered, then, they went to the dining room.

Marie was quietly happy, glad she had a new story, but now it was more than that. An easy feeling enveloped her, like a warmth that one feels in front of glowing fireplace. She coyly picked at her chicken dinner while studying her man, his face, hair, and eyes, 'he's so handsome,' she thought. But it was more than that she knew, it was his strength of soul that made him attractive.

Then she noticed something else, and had to ask, "why do you mix your peas with the mashed potatoes?"

"Easy," he said, "peas can be tricky to eat and roll off your fork. This way they get stuck in the potato's and you don't have to worry about them."

"Why not use a spoon?" She responded.

"I don't think it matters, since it all winds up in the same place anyway. Why do you ask?"

"I don't know, just curious about the man I'm going to marry, I guess." While thinking, 'yes, that looks logically efficient.'

Mick continued mixing his peas with mashed potatoes, while the lump in his throat exploded like a champagne cork. His eyes and ears were wide open to say the least, as he wanted to hear more good news and her plans.

Marie had mentioned marriage before and this time said it with a casualty that was meant to be understood; as in planned, but not officially engaged. Her beauty and caring ways move different men to distraction in such a way she didn't realize the real power she had over men with the simplicity of her smile.

Mick was more attentive and his heart pounded with her every move as they finished dinner. He did ask when were they planning on going to Hawaii but she didn't elaborate. Except to say, "sometime soon, after we finish the story."

After dinner they retired to their room. Marie quietly typed out the facts she had gathered on her laptop, while Mick stretched out on the bed relaxing and watching TV. There was a solace about the couple, actually an inspirit had been growing for some time now. Building blocks had been mortared, bonding agents hardened with time, but their hearts were soft, flexible, caring, nurturing life. She didn't want to hear any cheap "I love you's" after sex; she wanted the real thing and she felt she finally found it. She knew that kind of feeling is hard to find, but when it's found, it's understood.

When Marie finished typing her story she was enticed enough to start a new poem, but something was missing. She hadn't discussed her true feelings with Mick in a while because she was waiting, waiting for what she wasn't exactly sure. He had passed every test she threw at him and she was sure he was the real deal, reliable, faithful and trustworthy, what else does a girl need, she mused.

Then inexplicably she asked, as if to kick out any lingering doubt, "were you serious when you asked about adopting children?"

"Of course I was," he replied.

"We'll have to get married then," she said. "In Hawaii like you dreamed."

"Oh, of course Hawaii. The isle of paradise."

She had been sitting at the desk but now found the energy to take a flying leap of desire to join Mick on the bed to enter his soul. Not only did they enjoy the fruits of love in paradise that evening, Marie came and came up with a title for her next poem, "You're My Man Tiger." As she whispered it into his ear, she slipped the thought into memory bank #10.

The next morning while Mick was still sleeping, Marie typed out her poem while her spirits were high and jubilant.

The strength of my man

Tiger Possesses muscles that ripple

My love is bigger

My heart floats like a dangling participle

Did all the right things

Bodies we shared Satisfaction brings

Love—we cared

Yes, yes, feel like a mother

No need to hide

We love one-another

Feel the pride

Did you hear

Yes, love was understood

No one shed a tear Loving was good

The potency of my man

Tiger Possesses muscles that ripple

Glory the rigor

His kit's at my nipples

She was somewhat puzzled at the poem she wrote. It just flowed from her like a positive flood of thought. Wishful thinking,—maybe she wondered, intuition, sweet dream,—she reread her writing to make sure it was accurate.

"What ya doing now?"

Mick asked. Mick had awaken under the unmistakable soft clicks of her lap top, music to his ears, but Marie was startled as her concentration was disrupted by his question.

"Oh, I was just writing a poem," she said.

She closed her lap top, not that she was hiding anything or embarrassed by it. She didn't know how to explain what she wrote because she didn't quite understand it herself.

They readied themselves before checking out of the resort, plans included fishing, inquisitive fishing. The only other thing on Mick's list was to get some more spring water. "Why?" Marie asked. "Those woods are haunted," she chided.

"Because the water tastes good,—and the woods aren't haunted," he replied.

"That's logical," Marie said. "Then we can have another look at the animal compound?" She asked.

"Do you think they'll let us in?"

"I doubt it, but that didn't stop me the last time," she replied with daring confidence.

With their plans somewhat settled they checked out and stopped at a local sporting goods store for some gear. Mick wanted water containers to tote his spring water. Marie wanted to stop and ask questions.

The signs on the store window said it plain and clear, 'going out of business sale, 50% off everything.' They went in and found an elderly gentleman sporting a handlebar mustache behind the counter. He was wearing a round brimmed hat that was loaded with fishing flies, a flannel shirt and a 15 pocket vest.

"Can I's help you folks," he asked.

"Yes," Mick answered, "I'm looking for some camping water totes. An how's the fishing by the way?"

"Taint been no good lately, but thar's plenty out thar. Ya just needs the right baits 'tis all. I's got plenty on sale har. Just look about, I's give you a good deal on lures and such. Dem water jugs are over yonder."

"Thanks," Mick said.

Marie smiled at the man before she asked, "why do you need all them pockets?"

"Can't really tell. I's used to keep lures in um, but you know I'd keep forgotten which lure was in which pocket, den by the time I'd found what

I's was looken fer I's ferget why's I's was looking. So's now I's keep up empty."

Marie politely chuckled at his explanation, then asked, "why are you going out of business?"

"I's retiring."

"Why you look fit as a fiddle," she said.

"Thank ya, ma'am," he blushed sheepishly with his reply.

He didn't offer any other reason why so Marie had to pry further. "This is a beautiful spot for a bait shop."

"Yeah, buts I's got competition downs by the campground, and the critters down the road put most of the folk round here outs of work. Taint nobody got no money lef fer no baits. Sides—da moms got wind of dem haunted tales and grabbed up their childrens can get. Rubbish I's says. Dang rubbish, taint never believe in no Tiger Man's eaten up folks. Dang rubbish I's tell's ya.

Dem critters just don't want no more snoops around thar place tall's it 'tis."

"What critters?" Marie asked.

"Dem critters down at Cal-Con Health. Da ones taken advantage of children's labors."

Mick came back to the counter with two 3-gallon jugs and picked out an ultra-light spinning rod with a couple lures for prosperity.

The man rang up Mick's purchases and they said their "thanks." As they were walking away the man called out after them, "didn't mean to scare you ma'am, tain't no such thing as a Tiger Man." He thought he saw fear in Marie's face, but the reality of her facial expression was pure bewilderment.

As they drove past Cal-Con Health both noticed a new guard shack and barrier blocking the access road.

"I guess they do like their privacy," Mick said.

"Yeah, but that tells me they're still up to no good," Marie added. "Maybe, but let's not press our luck."

Mick pulled onto a side road that led to the lake access boat launch. He felt safe parking there and it was close to the spring that drained into the lake. The runoff was slightly more than a trickle and if a body wasn't looking for it, the spring could easily be by passed.

There were a few other cars and boat trailers in the parking lot, so everything looked auspicious when they began their trek. Mick carried his new fishing pole to avoid any suspicion as to their real intentions. Marie carried his camera to get some snap shots of the animal shelter, after the fact. She had strong feelings that Cal-Con Health was still hiding something, but Mick made her promise not to do anything foolish and there would be no trespassing this time. So she agreed to stay within the confines of the Lassen National Forest.

They found the aqueduct that channeled under the main highway. Unnoticeably small except for the fact that there was a 3' drainage pipe permanently graveled under the road, originally installed for storm runoff. After climbing the embankment they dashed across the highway and disappeared in the forest.

It didn't take them long to find natures path. The tire ruts Mick had made while escaping in the Humvee were already clogged with pine needles but the ground underneath was spongy and wet. They followed it right to the aquifer. The crystal clear spring sparkled invitingly like an old friend. Mick got on his knees and drank right from the source. The pool was bathtub deep there and he dipped his containers in the pool while Marie looked about to get her bearings. Slowly things filtered back to her, she remembers making love to Mick on the grassy mound just to the right of her before they were rudely interrupted with the sound of all those gun shots. Then they ran off to the north and climbed the mountain back to the ski chalet. But other things were still fuzzy to her. She was walking her mind back in time but still found some blank spots.

Mick had finished filling his containers and offered Marie a drink to quench her thirst. She took one. The sun was directly overhead and lit up the clearing perfectly. Her senses seemed to be in tune, she listened and heard the birds sing, she inhaled and tasted the sweet fragrance of natural pine, she looked at the spring and saw the blues and greens sparkling a wink at her. For a moment she thought of heaven and being so light and feathery she might actually be in it. Her spirit was being transported to another place in time. Actually traveling freely like no other time before. Then she thought of how nice it would be to go cliff dancing or hang gliding. Free as a bird is how she felt, in love without any harnesses or restrictions, in heaven with her Man Tiger. Then she thought it odd that in the middle of the forest, the clearing was here at all. She looked at her man and smiled.

"The animal shelter is this way," Mick said.

Her self-induced spell was broken and a new sense of energy and urgency awoke. "Yes, let's go," she said.

Mick left the water containers and fishing pole under a tree, no need to lug them around unnecessarily, he figured. They were both off in a stealthy trot and didn't stop until they saw the compound fence. Mick noticed right off that the fence had been repaired and Marie noticed all the empty animal cages.

They were hiding behind the second row of tree trunks and were satisfied there were no more animals on the property. Marie wasn't even going to bother taking pictures because the place looked deserted. Then they heard the unmistakable sound of a diesel engine fire up.

Marie hunkered down and readied Mick's telescopic lens. Then the garage door opened and a tractor trailer and its cargo pulled out. There were three men riding in the cab, she snapped off a couple pictures before it made a turn, then she took some more, carefully zeroing in on the license plates and logo.

When the truck disappeared they figured it was pointless to hang around any longer and melted back into the forest. They backtracked to the spring and picked up the water, while there a wind rustled the trees and wolf howls followed. Grabbing Mick's arm, Marie froze in her tracks. "What was that?" she whispered.

"Wolves. Don't worry, they want nothing to do with us," Mick calmly replied. They made their way back to Marie's Jeep and before Mick put the containers on the floor in the back Marie took another drink to quench her thirst. The spring water had a pleasant taste she noticed, perhaps it's void of chlorine and fluoride makes the difference, she thought.

Mick spotted some fishermen reeling in their boat upon a trailer and couldn't resist going over to them and asking, "How's the fishing?"

"No good!" The one said emphatically. "We see plenty swimming around on our radar scanner but they ain't biting on nothing. I've tried every lure in my tackle box and I was so aggravated at one point I was ready to throw the whole dang box in the lake until I realized how much money those lures cost me. Then I come to my senses. At least the weather is nice, a tomorrow is another day."

In the Jeep Marie speculated what was in the truck and where it was going, but realized they were powerless to find out. Then they decided to head home as Marie had delved into the story as far as she could for the moment, but still felt that Cal-Con Health was hiding something.

As Mick drove, Marie reclined in her seat and placidly melted into it. She still felt thirsty. Thirsty for water? No, she told herself, she just had some. She glanced over at the side of Mick's face and smiled. There was her answer. She was thirsty for love, thirsty for Mick. She closed her lovely eyes and transported her thoughts to a peaceful place—her house, their house, their garden, their paradise was wherever they were.

CHAPTER 24

Tree days in a row Tommy had commuted from Lake Elsinore and L.A. Every day he brought a fresh bouquet of roses. Three days in a row his pent up infatuation has been crushed. He couldn't understand why Marie wasn't home. He had to fix her window, she needed him, he thought. Whenever he was at her door he could swear he heard somebody snoring, but nobody answered his rings or knocks.

Even though he promised himself that he wouldn't take any more Comfitine, he needed them more and more. As his agitated frustrations were commanding him otherwise. Sure as the ocean tides flow, he would pull up to her house high with expectations, only to hear unanswered knocks and get the rejected feeling like being shoved down an outhouse pit. It was that damn snoring, the snoring coming from that house that made him take the pills to cure his ears.

After he settled down, he would go by the "kites". Those beautiful flying roses with extended pedals, he adored. His mind would float on air with them and he could watch the kites all day. He found solace there. One time when venturing up the mountain to explore their launching pad he discovered a side road with a dead end sign in front. It led to an old abandoned mine.

A perfect spot for shooting practice, he thought. As there was an area already littered with broken beer bottles and shot up cans. He vowed to clean that area, all's he needed was some garbage bags. But best of all, it was located partway up the mountain and was partially hidden by trees and under growth but he had a perfect view of Marie's house across the lake. The only telescope he had was on one of his rifles. When he took aim, he pretended he was like Cupid shooting his love arrows. The rifle had no bullets in it but every time he pulled the trigger he was filling Marie up with his love.

That was the perfect spot to set up his new campground, he thought. Still having to commute to Venice Beach to hook up with Boogie to sell his wares was consuming a better part of his day. Something he would like to eliminate, as he was tired of the travel already. He liked Boogie and felt things were going well enough to trust him with an extra front. He had already gotten his ass off the street and into a motel. That would cut his travel time down to every other day until Boogie made enough money to buy himself a car, then they could meet half way.

Boogie had moved a half case in the short part of a week plus business was destined to increase. At the same pace, Tommy figured he had enough pills to last for a year. But by then he figured he would be living with Marie and have enough money to buy his own property and open his own landscaping business and Marie would be adorned in roses.

Paul Dupree had been making his own house checks on Marie. First he noticed a broken window and assumed a burglar got in. Then he saw a bouquet of roses attached to her door handle and thought that odd. So he parked in his usual indiscreet spot down the road to watch for Marie as he didn't know where she was either. His bug plant has been silent for a week.

That certainly wasn't like him to know her every move. So now he spy's a teenager in a cargo van deliver another fresh bouquet of roses. Very peculiar indeed, Paul thought. Not so much as she was getting flowers, but FTD usually uses a delivery van. This cargo van was big enough to hold flowers for a presidential inauguration. The other thing was the way the kid paced back and forth on the front walkway.

He observed 15 minutes of knocking and nervous pacing. That was way too much time to spend waiting for a signature. So his shadow was born and the Oregon license plate copied. Paul was going to find out exactly who this strange young man was.

The cargo van was followed at a distance to the park parking lot but there were no hang gliders flying on this day. Tommy maintained his routine of cooking hotdogs and beans. Then he laid out on top of the picnic bench and gazed at the clouds.

All looked harmless enough to Paul who quickly got bored. Plus having better things to do, he slinked away without bothering to strike up a conversation with the boy. He didn't feel the importance or immediacy of disturbing the idle vagrant at this time. His curiosity of why the boy brought Marie flowers would have to be satisfied at a later date. After all, it very well may have been an innocent good will gesture by a distant relative.

Tommy on the other hand just appeared to be lazing the day away. His mind was fixated on one particular cloud. The cloud looked like Marie and she was smiling at him, her smile wasn't cloudy at all, it was picture perfect. Pearly white teeth, accented with delicate dimples, sky blue eyes cushioned by curls, perfect indeed. He further dreamed they were lovers and were walking hand in hand down an isolated beach until they happened upon a rose bush, he would pick her some flowers, and she would be so happy then.

As it was though, Mick and Marie had just returned home. She was upset about finding her window broken and puzzled to find roses in her door handle. With no card she privately thought, it was Paul's doings, and doubted it at the same time. That was certainly out of character for him, but who else could it have been, made her wonder.

Nothing was missing so they ruled out burglary. Mick busied himself removing the broken pane and when he was ready to throw the pieces into the garbage can he discovered four more bunches of roses. That was real odd they both agreed.

She had a sheet of plywood in the garage that Mick cut up to temporarily cover the window to get them through the night, until he could get the window replaced. Marie tried to stop him, declaring she could call a 24 hr. emergency board up service and explained to him that her home-owners insurance would cover the costs. But Mick knew he was perfectly capable of doing the job himself, for a fraction of the cost and she could profit the difference. Besides, Mick wanted to get that, 'needed around the house,' feeling. The internal satisfaction a handyman gets when a job is done right.

Marie called her insurance company regardless. She also called her editor and answered the messages left on her phone recorder. After she got off the phone Mick called to check on his RV and found out the side panel replacement parts had come in and it was just a matter of installation and finishing touches. He further asked about the breaks and found out the bleeding valves were loose and that is where the brake fluid leaked out from. Very unusual, Mick thought before thanking the man. He further called a glass company and made arrangements to get the glass cut to size and make the pickup tomorrow.

The next day Marie begged off the glass trip to LA, she had plenty do around the house. He kissed her goodbye and threw in a, "I love you," and "I'll be back in a couple hours." With that Mick was off.

He had removed the entire window frame and laid it down in the bed of Marie's Jeep Cherokee. He had calculated for everything. His mind was busy with the necessities that go with repairs but neglected to consider that he was leaving Marie at home alone, when he should have known, someone with a bouquet of roses was on his way.

CHAPTER 25

Some men have no bounds when it comes to greed. The Holy Hunter was still a multi-millionaire, even though, by his account, he should have been a billionaire. If only Terrance DeVour hadn't given him the slip and the shaft. Not with standing, so resentful that they couldn't still deal together.

Cal-Con Health was going through normal bankruptcy proceedings and by all accounts the only real losers were going to be the stock holders. Company restructuring was in the process, after all the health insurance part of the business was the only part of the company that made a profit and showed plenty of black ink.

Since Terrance DeVour had sold or closed all but one of its off shore holdings, the losers on the ledgers were gone. Now it was just a matter of restructuring the debt load. Never mind that the debt was more than all the assets combined, and it would take a decade to pay it down enough to eke out a profit, as the company has already been thoroughly looted.

Among other things, the manufacturing of Comfitine was running full bore at the Eagle Lake facility. Illegal aliens filled the void nicely and at this very moment a piggyback truck trailer was being loaded onto a cargo ship destined for a port in Greece.

In L.A. Comfitine was all the rage, the hippest designer drug the town had seen in ages. The DEA hadn't got wind of it yet though, and the cops have been busy with corpse's. A sudden rash of dead junkies have caused a shortage of body bags.

Blood tests were backed up in technicians labs but all preliminary findings were, heroin overdose. Fact was, the labs weren't capable of testing for Comfitine. Comfitine was a complex and complicated compound of opium and synthetic drugs. But when added to heroin, the heart slowed down to a point where oxygen and blood circulation to the brain effectively shut down vital body functions, resulting in death.

The chemists that designed Comfitine did so with the aim of replacing heroin. In effect putting terrorist drug dealers and poppy growers out of business. They had a grand design of a peaceful resolution to the ills of third world and industrialized nations. They were sure Comfitine would replace heroin as the drug of choice among addicts.

Visions of grandeur and ideology prodded the chemists during Comfitine's development. For the junkies who mixed the drugs, there was no such considerations, and the lethal results were not part of the equation. The ideology of a perfect Socialist Society where drug abusers could be controlled in a non-violent, utopian world were the desired results. A very realistic goal, they thought, but not very realistic in practice.

Their experiments with the children at Cal-Con Health was a complete success as far as they were concerned. They had taken the most disturbed teenagers America had to offer and turned them into productive sub servants. That was until the government intervened, and now they were doing a repeat performance with adult illegal aliens. Originally signed on for two weeks labor, turned into a full year contract, 100% re-enlisted. They willingly gave up their families, heritage, dreams, desires and plans for a vitamin pill, Comfitine.

Terrance DeVour had to prepay for his first shipment of Comfitine. 'Nothing personal,' the Holy Hunter explained, it was the fact that CalCon Health needed a quick infusion of cash. The money was logged under a health care insurance entry for a Nigerian Granite Company, and there would be no pay-outs because the employee's will have no idea the insurance policy exists. So the money games continue and all's well at CalCon Health for now.

Paul Dupree and his financial forensic team had wound up a meeting in which 85 financial transactions worth billions of dollars total, appeared to be fraudulent. The ledgers that Paul had copied in Marie's office were damning alright, but the FBI would still have a hard time proving intentional fraud. Most of Cal-Con Health transactions were with off shore companies, some were set up in Bermuda, some on other obscure islands. Still others were set up in Germany, and a variety of others were all linked up with Swiss controlled banks. Banks and vaults that are filled with dark secrets, it would take more than dynamite or subpoena's to open. Connecting the fraud dots was a daunting task.

Talking about fraud, the running jokes between department heads was about the FBI's own new Trilogy Computer System. Designed to make case files more accessible, was still not up and running smoothly, months behind schedule and 200 million dollars over budget. The original price tag was 380 million, now has topped 626 million and rising.

It was suggested to Paul that he find a leaker, someone with inside information. A willing whistle blower. Loose lips still sink ships and corporations faster than anything else. Paul knew exactly how to do that too. Collect some unrelated garbage and dangle it in front of the victim and wait for them to take a bite. Then cut a deal to drop the trumped up garbage for the information to indict the real deal. 'Spring the sting,' he called it.

Two bodyguards in black uniform suits that the Great White Hunter had left behind, were talking to him via satellite. Using un-discrepant terms, they explained the near-miss RV accident to him.

"Keep after them," the vengeful Terrance DeVour demanded. "But do the best you can to make their demise look like an accident" was their standing order.

Actually he could care less if their deaths looked like an accident or not, anyone who messes up his business plans like those two did, deserve to die, and that was all that mattered. It wasn't the first time people have been eliminated by his hand and it won't be the last. The blood lust for business and mayhem catapulted him into the success he is. Nobody or nothing gets in his way. As a matter of fact, as soon he got off the phone with his men he went to the refrigerator and retrieved some lion's blood and drank a toast from his new silver chalice, to the assured premeditated deaths of Marie Sweet and Mickey Swift.

CHAPTER 26

Marie answered the pounding at her front door. She barely recognized Tommy. She remembered him looking neat, wearing a blue jumpsuit and bib gardener coveralls. Now he was sprouting a patchwork of adolescent peach fuzz, and wearing a wrinkled T-shirt and dirty jeans.

Temporarily dumbfounded by the sight of him standing there holding a bouquet of roses, she finally spit out, "what are you doing here?"

"I brought you some roses,—see." He held them out for her to take. "You shouldn't have done that," she said with an ungrateful tone.

"It's alright, I owe you for helping me." He held the bouquet out further for her.

Marie wasn't exactly sure how to handle the situation, so she took the flowers. "How did you find my house?" She quizzed.

"Oh, I forgot—I found your wallet and driver's license. I got them in the van, I'll be right back." With that he turned and trotted off to his van.

Upon his return, Marie instinctively had her nose sniffing at the roses. She smiled at Tommy and thanked him for being so considerate. "Won't you come in?" She politely asked.

She led him into the kitchen where she immediately took one of her vases and filled it with water for the roses. "Do you want a pop?" She asked.

"Sure," he said, while putting her wallet down on the kitchen table.

She fetched him a can from the refrigerator, but this time, in closer quarters she got a whiff of his manure like body odor. She frowned somewhat and took a step back, then asked, "what have you been doing with yourself lately?"

"Nothing much," he said. Then he added, "I've been watching the guys flying in the kites."

"The hang gliders," she corrected him. "Yeah, that's them."

"Where did you get the money to buy flowers?" She wanted to know.

"I do gardening work in L.A. sometimes." He didn't want to tell her the truth. "I'm a real good gardener," he added with pride, to make his statement a half lie. He had a talent for being convincing.

"Where have you been staying?" Marie's prying questions were unexpected and all he could think of saying this time was the truth.

"Up the mountain on a dead-end road by a closed mine," he answered with a bit of embarrassment.

"When's the last time you had a bath?" Her nose forced out the rude question.

"Couple weeks ago, I guess." He was puzzled at that question too, his nose was numb to himself.

Marie felt sorry for her visitor. His disheveled appearance boarded on disgust. But she wanted to thank him for returning her wallet. When she glanced inside and found her money still there, she couldn't send him away like she was ungrateful.

"Are you hungry?" she asked.

"Yeah!" he said with unmistakable excitement. He was elated that she would actually cook for him.

"You'll have to get cleaned up then," her motherly instincts took over. "Do you have any clean clothes?"

"I have some in the van, but I don't know how clean they are."

"Well, go get them and I'll stick them in the washer while you're taking a bath." That was the least she could do for him, she thought.

He ran back to the van and got a duffel bag full of soiled laundry, and one K Mart bag that had new briefs and socks inside. Marie was relieved to see that at least.

She led him to the bathroom and put out some clean towels and a robe for him. Then she dumped the smelly contents of the duffel bag in her washing machine.

Soaking in a hot tub made Tommy feel good, but it wasn't the hot water that heated his soul, it was Marie's warm heart, her caring ways, he was in love. He smiled to himself as he soaped. He felt like singing a song, but all's he could remember was, 'rub a dub, three men in a tub.' That's the one his mother used to sing to him when he was little. He didn't remember much about her, but he surely remembered that, and that made him happy.

Mick had returned with the glass and greeted Marie in the kitchen. She was boiling water and simmering spaghetti sauce. "Who's cargo van?" He asked.

"We have company," Marie declared. "Oh, who?"

"Tommy, from Eagle Lake."

"What's he doing here?"

"He returned my wallet. Wasn't that nice of him."

"Yeah, where is he?"

"Taking a bath."

"Oh." Mick thought that odd but didn't press any further. "I got the glass and they put it into the frame and everything for me. So all's I gotta do is put it back in the window, but I think I'll wait until after dinner, smells good."

Marie stirred the sauce, then Mick noticed the roses, "where did these come from?"

"Where did these come from?"

"Tommy brought them."

"Oh, so he's the one. Is he living around here now?" Mick wanted to know. "He's been staying in an abandoned mine up on the mountain," she explained.

He had just gotten out of the bathroom as if his ears were burning. He stood at the hallway entrance until Marie acknowledged him. "There you are," she said. "Dinner is almost ready."

He stood there for a moment in the bathrobe Marie had provided, staring at Mick. He had forgotten about him, his smile was gone.

"Hi Tommy," Mick said.

"Hi." His begrudged return went unnoticed. He was sure Marie would have gotten rid of the old snort bag by now, he thought.

"Your clothes are in the dryer. Why don't you sit down, the spaghetti will be done in a minute," Marie said.

Over dinner Marie tried to pick Tommy's brain with more questions about Cal-Con Health, but his responses were mundane, 'I don't knows.' A sullen spirit hovered over his evasive answers. Marie didn't notice what Mick saw.

When they finished their meal Mick, still having plenty of daylight, excused himself by saying, "I'll go fix the window now."

Tommy inexplicably blurted out, "I was supposed to do that."

Mick and Marie both raised an eyebrow but it was Mick that asked, "do you know how it was broken?"

"No," he immediately replied in his confident tone, "I just wanted to help Marie."

Mick read a lie on his face but again didn't press, he went out to the garage for tools to finish his chore, but thought Tommy was acting a bit strange. Marie took it all in with a smile, like a cubby bear with a honey pot. Not that she was a gullible person, it was that Tommy had no reason to lie to her.

His clothes were still tumbling in the dryer and Marie started to clear the dishes from the table. Tommy perked up in Mick's absence and insisted on helping. "That's not necessary," she said.

"But I want to help," he insisted. So she let him load the dishwasher while they chatted about his life at Cal-Con Health.

After that information gathering session, she inquired, "what are you going to do tomorrow?"

"I have a job to do in L.A.," he said. "Where are you going to sleep tonight?"

"In the van, I guess," was his meek reply. He was unsure of how to express his true desires. His thought process was all garbled, what he really wanted was to sleep with Marie.

"You've been living out of your van," she asked. "Yeah," he said.

"And how long have you been doing that?"

"A couple weeks,—but I don't have to. I'm just saving some money until I get my landscape business going," he boasted proud as a peacock. He actually thought that his gardening plan would attract her. "You need some rose bushes in front," he proposed.

Marie ignored the statement but offered, "you can spend the night here if you want. I have a pull out bed in the den's sofa." He took it, anything to get closer to Marie.

Mick had finished the window installation and was sliding it up and down to make sure it didn't bind anywhere, when Marie slid up behind him and wrapped her arms around his waist with a loving hug. "Nice job," she said.

"Thanks," he returned smiling.

Tommy saw the congratulatory tenderness and seethed. He was supposed to fix the window. Marie was supposed to be hugging and kissing him, he thought.

Then Marie told Mick Tommy was spending the night in the den. "Ok," was all he said before going about his business of putting away all the tools and placing the plywood back in the garage.

Marie was taking Tommy's clothes out of the dryer and he was gazing out the kitchen window at some colorful gliders in the garage. "You fly on those things," he asked while pointing. "Yes," Marie answered.

"Can you teach me?" He enthusiastically asked.

"I don't see why not," she said with an armful of folded laundry. "Maybe someday," she added as an afterthought.

She's taught other people how to hang glide before, her hesitation wasn't about that, she was expecting to get busy again when her editor calls. She didn't want to promise away time she didn't have and for the first time she shuddered at the thought of him getting hurt. She couldn't explain that odd flitting feeling even to herself, all of the sudden it was there and then gone.

Marie gave Tommy his laundry so he could dress. He thanked her over and over profusely to the point of aggravation. 'Enough already,' she thought. She escaped the gratitude by walking out to join Mick in the garage. She was wondering what was taking him so long anyway.

"It smells like rotten eggs,—or a dead rat in here," he answered when she asked what he was doing. It was a normal two and a half-car garage with one automatic door and one side man door. Two windows on both sides with a long wooden work table. The hang gliders and trailer took up one parking spot and she rarely used the other one. There was a lawn mower and various other gardening implements in the back by a special cabinet for her ceramic supplies. She never locked the man door because of the close-nit neighborhood, nobody really feared burglars.

Marie sniffed at the air a few times but couldn't differentiate the aroma Mick thought strange. "It smells like a garage to me," she said.

Tommy appeared at the garage door. He was looking for Marie and wanted a closer look at the gliders. Their conversation was interrupted and Tommy's eyes were open wider than an eagles. His eyes reflected the fancy colors of the silk like glider fabric. His voice sparkled like a kid with a new toy. "I can't wait to learn how to fly," he said.

Marie's misgivings were moot. She didn't want to disappoint the kid with glittery eyes. How could she refuse a simple request after he came all this way to return her wallet. That's the least she could do, honor a simple request, she thought. But that danger feeling crept to mind again, how to gracefully wiggle out she wondered. "I thought you had to go to work in LA?" She tried.

"Yeah, I do but don't. I can take a day off. I got plenty of money."

Strong statement for a kid, Mick thought. He was penniless a month ago,

and where did he get the money for the cargo van? Maybe it's stolen? He privately wondered.

"Ok, tomorrow then. In the afternoon, after the sun heats up the air." 'Too late to back out now,' both Mick and Marie thought silently. They were so in- tune with each other, they were starting to think alike without prompting.

Marie started to explain to Tommy the aerodynamics of the glider, how to steer with the body and how to land and take off on the run. Mick was distracted enough to forget about the odor source, and closed up the garage when they were finished chatting.

At the kitchen table he took out a newspaper he bought while waiting on the glass. He wanted to show her the AP article she wrote, but she wouldn't read it. She explained that, the way her editor cuts and dehumanizes her stories to pure reporting, she always feels disappointed. So then Mick turned a page to show her a story about a man who got thrown in jail for fourteen days because he burned a flag.

That irritated her to the max. "They can't do that!" she fumed. "In 1989 the U.S. Supreme Court ruled that flag desecration laws were unconstitutional. It violates the First Amendment, freedom of speech."

"I know, I know," Mick said in a soothing tone. Then he went on to explain that the guy was from Jonesboro Illinois and was made to pay court costs, then submit DNA samples to the state police.

"That violates the Constitution too! Let me see that article." As she read it for herself, her face was getting red like mercury rising in a thermometer on a 100 degree day. When she finished, she threw the article on the table and said, "assholes!" Before she stormed out of the room.

Mick was somewhat taken aback as he never heard her swear before. Tommy looked on puzzled as to why Mick would upset his lovely flower like that. Being a few peddles short of a full bud himself, he was incapable of comprehending that Marie wasn't upset with Mick at all. She was upset because some government officials have no respect for the US Constitution. They view it as an obstacle to the power they want. The checks and balance system is so tilted for the rich, it's teetering on self-destruction.

Marie's dander was raised to the point that her hair felt like a static filled Halloween cat. She went to the bathroom to brush out her frustrations, stroke by stroke. Mick went to the fridge and popped open a beer. Tommy didn't like that smell, it reminded him of his father. He didn't like Mick at all. He made Marie mad. He actually felt like punching him but didn't dare. He was so much bigger than him.

Marie returned refreshed and suggested to Tommy that it was time for bed. "It's too early," he protested like a child.

"Not if you want to go hang gliding tomorrow it isn't." She hung over him like a mother, she had other plans, loving ones.

He relented but couldn't sleep, he laid there staring at the ceiling. Excited about the prospect of flying in a kite made him happy. But he was sad that Mick had made Marie mad. He was still staring at the big movie screen overhead and saw himself spreading his colorful peddles, floating on the wind like a kite. Then he heard the pop, pop of beer cans, followed by laughter. All the sounds resonated down the hall from the kitchen. He's getting her drunk, he thought.

He stared back at the ceiling trying to concentrate the noise away. His vision was gone, the ceiling was colorless and gray. He missed sleeping in his van, he felt comfortable there, but what he really wanted was to sleep with Marie. He stared at the gray ceiling, beads of perspiration formed on his forehead. Grey shadows on the ceiling started to move in a circular pattern. He felt dizzy. He closed his eyes.

His eyes were closed but he could see better than ever. He saw red spider veins in his eyelids. He saw things he didn't want to see. He heard whispers that no child should hear. He saw things that were going to change the rest of his life. He saw his father's head split open like a watermelon, he saw blood splattered by a baseball bat. He heard snoring.

He opened his eyes and sat up in a panting sweat. He looked around and focused on the fireplace, there was no fire but the poker was glowing at him like a happy smile. He put his hands to his head to cover his ears, he still heard snoring, like echo chambers rattling around in the deep membranes of the cranium.

Getting out of bed and going by the fireplace he grabbed the cast iron poker. More lethal than a baseball bat, more lethal than a knight's lance, he thought. It was pointed at the tip and had a treacherous hook on the side. A wry smile grew on his face. He had to stop that damn snoring, that snoring.

Sometimes Tommy heard and saw things that weren't really there at all. But this time he was hearing the sounds of passion. Mick and Marie were making love. Poker in hand, socks on his feet, he silently, slowly crept down the hallway. He paused to put his ear to Marie's door, the snoring was loud and getting louder. He reached for the doorknob and slowly twisted it.

He figured Mick was doing all the snoring and he could help save Marie from the drunk. Marie would surely love him then. All's he had to do was get the jump on that snort bag and whack, then, they could live in peace and quiet. He looked down at the poker by his side. Twirling it slightly, the dim light reflected menacingly off the cold steel, but Tommy's dementia thought the shine was smiling at him.

Tommy had twisted the doorknob but it wouldn't open. He tried twisting slowly in the other direction and it still wouldn't open. It was Mick that locked the door. His ears were full Marie's rapturous groans. Still he was perceptive enough to look at the doorknob he heard jostle. To close to climax his attention went back to his partner as whatever the disturbance was fell silent and Marie, his main concern, was bucking in ecstasy.

Now Tommy was befuddled. He hadn't planned on a locked door. Confounded, he removed his hand and dejectedly walked back to the den. He leaned the poker back on the fireplace before climbing back into bed where he started to cry. Blocking his ears with a pillow, he still couldn't get that snoring out of his head. His failure to save Marie reverberated there too.

Crying did nothing to ease his pain. He shivered with sweats. He looked out from underneath the pillow, synthetic Comfitine ghosts continued to haunt him. They floated up the gray walls, then, spun on the ceiling like a fan. He thought about shooting them, then, he remembered the handgun he had in the van under his bed. Tears still blurred his vision but he got up and ran out the front door anyway.

Cold steel trembled along with his hand. Perspiration still dripped from his forehead. Boldly he walked back to the house, determined to get rid of that snoring and save Marie. He must, he couldn't help himself. On the concrete walkway he had to pass the window that Mick replaced and saw his reflection in the moonlight.

He saw Mick snoring at him through the window. He raised his arm, trembling gun in hand, "you snore," he cried before pulling the trigger. Click, the snoring got loader, click, now he was laughing at him, click, click, click. The gun had no bullets in it.

Tears still blurred his vision, then, the most beautiful deity appeared in the window. She smiled at him and asked in the kindest voice asked, "why are you standing outside in your stocking feet?" He looked down and felt the cold concrete permeate his socks. The concrete was hard and sobering. He lowered his extended arm in disgust with himself.

His body shivered again in the cold night air, "Marie," he cried out as the wispy deity disappeared from the window. 'Bullets,' he thought irrationally. 'I need bullets.' He looked down at his feet again, they were cold and hard, running back to his van he was planning on getting his bullets. He spied his jar of Comfitine first, his body shuddered and he took a pill. Heat immediately pumped through his veins. That ever so comfortable warmth, there was his bed too. His tears dried up, the snoring stopped ringing in his head and he couldn't remember what he was looking for. He crawled underneath his sleeping bag and was sound asleep in a matter of minutes.

CHAPTER 27

Lucky for Tommy that he took the day off, because his buddy Boogie got busted. A vice squad was hot on the trail of who was supplying heroin to a certain movie stars son who had over dosed. After interrogating friends of the deceased, the cops had a good idea of where they could find the supplier.

Tress Tree's was a popular lounge on the boulevard. With a state of the art sound system and a huge dance floor, this was where all the famous and wannabe's show off their gyrating dance moves. There always was a line to get in. It was here that Boogie sold his wares. Once he sold out his entire stock in one pass. Two hundred dollars profit in five minutes, not bad for a day's work, he thought.

That was until he got stung. The cops thought he was pushing some kind of prescription drugs on first examination. During interrogation they found out otherwise. Boogie called them vitamins; the cops didn't buy the story. They had 24 hrs. to hold him while they sent one pill to the lab for analysis. The lab didn't know exactly what they were looking for but came up with an opiate base. That made it a narcotic and illegal to distribute without a prescription. So read the charges.

Threats of a life sentence scared Boogie enough to flip on Tommy. He was honest with the cops when he told them he didn't know anything about his supplier other than his name. So the cops toke him for a ride to meet him. But when Tommy didn't show up for their usual rendezvous, the cops were pissed off for wasting their time and threw Boogie back in the slammer with new charges of obstructing justice.

The L.A. street gangs were now selling in quantities and that made Boogie miniscule. Not only were the pills being distributed in LA, they were being sold to cities around the country, courtesy of the U.S. Mail.

Money was talking to the Holy Hunter. The L.A. street gangs already distributed three truckloads of Comfitine and wanted more. Cash profits were rolling in for Lawrence Marsi. Profits, that weren't logged into any of CalCon Health books. He was charging the LA street gangs a premium price, far more than he was getting from the Great White Hunter.

That fact put Terrance DeVour and his Grand Granite Pits on the back burner. Still he had enough production output at Eagle Lake to keep up with demand. That is, if demand for Comfitine didn't expand beyond his capabilities to produce. The solution to that kind of blessing is simple as raising prices. Comfitine was still a bargain compared to heroin and he figured it wouldn't take long before his drug over takes heroin in popularity.

Marie was puzzled at the sight of the empty sofa bed and Tommy's shoes beside it. Mick wondered why the fireplace poker was out of place, especially when they didn't build a fire last night. His van was still parked outside so they know he couldn't have gone too far.

She whipped up a pan of scrambled eggs and popped some English Muffins in the toaster. While the coffee brewed, Mick checked out the van by peering into the window. He located the sleeping teen.

"He's sleeping in the van," he reported back to Marie. "Did you wake him? Breakfast is ready."

"No—Let him wake in his own time. Strange one that kid is." He said, somewhat concerned.

"He probably just missed his own bed," Marie explained.

They ate their breakfasts and Marie covered a plate for Tommy, whenever he came around. Then looking out to her patio at the kiln, she remembered the mold she had made of Mick's masculinity. A sly mischievous smile crept across her face. She has really come to appreciate his maleness full heartily. She would finish step two of her project that morning.

Tommy didn't wake up until noon. The sun had heated up the inside to well over one hundred degrees and he lay in a pool of sweat. Other than that he felt great. He himself wondered why he was sleeping in the van. He vaguely remembers going to bed in Marie's house, but that didn't matter, he did remember that he was going fly in a kite, and that made him happy.

He stepped out of his cargo van and looked at his stocking feet. His T-shirt was drenched through and through. Realizing he left his shoes inside with his laundry. He ran back to the house, whizzing by his nightmare window with nary a glance. Entering the front door, grabbing his shoes and a change of clothes, he went into the bathroom.

Marie had heard the commotion and went to investigate. She had finished step two and her work was back in the kiln. Mick had busied himself with neglected yard work.

When Tommy reappeared, Marie quizzed him as to what happened. He explained her inquiries with the likes of, "the bed was too lumpy," and "I felt more comfortable in my own bed." Excuses plausible enough, and read with a sincerity that fooled Marie again. Truth be told, he had no clue as to why he slept in the van last night.

"Can we go flying now?" he asked.

"Yes," she said. A Deja vu illusion of a, 'don't do it,' voice dashed through her frontal lobe with such speed, she didn't hear it. It wasn't a haunting voice, it was more mystic, beyond reality. Fast and fleeting, the thought was gone before she could file it.

They walked outside and saw Mick washing the dirt off the driveway with a garden hose. 'Stupid,' Tommy thought, 'water is for roses,' but he said nothing. The disgust he felt about the way the landscape was done magnified his disdain for Mick. There wasn't even one rose bush planted. Nothing but sun baked grass and cactus 'yuck.'

Mick wrapped up the garden hose on the reel while Marie hooked up the glider trailer to her jeep. Tommy climbed into the back, noticing Marie's climbing gear in the rear bed and the jugs of water on the floor. He didn't know what all the ropes were for but had to ask, "what's with all the water?"

"Oh,—that's spring water from Eagle Lake," Marie answered.

"That water is good for roses. It has a lot of minerals," he said proudly with airs of, he's an expert with roses.

"There's some in the canteen in back," Mick offered.

Tommy turned down his goodwill gesture. He was in a mindset to rebuff any of Mick's friendly overtures. If only Marie would have said that, he surely would have partook. He would have emptied the whole canteen in one gulp to impress her.

Then they were off down the road. Marie was preaching proper procedures most of the way, emphasizing safety. Tommy naturally mistook her concerns for love. Then Marie gave Mick instructions to pull over on a grassy area at the base of the mountain.

"Why are you stopping here?" Tommy asked. "You're going off the beginners hill first," she said.

Tommy instantly pouted. He didn't like the term beginner, even though he was one. It was a male macho hormone that all, 'I can do it,' teenagers have. He wanted to go right to the top and take a flying leap, fly as high as he could go, just like a kite. Marie recognized his childish behavior and soothed it by saying, "this is the same hill I learned to glide from."

That made all the difference in the world. The connection, the bonding, it was the same hill, no longer a baby thing to do, Tommy thought, if she did it this way, then he was all for it.

So they took one glider off the trailer and carried it up the hill. Once there, Marie unfolded the delta-shaped flexible wings like a pupa turning into a butterfly. The hill was perfect to learn from. Being only 50 ft. high with a gentle slope, there was little chance of being hurt if one crashes.

He listened intently like a student while Marie once again explained to him how to use his body weight, the parallel bar control, and how to land in a fast walk, just like taking off.

"I know, I know, I've been watching them all week." His macho eagerness to take off was in a hurry. Marie slipped on his safety helmet and adjusted the chin strap for a snug fit.

Mick was at the bottom watching. He was about 200 yards out on the flat land sitting on the trailer. Marie explained to Tommy that he should be able to glide at least that far and she would meet him down there.

With a, "good luck," and a smile, Tommy started his run and leaped into the air. Marie watched his form with an experts eye, as he glided just like she instructed him. She stood there motionless until she was convinced Tommy was in complete control. Then she started a fast jog downhill.

Tommy had landed perfectly too, actually going 20 yards past his target, and that was fine with him. He surely enjoyed the rush and couldn't wait to take off from the mountain.

Mick doubled over with laughter at the comical sight of Tommy running back to the trailer with the glider still on his back. The wings were bobbing up and down in such a fashion that reminded him of the flying monkeys from the Wizard of Oz. Or maybe it was the early flying machine contraptions featured on the old time news reels reveling man's first attempts at flight. The sight sure struck Mick's funny bone.

Tommy didn't think of it as being funny as he struggled though. He thought it contemptuous of Mick to be laughing at his first successful flight. Good thing Marie jogged up to help Tommy out of his harness. "Good job," she said in praise.

"It was easy," he replied in a boastful tone.

"Do you want to try again?" Marie asked the dumbest question of her life. "Yeah,—but off the mountain this time."

Mick had stopped laughing as the two of them figured out what to do next. Tommy insisted he was ready for the mountain, Marie wasn't so sure. She won out with a compromise. "So Mick can take a picture and you can practice more turns," was the way she put it. One more flight off the hill, then the mountain, and so it was settled.

Mick had his camera out for the second test flight and snapped off a few pictures in the sport mode. After another success, they folded the wings and put the glider back on the trailer for the trip up the mountain. On the way there they passed the dead end road that led to the mine and Tommy let the information slip out, that was where he was staying nights. He came to realize, learning information made Marie happy, and he was willing to do anything to fulfill her wishes.

But he was repeating information she already knew. Tommy was jabberjawing to be talking and looking for Marie's approval. Mick was soaking in all the extra information that made him feel Tommy was weirder than he realized.

There were other gliders there and Tommy was ecstatic about the event. Like a bikers club, hang-gliders hung out together. There were coolers of beer atop and barbecues fired up below. The club women who weren't flying had a blast throwing delta wing tailgate parties. Walkie-talkies and cell phones aided communications. But mostly the club members that made the trip from San Diego knew who was gliding by recognizing the variety of colors of wings and they just started to take off.

Marie again explained to Tommy that the air currents are stronger up here because of the updraft and that all he has to do was sit in the harness steer with his body and relax. Tommy assured her that he would be alright.

Her cautious pampering was beginning to irritate him a little and his tone showed it. He just wanted to fly like a kite and couldn't wait until it was his turn, and then it was.

Mick took up his favorite picture position to record the, 'historic event.' He teased. Tommy could care less about pictures and he gave Mick a snide smile before he took his flying leap. He was in heaven now as he floated on the air. His grin was now as wide as it ever had been. An eagle size view of the valley below and he was relaxed and poised. Then he felt the updraft lift him higher and higher. He turned the glider and completed his first circle.

Marie was ready to take off next. Mick had his routine down, take some pictures and drive back down to pick them up for another turn. Mick was atop a boulder off to the right of the launch site, he had an eagles view of the valley below too. Only this time when he peered down at the landing area he spied something that bothered him.

It was that black sawed-off Brinks truck. The ugliest vehicle in the world, or so it seemed to him. That black Humvee was down there. He spied down there with his telescopic camera lens. Two men in suits got out with binoculars. He snapped off a couple pictures by instinct.

Instinct is a funny thing sometimes. It tells you things that don't always immediately register, warning. After all, they were way down there and he was way up here. Why should he be afraid of two suits with binoculars? But they looked like the guys he saw after the RV crash. And they resemble the dead guys from Eagle Lake. Bad things seem to follow those guys, he thought before it sunk in.

He was about ready to yell 'stop,' at Marie but it was too late, she took off. Mick's heart-beat took off too, faster than it ever raced before. He looked out at her floating on the breeze. She looked perfectly fine. He looked back down the valley and saw the suits climb back in their Humvee.

He focused his camera on the Humvee again and snapped off a few more pictures as it pulled away. Then focusing on Marie again, everything appeared normal. His instinct and heart told him she wasn't. That smell, that smell permeated his senses. He felt stomach pangs.

He gathered himself and made a bee-line for the jeep. Hurling down the mountain as fast as he safely could, or so he thought. Thinking and driving don't necessarily mix, especially thinking about the things he was thinking of. Mick knew they could aloft for an hour or so if the air favored them. But he could no longer see them as he tore down the mountain. His grip was tight on the steering wheel, tighter than it should be.

Not being able to see them tormented his suspicions. That smell, that smell, what was it? He tried to think. He didn't know, that fact fueled his apprehension. Feeling the trailer bouncing and swaying with reckless abandon, he let up on the gas. 'Calm down,' he told himself. A useless feeling enveloped him. He sucked in an extra-large gulp of air. 'No sense in crashing,' sparked a sedate message through his nerve center. He was helpless and realized it. Foreboding anxiety and tranquility messages were battling out for position. Nanoseconds of electric nerve data were bombarding his brain. His strangle hold grip on the steering wheel relaxed. A lone tear trickled down his cheek.

Tommy was having the time of his life. He knew he could fly like a kite. He liked looking down on the people in the valley. Gliding in a huge circular pattern he pretended he was a California Condor hovering over his prey. Feeling all powerful, circling over and over like the vultures in western movies.

He wasn't skilled enough to recognize the powerful updraft and ride the wind like a surfer picks the big wave. So his decent was a little faster than that of a more experienced flier. He heard the wind whistle through the ear holes in his helmet and he was pretending to catch prey in flight like a hawk now.

Marie was circling high over-head, keeping an eye on her young student. She remembered her first flight and the swell time she and her friends had. She considers herself a champion glider pilot. She had won numerous competitions, one for efficiency, for which she is most proud. The competition was for the longest time aloft over the Pacific Coast cliffs. She had a very maneuverable glider. Modern designs and improved safety were brought about with the strongest lightweight materials. Flying a glider was one of the easiest aviation sports she knew. That was one of the reasons she let Tommy go gliding with her. She was proud of herself, Tommy looked to be enjoying himself thoroughly.

Mick had pulled into the landing area and was relieved to see they were still gliding away. 'Paranoid asshole,' he cursed at himself. His relief was short lived, however. Tommy had decided to play like he was a jet fighter in a dog-fight. He was bored with flying in circles. He wanted more speed. Starting to weave in a straight line, banking left, then right like he was on some kind of carnival ride and flying over 50 mph.

"What's that asshole doing now?" Mick asked himself. He had asshole on his mind, a natural mental reaction when people don't do things the way the thinker would.

Then it happened, Tommy had built up the extra speed he wanted but when he pulled up to raise the glider a nylon twine snapped. The cord supported the steering seat and the sudden G forces ripped Tommy's hands from the parallel bar. He was wrapped up in the remaining seat harness but wasn't able to steer the craft. Imitating a tornado ready for destruction he went into a dizzy tight spiral spin. He did scream as he struggled but nobody could hear him. Observers only had time to drop jaws and then it was over.

With a crash and a thud Tommy had landed in sage bushes on the bottom side of the mountain. The out of control glider had a slight parachute effect and free fall speed was reduced. His lifeless looking body sent rescuers running but they all expected the worst, death.

Marie witnessed the event from above and cursed herself. She wanted to end her flight immediately. She dipped her delta wings and sped to the landing area. She didn't know what happened to Tommy that made him lose control but was going to find out as the nylon twine that supported her steering harness snapped under the extra tension.

Her body shifted but was able to hold on to the parallel bar. Faster and faster her out of control glider went. One hand slipped off the bar as she struggled with the grip. She could no longer steer her craft.

Mick had been running with the others to the aid of Tommy but now witnessing Marie's distress, he stopped in his tracks. 'Oh no, oh shit,' were the first things that his mind transmitted as he witnessed Marie disappear into a grove of trees. 'God damn motherfuckers,' was the second.

Paul Dupree witnessed it too. He was on the run also. He was spying the events from the parking lot and was much closer to Marie. He had cell phone in hand and was already communicating for emergency services.

Marie's glider was all bent out of shape and stuck in some branches. She dangled upside down. Feet in air, and strapped in the seat, her head scrapping the ground. Paul had a pocket knife out and was cutting away at the harness to free Marie as Mick and others ran up to lend assistance.

Mick was crying, "Marie, Marie," trying to get her attention, as her chest heaves indicated she was still breathing, but was unconscious. Mick cradled her in his arms and picked her up as Paul sawed at the harness freeing her. Now entirely in his arms he tearfully whispered, "Marie, Marie."

"Lay her down," Paul demanded. "I have paramedics on the way."

That done, Mick made a move to gently remove her helmet. It was cracked and only held together by the glued foam pad.

"Leave it on," Paul instructed. "Don't move her any more than needed. She needs to be hospitalized."

That was obvious, her lower rib cage was bloody. Shirt torn, her exposed stomach was red with blood and welts. She likely landed on a branch.

Mick knew Paul was right but said and did nothing. Helpless again, he was out of sorts, somewhat ill, gazing at her every shallow breath like it might be her last. 'God damn those dirty motherfuckers,' were his cursory thoughts. He got off his knees and looked at the carnage stuck in the tree above.

He smelled a rat, a dirty stinking dead rat. The same smell that was in the garage. Grabbing the cord that had snapped, he examined it while dangling from the tree. It looked melted and stretched like it was burned by flame. He smelled that stench when he put it under his nose. "Sabotage," he said aloud.

That word got Paul's attention. "I'll have it sent to the lab," he replied automatically.

"Who are you?" Mick asked.

"I'm with the FBI. What do you do for a living?"

"I'm a photographer." They exchanged fuck you glances and nothing more.

Mick didn't trust suits, no matter what style they wore. Paul didn't like Mick either because he was doing his girl. He wouldn't have cared if he was the president himself, he would still hate him. But the facts at hand lent to an unspoken moral truce and prejudices mote. Both were helpless, but Paul had clout. Fact was he had a medivac helicopter in-route.

The fire department paramedics siren could be heard in the distance. Getting loader by the second. Other people had called 911 after seeing Tommy crash. Barbecues were abandoned, char-burgers were blackened, crowds huddled. Nobody had ever seen such a horrific spectacle before. The men had removed the wreckage that was covering Tommy.

It was a miracle he was still alive. The sage bush had cushioned his fall they all agreed. Lucky he was wearing a safety helmet others observed. He had landed on his back, helmet dented the sandy soil, blood lined his lips.

The paramedics located him first as they saw the crowd from the road. They checked him for vital signs. He had a pulse but was unconscious. Using all their skills they carefully placed him on a stretcher and carried him to the ambulance.

Paul was on his cell phone and directing the heli-medivac to the closest landing area. Mick was on his knees again. He held Marie's hand while caressing her arm and repeating, "You're going to be alright. I guarantee." Consolatory terms that comforted him all the while hoping she would awaken and give him a smile.

Trying to stay positive, watching her every breath, his already cloudy mind started getting darker, like a storm brewing. He had been so content with her companionship. The peaceful easy feeling that encompassed their life sharing. All of that was fading as the dark clouds of hatred covered their Garden of Eden. He couldn't understand why anyone would sabotage his RV and her gliders. His brain was boiling, sabotage was a small fraction of thought that was causing friction within. The mental friction was getting hotter and hotter, no matter how many times he said, "you're going to be alright,—I guarantee."

The chopper blades whirled the air but he took no notice of it until the paramedic said, "excuse me." He laid her arm back down by her side, stood and backed away while the experts went about their business. He walked behind the gurney to the helicopter. Paul was already seated next to the pilot. He tried to enter the rear with the paramedics and Marie but was stopped.

"Immediate family members only," were Paul's orders.

"Where are you taking her?" Mick screamed over the copter's noise. "St Michael's," the paramedics replied.

Mick had to back up as the copter blades sped up. Even with the grassy field, the speeding airflow kicked up every speck of dust and flung it violently about. Mick cowered from it all. He couldn't stand to look anyway, Marie was being taken away from him again.

The fire department paramedics already removed Tommy and were streaking to the hospital. The local police were gathering statements from eye witnesses and gathering the pieces of wrecked gliders.

Thunder clouds were now clashing in Mick's body. He wasn't in an interviewing frame of mind. Someone had offered him a beer, but he declined even though he was thirstier than ever. He wasn't normal. He kept on walking to the jeep, and unhooked the trailer. He wouldn't need it anymore.

Sitting in the jeep, he took a much needed drink of spring water from the canteen. Thinking, thinking, alone again, and what to do next? Perspiring with anger, the mental thunder clouds opened the flood gates with a down pour. His mind was flooded with hatred, he wiped at his bone-dry brow in angst. He took another drink from the canteen and decided next to Marie was where he belongs, and St Michael's was where he was going.

CHAPTER 28

The Great White hunter had received his shipment of Comfitine and it was being distributed to his workers at the granite pits. Vitamins, the workers were told, and they started the day with them. A healthy worker, is a happy worker, was the propaganda they used. In a weeks' time, all the workers were now addicts. Desensitized, resentment of interrupted tradition, Qat chewing the narcotic leaf, went unabated.

Comfitine didn't make the workers any more productive. Other than, now they had to come to work every day to get their fix. Production was increased however because the granite pits were in operation 24-7.

As for Terrance DeVour's aphrodisiac fix, he was going on another safari. He was sourly out of beast blood. This time though, the president of Niger was so grateful, arrangements were made and once again, caged animals awaited their destruction.

Time and comfort were priorities. The Great White Hunter didn't want to waste time traipsing through the jungles or plains for his meat. Once was enough for him. He wanted everything handed to him on a silver platter, and he wanted to drink his blood out of his silver chalice.

There were diamonds to smuggle and the Mediterranean Sea to be cruised. Then again, there was a new venture to be looked into, plastic explosives. For oil or gold, there was always a black market for explosives in the Middle East. And Terrance DeVour was an expert in all.

Meanwhile his state side bodyguards apprised him, via satellite cell phone, of the situation. There seemed to be an accident involving gliders in Lake Elsinore, but one Mickey Swift escaped unharmed.

"Finish the job," were their orders.

Then there was another matter reported. Comfitine was the rage, the designer drug of choice in the LA clubs. Terrance DeVour pondered over the information a moment, then said, "go back up to Eagle Lake and see what's going on, then finish the job.

The Holy Hunter was now in charge of day-to-day operations at CalCon Health. Bankruptcy was immanent, or so Terrance DeVour thought. That was why he sold all of his stock and gave up control. He also knew what a great hustler Lawrence Marsi was. If anyone could save the company, he could. He was such a fantastic liar, so cleaver he could skin a grizzly bear in hibernation without waking him.

Problem was, the Great White Hunter didn't like giving up control of anything, even junk bonds. If there was a way to squeeze a dollar out of a penny, he would find it. He wasn't a bloodsucker for nothing. Then there was the matter of that villa he wanted. The one he just bought on the Greek Isle of Capri was fine. But now he wanted one on the South of France too. He belonged with the Royalty of Monaco, he figured. And if he found out Cal- Con Health was still making a profit, he could squeeze out 10 or 20 million more in the golden parachute he deserves.

The Holy Hunter wasn't stupid either. None of the Comfitine cash profits were on the books anywhere. Fact was the money was being funneled into a Texas Estate, a thousand acre ranch with the main house as big as an airport hangar. Funny thing about bankruptcy laws, they vary from state to state, but in Texas and Florida, if a CEO drives their company into bankruptcy, the CEO still gets to keep his main residency out of court proceedings. No matter how much money the stock holders lose, and that was just fine with Lawrence Marsi.

CHAPTER 29

Mick had made it to the trauma ward at St. Michael's hospital. He had to lie to get in by claiming he was Marie's brother, afraid they wouldn't let him in if he didn't. He felt like saying husband and wished he was. He had been planning on marrying her anyway. So his concerned look carried the slight fraud. But he was forewarned that she had a concussion and in all likelihood would be unresponsive. He insisted on talking to the doctors, regardless.

"Follow the red line down the hall," he was instructed. The floor was lined with colors, red, blue and green. Signs were everywhere, not much of a chance getting lost. Still he gingerly walked down the hall. He noticed people in hospital gowns sitting in wheel chairs all depressed looking, a reminder that going to the hospital is not about having fun. Then there was that that unique odor, sanitized death. He shook the thought away. "You're going to be alright. I guarantee," he remembered his promise. 'Think positive,' he reminded himself.

Still he noticed how slow he was walking. Was it because he was in no hurry to hear bad news? That wasn't his attitude when he was speeding to get here. He only missed the one turn, when he saw the hospital sign it was too late to slam on the breaks. So he had to go down a block before he turned around. Or was the visual being in a hospital depressing period. That didn't seem to bother the doctors or nurses that were scurrying around though. They must be hardened to their environment, he thought.

Following the red line led him to a corner and he turned. The souls of his gym shoes squeaked on the ultra-clean floor. It was ear piercing, or so he thought, nobody else seemed to notice. He slowly moved ahead.

Getting closer now, he could see the trauma sign. He walked slower yet, he didn't want his shoes squeaking anymore, he didn't want to hear any bad news. His walked turned into a turtle crawl.

'Why did he come here?' He uneasily asked himself. 'Why did you volunteer to do this?' He had to see Marie he told himself. Then he had a vision of seeing her with all kinds of tubes attached to her, intravenous catheters dangling from a mobile stainless steel mast.

He stopped outside the door, he didn't want to go in. It didn't seem to long ago that he walked through a similar door at the morgue. He didn't want to walk through that door either. He was frozen solid then and he was frozen now. He stood and stared at the door.

"Hospital personnel only,' was looking straight at him, it took a while for the sign to register. His mind was preoccupied, body enema'd of feelings, except for that smell.

Mick peered through the glass in one of the double doors. Tommy was laying in a bed next to Marie separated by a curtain. Both were hooked up to an EEG machine. Wires were taped to their heads. He could hear the blips and see the sine waves on the screen. Two doctors and two nurses were monitoring the equipment and their patients.

"You can't stand here," a nurse entering the room with a cart full of needles and drugs said.

Mick took another position and leaned against an opposing wall. He would wait for a doctor to come out and then inquire about their conditions. Helpless again, he was uncomfortable, shifting his weight from on foot to another every second or so. To a casual observer it would appear he was trying to rub the paint off the cinder block wall with his back.

Time flies when the mind is occupied. Mick had been scratching his back for so long now, the paint should have been gone by now. He would take a gander in the room whenever a nurse would come in or out. This particular time a nurse came out with a panic look about her and both doctors were hovering over Tommy. Back the nurse came hurriedly pushing a defibrillator. Mick noticed one of the EEG machines had a flat line on the screen.

Tick, tick, tick, Mick looked at the clock on the far wall over the nurses station. He was temporally paralyzed by the second hand. Tick, tick, tick, every second now was somehow more important than the others. The clock was battery operated and didn't make any noise. But Mick's mind cut through all that silence, tick, tick, he heard every second load and clear.

He couldn't look anymore, 'how's Marie,' started to bombard his brain.

He felt like bursting through the double doors to see if he could help. But the sign said, 'hospital personnel only,' he was wallowing the self-pity of helplessness. He was pacing now, over the multi-color lines on the floor. He was staring at the lines as he paced, but he didn't see any bright colors, he saw only gray. The fancy colors on the floor were designed to give directions and reflect joy. He only saw gray, deaths gray, Tommy was dead.

The doctors were baffled. Tommy was younger and had less injuries than Marie. They put them into a barbiturate induced coma to protect the brain from further damage. The first hour is especially critical for concussion victims. Bleeding and swelling can choke off vital oxygen supply. Marie was given the same dosage, plus she suffered from fractured ribs and a miscarriage. Tommy's heart gave out, an autopsy was automatically ordered to find out why.

Mick had finally cornered a doctor to find out what was going on. He was reluctant to talk about what happened to Tommy. The main reason was because he didn't know. Regarding Marie he said, "she had a miscarriage in route, caused by the fall. Her brain is effectively anesthetized so it will require less oxygen."

He further explained that she would be given a CT scan and an MRI and would be transferred to an intensive care unit. "She will remain there for the next week, or possibly up to a month, brain injuries can take a life time to diagnosis."

"She's lucky she was wearing a helmet, or she would be dead too," was the last thing the doctor said.

Mick was in a confused quandary. Miscarriage? He might as well have been in a coma too. What was he going to do without Marie? Was his main question. What would Marie do if the situation were reversed? Was his second. The answer didn't come to him until he reached the jeep and took a drink of spring water from the canteen. 'She would go get the complete story,' was his answer, and that was what he was going to do.

When he reached Marie's house he entered the rear door. He stood in the kitchen of emptiness, or so it seemed. Sure there was a refrigerator and stove, a counter, table and chairs, toaster and microwave too, but the house was as empty as his heart, Marie wasn't there with him.

Ghosts of emptiness past were haunting him. The patter of little feet from a long time ago, were following his every move. The echo in his ears told him a house isn't a house when it's empty, he thought.

A promise to another woman followed too, 'adoption, this house deserves kids.' Why didn't he press Marie to marry him earlier? Why didn't he press Marie to start adoption proceedings sooner? This whole episode could have been avoided. She would be home now he reflected.

His nerves were on edge. He was playing a dangerous blame game.

Remembering the same thing happened not too long ago. The sadness.

He went to the refrigerator and plucked out a beer and sat at the kitchen table in front of Marie's laptop. Opening it up, turning on the power, then read what she had written while sipping at his beer.

One line at a time, one poem after another, rhyme after rhyme his heart twanged. When he finished the last poem, he wished she was there so he could tell her how good they were. Reflecting the ponderous, then closing the lid on her laptop, he closed his face in his folded arms on the table, and cried in heaves of agony.

CHAPTER 30

On the rise of the next day Mick's mind and body were refreshed. He made himself a pot of coffee and fried up some bacon and eggs. Then made a phone call to check on his RV, it was ready.

While waiting for a cab to pick him up, he thought to rummage through Tommy's cargo van to see if he could find a relatives to inform them his vehicle is here and it had to go. The door was unlocked but the keys weren't in the ignition. 'Must be in his personal effects at the hospital,' he deduced.

Looking about in the back, right on the floor next to the raised bed, Mick spotted a gun. That made him recall a thought that the van might be stolen. Upon further inspection he spotted a rifle butt sticking out. He lifted the moving blankets and sleeping bags to further discover cases of Comfitine. The cases were stamped with the Cal-Con Health logo. One case was already open, he popped open a lid and saw the pink pills. He was wondering what they were for and what they do, when his thoughts were interrupted by the horn from the cabby. He mulled things over good on the ride and came up with a few different scenarios.

It felt good to get back in his captain's chair. He thoroughly enjoyed his trip home. Once there he removed Marie's mountain climbing gear from the jeep and put it in the storage compartment under his RV. He had a quasi-plan and he was going fishing at Eagle Lake. But he also suspected he had another one of life's mountains to climb.

He packed and readied himself for the trip. Wanting to hit the road as soon as possible, not a moment was wasted. Even the most unlikely thing, he called Paul Dupree to report things of interest in Tommy's cargo van, then he was off.

Paul Dupree did indeed hustle over to inspect the cargo. The FBI lab had found an acid on the glider cords. Tommy's death was ruled a homicide. State and local authorities were investigating.

The FBI already had a vested interest in the financial goings on at CalCon Health and now Paul had drug samples to be lab tested.

The cargo van was confiscated and removed for firearm violations.

Paul had wanted to interrogate Mick and seeing Marie's jeep in the drive way was surprised when there was no answer to his rings. It wasn't until he saw the double wide tire tracks on the drive way did he surmise he retrieved his RV. But where Mick was or where he was going was a mystery to him. Back where he came from, he hoped.

The L.A. street gangs that were distributing Comfitine were becoming addicts themselves. The drug was to die for and many of them did. Especially the ones that searched for the ultimate high, took multiple pills or mixed with heroin. Street level dealers were the first to drop. Replacements were readily available.

The scientists that created Comfitine didn't plan on adverse effects. The drug was designed to replace heroin, not to be mixed with it. Then there was the other idea that doomed it for failure. The notion that drug dealers would be willing to give up their guns for a Comfitine fix was a complete fallacy. Reason being, they were in control of distributing the drug. They knew where it was being manufactured and they were making plans to wrest control over operations from the Holy Hunter.

Part one has been established. Gang members were already in place as hired armed Cal-Con Health guards. Security was so tight even the Great White Hunters assassins were rebuffed at the front gate, 'no pass, no entry,' were the standing orders.

The assassins were pissed off, not so much because they had to turn around, it was because of the punky looking guards at the gate, their black leather berets and smart aleck expressions.

"Those punks don't know nothing about nothing," the one said to the other. "Yeah, for two cents, I would have plugged them both. And what's with the Uzi's they're packing?

They act like their guarding Fort Knox or something." They both looked at each other and thought the same thing, 'maybe they were.'

On the cell phone immediately, they informed Terrance DeVour what had transpired so far. He instructed them to hole up at the Eagle Lake Resort and wait for his return call.

Terrance DeVour called the Cal-Con Health headquarters and was conferring with the Holy Hunter. First order of business was to get another order of Comfitine. The second was to find out why his men were denied access to the manufacturing plant. He was advised that the production manager had quit the previous day because of family problems and couldn't elaborate. But assured him, he would personally see to it that he got his Comfitine shipment.

The Holy Hunter had a new set of problems. His only production manager quit, and as far as he knew he didn't have a family. The lab scientists that developed Comfitine were reassigned in the organization or laid off. They didn't know about production equipment anyway and he already possessed the formula. Illegal aliens made up the work force and could carry on until a machinery part broke. Then there was the LA Flat Hat street gang who had taken over the guard duties and a skeleton crew of paper pushers was all that was left.

But now he knew the Great White Hunter had his men in Eagle Lake to spy on him. He didn't like that scenario one bit. So now he knew he would have to return to the old hunting grounds and take care of business himself.

CHAPTER 31

Mick pulled his RV into the boat access area. He noticed a black Humvee in front of the resort when he drove past. First thing on his agenda, was to fill the RV's tap water tanks with pure spring water. Oh, how he loved the flavor and the way it made him feel.

A mile trek adds up when water is being carted gallons at a time. After his third trip his arms felt stretched to the point that his knuckles felt like they were dragging on the ground. But he felt it was worth the extra effort.

Then he took a bike off the rack he wanted to ride back to the one hour film developer to pick up the film he dropped off. He was more than curious to find out if the license plate pictures he took in Lake Elsinore and the ones at the resort were the same. He had a feeling they were.

Pictures in hand, license plate memorized, he decided to pay a visit to the resort lounge to eavesdrop on his adversaries. Doubting the bartender would recognize him, because all's he did was stare at Marie's cleavage the last time they were there.

By the time he cycled back to the resort lounge there were two black Humvees, and one of the plates numbers matched the set embedded in his mind. Stopping short of entering the lounge because five black suits appeared to be having a meeting at the bar. Looking through a glass pane, he changed his mind about any confrontation, he knew those men were dangerous. If the bartender did recognize him after all, or maybe the men in the Humvees already know what he looks like. They seem to be following him everywhere. He felt his every move was being monitored, his life being torn apart. Marie's too, miscarriage? Was he targeted for elimination? But why, he wondered. The answer came to him in seconds. It lay at the doors of Cal-Con Health.

But for now it was time to go fishing. It had bothered his subconscious that the fishermen had complained about the fishing. With dusk about to settle in, the time was now.

After hooking the bike back on the rack, he got his fishing gear and went out to the boat launch peer. There he took out his favorite crank bait and started casting away. After a half hour of fruitless casts, the sun was set and the water flat as glass except for a spot a hundred yards down by the spring feed. There were all kinds of fins breaking water. He walked over and on further inspection it looked like the fish were going through a mating frenzy. But the spring feed was to slight for a single fish to get upstream, and he knew it was too late in the season for that. He cast his bait out into the middle of the action.

Nothing, not a bite, over and over he cast into the skirmishing fish. He couldn't believe they weren't taking the bait. The thought occurred to him, that he would have better luck scooping the fish out with his hands. The idea struck his fancy and he put down the pole, took off his shoes and socks, grabbed his fish net and waded out two feet. Dipping his net in the water he caught two trout in the one scoop.

Somewhat befuddled at his accomplishment he traipsed back to shore with his catch. Putting his shoes back on first, then picking up his tackle box and pole, he headed back to his RV for supper. Trout was one of his favorite eating fish besides Walleye. He had them filleted and in the frying pan in no time.

Delicious, he thought, and oh how he wished Marie was there with him to enjoy. He only ate one before a full drowsiness overtook him. He was still thinking of Marie when his unawares were violated. Transgressions of the supernatural walked through his skin. His sights were affixed to how lovely Marie looked dancing on that cliff face. Someway he saw himself next to her dancing on the mountain wall together.

Sabotage joined his thoughts along with miscarriage. How dare those guys hurt Marie like that, followed. Thoughts like that tend to keep Mick awake at night. Poisonous hatred was causing a neurochemical imbalance, it was like walking through death with courage. An unrecognizable hallucination, intelligent, yet unconscious kind of magical meditation, contemplations of abstruse concepts flowed like pure spring water. Skin walking with the heat of hatred, fingers wanting to claw, but his body was so relaxed, so confident he could climb any mountain.

He strapped Marie's rappelling harness taut. The girth feeling. He then perked his ears and flared his nostrils. The call of the wild was in the distance, the smell of rotten eggs in the air. He headed out to through the forest.

Marie's spirit was with him, she was atop a steep cliff. Mick labored with ropes, carabiners, pitons and the rappelling harness. He wasn't exactly sure how to climb that cliff, he only knew he had to, he had to reach her.

It was a witch black night but her face glowed like the shimmering full moon, giving Mick guidance. The cliff was icy slick. He held the rope fast as he scaled. He had no fear as he bound atop a flat gravel surface, spongy underfoot, but sturdy.

Marie was whispering to him now, soft as a breeze she was. Nowhere near as brutal as helicopter blades, nowhere near as rude as the blades that took Marie away. He knew where he was now, right above a rotten smelly egg hatch. He opened the maintenance service door.

There were big brown dinosaurs standing as rigid chess pieces. Some hoppers were filled with dry powder, chemicals seemed to be everywhere, liquid tanks resembled missile silos. They were all asleep now, shadows were highlighted by emergency star lights. Mick's pupils opened cat eye wide to soak it all in. He recognized cases of Comfitine with the Cal-Con Health logo stacked on pallets ready for shipping. They were the same boxes Tommy had in his cargo van. He also knew they were the reason his RV and Marie's gliders were sabotaged.

Still that smell led him to rows of drums, clearly marked with skull and cross bones, acid the label read. A set of two red eyes from the monsters brain box kept blinking at him. "Be with you dinosaurs in a minute," he said in a warning tone.

Marie was whispering with enthusiasm now. "You can do it, you can do it,"

"yes I can," he responded. If there was one thing Mick knew, it was his electricity. His specialty was repair, but he also knew how to destroy. Swiftly like a cat in the night he prowled over to the repair shop and borrowed a wire stripper and screwdriver.

Going to the dinosaurs control panel, he was going to make sure the eyes stopped blinking at him and that they didn't spit out any more pills tomorrow. He cut and peeled back a wire. Then jumpered it to a power source, effectively short circuiting the machines computer control. Then he repeated the steps on the other pill pusher.

That accomplished, but worried that the machines could be easily repaired by replacing parts, so he smoothly glided back over by the repair shop. There were acetylene and oxygen cylinders there chained to the wall in the welding shop. He removed the safety caps and cracked opened the valves causing a slow leak of combustible gas. Then grabbing a box of old oily maintenance rags, and placing under the acid drums. Proceeding to finish his business, in a fluid motion, he jumped on a pallet mover fork truck and repeatedly punctured the drums with the forks.

The acid mixed with the oily rags and started to smolder a toxic fume while most of the other acid ran out on the floor, peeling the coating on the way to the drain. Driving the fork truck to the stairs that led to the ceiling hatch, he started his climb. Taking two steps with every bound, swiftly he was back on the roof, then over the side. Rappelling down was easy, just like Marie had taught him.

Working up a massive thirst, he took a jaunt over to his favorite spring. Lapping up his fill of water, then he rolled into the shallow pond, rappelling harness and all. He wanted to wash that rotten egg smell off everything. While his head was under water, *"KA-BOOM!!!"* The roof of Cal-Con Health's lab blew off.

The light temporarily matched that of the rising sun. The sleeping guards in the shack were showered with debris. The alien workers in the dorm rooms were rattled awake too. The wolves and the coyotes howled their approval.

Mick pulled his head out of the water and slicked back his wet hair. He didn't even flinch at the dull thunder, the water had muffled the explosion. Now he had Marie's sweet scent in his nostrils and her wellbeing on his mind. The scent was strong and over bearing. Giving him more strength than ever. He knew his job wasn't finished, and he went back to his RV. "Get the story," he told himself. That's what Marie would do.

Upon entering, he sat right down at the kitchen table, opened her laptop and a new file. Typing like he was possessed, not noticing his damp clothing or any hatred, words flowed from his fingertips. Oddly enough, he wasn't writing about Cal-Con Health at all, his story was about the fishing at Eagle Lake. Once finished, exhaustion overtook him and he curled up on the bench seat to sleep.

CHAPTER 32

The explosion was heard halfway around the world. As the Great White Hunters assassins reported the chaotic scene. The volunteer fire department was there putting out debris fires on the edge of the forest. The explosion robbed the building fire of oxygen and extinguished itself with the help of mangled fire sprinklers. Still the rubble resembled being hit with a five hundred pound bomb.

Furious set the tone of Terrance DeVour's cell phone conversation. He was having a peaceful evening cruising off the coast of Southern France. But he made everyone on board aware that something was seriously wrong when he started yelling, "kill, kill, kill the motherfucker who's responsible for this, and after he's dead, kill him again. Dismember him, I want his head on a silver platter. But more important, check the Exotic Wildlife Sanctuary warehouse. I need the rest of the Comfitine and I need it now!"

In a different conversation he also informed Lawrence Marsi he needed a shipment of Comfitine. Their granite pits in Africa needed it.

"Impossible", he was told. He reminded Terrance DeVour that CalCon Health was in bankruptcy and even with the insurance money it would be highly unlikely they could rebuild without a substantial cash infusion. He further explained that the top half of the building was completely destroyed. The metal siding walls were gone as if a tornado ripped them off. The roof had collapsed with the joists and only the Ibeams remain. He estimated building repairs to take six months.

Then it was suggested that it would be faster to salvage the equipment and move to another location in L.A. That affirmed, the Great White Hunter decided to return stateside to supervise the operation. Not that he didn't trust the Holy Hunter, because he didn't, and for good reason. Terrance DeVour wanted the Comfitine stock pile and Lawrence Marsi wasn't going to give it to him. The drug was now scarce, too valuable and the price was about to triple.

The Great White Hunter's men tentatively searched the perimeter of what was the Cal-Con Health building. Around the back, in the early morning dew they were looking for a man's foot prints but found what appeared to be tracks of a big cat or bear, they thought. But even with guns and bulletproof vests they didn't even dare venture into the forest. What had happened to their colleague's was still fresh on their minds. Then there was the eerie, 'dare you to come in,' howl of the wolves that spooked them too.

The assassins excused themselves with, 'the guy's got at least an hours head start on us,' and 'we'll never find him in there, if he's in there, besides we have our suits on.' Then it was, 'yeah, we better check on the warehouse and see what's going on like Mr. DeVour said.'

They had to walk past the Holy Hunter and his men who were conferring with the fire chief and sheriff in the parking lot. Lawrence Marsi gave them the evil eye as they passed. When they got into their Humvee and took the access road to the warehouse, he nodded a head signal to his men, who picked up the cue to follow.

The illegal aliens who had emptied the dormitory building were instructed to clean up the debris from the parking lot and lawn. They were further ordered not to enter the Cal-Con building, as it was deemed unsafe.

The Flat Hats were busy in the warehouse loading a semi-trailer with Comfitine, when the assassins walked up and drew their guns from their shoulder holsters.

"What's going on here?" One of them asked.

"Who the fuck are you?" One of the Flat Hats replied.

'Bang,' one shot, one dead. The bullet went right into his forehead, knocking off his black flat hat before his shattered head slammed into the concrete warehouse floor. Blood soon collected in a crimson pool under what was left of his skull.

The Flat Hats had made a serious error by hanging their weapons up while they worked.

"Anyone else want to smart off?" the assassin asked. "Keep loading the truck," the other said.

The assassins were still outnumbered, four to two, but the Uzi's were gaudily hanging on a coat rack out of reach. At first the Flat Hat's looked at each other, arms held out in a shocked, 'hold it man,' body language. They instantly recognized there was nowhere to run. Then the one assassin repeated himself, "I said, keep loading the truck." They had plans on hijacking the truck load and more.

Then the Flat Hats fell in line and resumed loading. The gunshot that was fired was somewhat muffled being inside the building. But the Holy Hunters bodyguards heard it. They had just exited their parked Humvee. Now their chore was to get the drop on the assassins unawares.

Spying through an office window, they caught a glimpse of the assassins taking the automatic weapons off a coat rack. The Flat Hats were almost finished loading the semi when, 'rat a tat, tat. Two of them never saw it coming until the bullets that entered their backs exploded blood out their chests onto stacks of Comfitine boxes. The other two tried to scatter, but just ran into the bullets being fired at them.

"Any more questions," the assassin asked the dead men through a haze of gun smoke.

Two of the bodies were already in the trailer, two were on the dock plate, those were the ones moved into the trailer first. The fifth one was being dragged toward the pile until one of the assassins noticed some movement out of the corner of his eye.

Shots rang out, a bullet entered his temple effectively knocking the eye out of its socket. The other dropped the body and jumped off the truck dock and scrambled behind the tandem wheels. His vest had already caught two bullets and the tires he was hiding behind caught two more. The hiss of escaping tire air masked the assassins own rapid breath. His heart was pounding, nerves rattled like a snakes tail, fear struck his eyes, yet he looked for an escape route.

An army of bullets kicked up chips of concrete and punctured two more tires as he cowered. The trailer started to list above him. The Holy Hunters men split up to form a cross fire while the assassin tried to escape out the other side. He took a bullet in his leg first, then one through his shoe, exploding his foot. On his knees, reeling in pain, he fired his 9mm at one then rolling on his back fired at the other. Desperately trying to keep them at bay. Another bullet entered his shoulder, the frightful pain and constricting muscles forced him to drop his weapon.

The Hunters' bodyguards all used to be comrades in better times. Back when the Hunters were together. The good times, when wine, women and money flowed like no tomorrow. But now the assassin lay helpless on the concrete pavement, and he knew the rules of the hunting game.

The assassin was in so much pain he almost welcomed the Holy Hunter's men. They were walking toward his writhing body with weapons pointed. There would be no words exchanged, no good-bye's, no nice knowing you, nothing but a bullet. Bang, his lights were out. His head bounced once off the concrete with a splat.

CHAPTER 33

When Mick awoke he was in a fantasy daze. The daze had some dazzle, the kind that comes with a fantastic dream. Orange and black stripes glazed his eyes like crusty sleep. He was still curled up on the dinette bench seat and the first thing he saw was the bottom of the kitchen table. Stretching his legs out into the RV's aisle and getting his bearings. Every muscle in his body seemed to ache. He chalked it up to sleeping in tight quarters. Why he slept there, he didn't know. He vaguely remembered writing the fish story. But there it was, right on Marie's laptop. He sat back down and read it to refresh his memory. "Not bad," he said to himself.

Off to the shower he went, then with a change of clothes he felt whole again. In a determined state of mind, Mick didn't even look at the destroyed Cal-Con Health building. It was as if nothing had ever happened, ground zero, clean mental slate, sharp and focused, cruising in his captain's chair, headed for Marie. He had a story to show her.

The RV drove straight and true, it was in automatic and so was Mick. Not one stop would he take, not for gas, not for wine or food. The gas tanks were running on empty when he pulled into the driveway, but Mick was full of apprehension. But still, he would have to suffer through a night of his own anxiety.

Being late, weary from the long drive, and wary for Marie, frustration set in from his own inability to do anything to help her. Endorphins drained, pain struck at his heart, exhaustion over took his body. He went to lay down on the couch. Mental neurotransmitter's needed recharging along with his body. He sunk deep into the abyss of comfort on Marie's couch. He was home again. Closing his too tired to dream eyes means nothing in the spiritual world, because he did anyway.

A warmth enveloped him like a mom's knitted comforter. Moments of doubt and pain vanquished. Positive spirits resonated with a single glowing aura. Mick was drawn in on metaphysical Mercury wings. He floated into the glory.

There he saw a bearded man in a white gown with world wise blue eyes. He stood there on a sea of dead water casting a net. His mesmerizing face was sad. With each cast dead fish appeared in his net. Then with a single breath there was life again. Over and over he did his magical chore without complaint. Confidence was his faith, peace was his allure.

Then the glowing glory was replaced with a deep green, forest green. Mick was traveling in a different direction of disparate dimensions. A dark hole paled a galaxy of fir trees. It was a gory manmade hole. Like a vacuum, red crimson coated men were being sucked into it. There was no escape for them, it was a cold, damp, dark hole in this galaxy. Coal black suits were influencing the celestial bodies and events.

The big bang happened, the explosion was real, and now the dense core was rapidly cooling into other states of the ever expanding universe. The core of the cosmos was cracked, no longer orderly and harmonious. Dispersion between different wavelengths in the spectrum was absolute. Then with a shovel of crust everything was as black as burnt toast again. Mick finally entered a deeper sleep of dementia.

Refreshed like the dawn of a new day, he called Marie's editor to report his story about fishing at Eagle Lake. "Interesting," he was told before the rejection. He was getting a lesson on how difficult being a freelance writer can be. But the editor was nice enough to explain that wasn't the kind of story his readers are interested in. He recommended submitting it to a sports magazine or if he had more scientific data, or details from a government agent like the EPA, then call him back.

Thanking him for the information and suggestions, Mick figured he would call in a report to the EPA and forget about selling the story to a sports magazine. A more important thing was on his agenda, he wanted to go back to the hospital to check on Marie.

He called the hospital asking for the attending physician. That wasn't possible he was told. He was further informed that Marie was still in a coma in intensive care and visitation would be fruitless at this time. Nonetheless, Mick insisted on visiting during regular hours.

CHAPTER 34

Bingo Bonnie and Joan were at Marie's bedside when Mick arrived at the hospital. Bonnie was applying some cream to her face and was caught a bit off guard at the sight of him.

"How is she?" was the first thing he asked. "She's still in a coma," Bonnie replied.

"And where have you been?" Joan asked in a scolding tone.

The girls were at the hospital every day since they found out their friend was there. In spare gossiping moments they conversed about Mick pulling a, 'slam-bam, thank you ma'am. Then when the going got tough, took off. Which naturally led them into a bigger state of depression.

Mick didn't know how to respond to the rudeness, so he ignored the question. He had enough experience to recognize a trap with no possible correct answer. Even if he told them the truth, going off to get a fish story would just open another can of worms, in the form of another line of questions he had no correct answers for. So he politely asked, "what did the doctor say?"

"They expected her to come around yesterday, but there may be complications they haven't been able to diagnose. Her swelling is down and the MRI shows no abnormalities. Meanwhile the doctor said to talk to her normally, it may spark a response." Bonnie answered.

With that said, a man entered the room. He had shoulder length light brown hair, with a neatly trimmed beard. He wore a white frock and had a stethoscope draped around his neck. More strikingly were his deep blue electrifying eyes, they literally lit up his face. Mick could have sworn he saw him before, but didn't recognize the doctor.

"You'll have to wait outside while I examine the patient," he politely instructed.

Mick studied the man a moment as the girls filed out, then he followed. They huddled in the aisle. The girls shared sets of bloodshot watery eyes.

Lack of sleep wasn't the cause and the sniffling wasn't from colds. Both were on leave from work, they had been visiting their best friend religiously for days. Despondency grappled their spirits after the first visit, only to be amplified by Marie's missing vibrancy. They returned to torture their souls anyway. Talking into a vacant void drained their psyche like sand in an hour glass but they continued to believe they were helping Marie.

Whenever love is emptied from the heart, loathing naturally flows in one's veins. Joan had such a case of hard heart and couldn't stand Mick's presence. She blamed him for Marie's misfortune. Bonnie was more forgiving, she had agreed with Joan when Mick turned up missing, but now that he returned, made all the difference to her.

Then Joan said, "come on Bonnie, let's go, I'm hungry."

"Yeah sure," then turning to Mick Bonnie said, "we'll be back tomorrow."

See ya later," and they were gone.

Mick waited in the aisle patiently for the doctor to finish his exam. He had all kinds of questions for the doctor rolling around in his head, practicing for the encounter. But mental preparation is different from reality. As when the doctor reappeared, he only rattled off two.

"How long is she going to be in a coma?" was his first. "Nobody knows but the good Lord."

"What can I do to help?"

"Just talk to her, familiar voices can only help, and say your prayers."

The last answer didn't sound so good to Mick. Brain freeze struck him as he contemplated the doc's answer. Part of the mental congestion was because he hadn't said any prayers since he was a kid. For all the prayer memorizing was in the distant past, so distant in fact that he didn't think he could recollect one in its entirety. But being in a religious hospital, he made a mental note to stop at the chapel for a prayer card on the way out.

That decided, he went to Marie's side and sat. It took him awhile to get comfortable, but once he did, he started to tell Marie about his fishing story in a soft monotone.

When he finished the story he asked her, "I bet you didn't think I could do it all by myself?"

He looked at her blankly for a reply that he wasn't going to get. So undaunted, he started at the beginning and repeated the fish story. But this time he reached out and held her hand as he did.

He told the same story over and over until the nurse came around to announce visiting hours were over. It was a good thing too, unbeknown to him, depression was starting to set up shop in him too. The constant repetition of the same old story with no reply was as aggravating as a phonograph needle being stuck in a scratched album. When he looked at Marie's vacant face to tell her he would be back tomorrow, he had to swallow a dry lump, pent up pressure was building in the aqueducts, then along with the words, "see you later," tears roiled. The terse pressure was relieved.

Meanwhile the EPA was busy taking water samples from Eagle Lake. The first call they received was from Mick, but since then the agency was under a deluge of complaints. The towns people and sportsmen wanted to know why a multitude of dead fish were washing ashore. Not only was the scene putrid, the stench was horrendous.

The EPA had found the source of the hazardous industrial poison coming from a trickle of a stream that led to the Lassen National Forest. Sewer water contamination that seeped into the spring water was the obvious conclusion the EPA experts agreed, and the culprit had to be from the recently destroyed Cal-Con Health building. But further tests would be needed. Criminal complaints were in order.

The ATF was called out by the sheriff to help investigate the explosion. The FBI came out because Cal-Con Health was already under investigation. Now with the EPA on the scene, normal government infighting was the rule of the day. Nobody seemed to know what was going on and who was in charge. Along with that confusion, scores of reporters were investigating right along with them. At least the sheriff knew what he was in charge of, mountains of traffic.

Fact was, by the time Marie's editor read the AP news wire report about the EPA and Cal-Con Health, he had tried to call Mick back about his fish story but couldn't reach him. He was telling Marie about it at the time. He did however leave him a message on the voice mail to no avail.

Alas, hour old news is as good as recycled print, garbage. News is a competitive business, and being first with the story matters. Timing is everything in most businesses, the press more so. Mick missed out on his opportunity, but he could careless now, he was preoccupied with more pressing priorities.

CHAPTER 35

The next day, Bonnie and Joan had curling iron and brush in hand and were doing Marie's hair. "Can't a girl have some privacy," Joan badgered at Mick's intrusion. Mick apologized and turned on a dime.

He knew he would need a mountain of patience to survive the attitudes. So he waited out in the aisle for the right moment to win back the girls esteem. He didn't have to wait long before Bonnie came out and got him, "excuse Joan," she said, "we've had a tough week."

"Hey, no problem, I understand," he said.

But before they reentered, they saw Marie's doctor approaching and froze in their tracks by the door. They both felt in awe at his presence. They both knew he was key to Marie's recovery.

"Good afternoon," the doctor said, as they silently backed away to let him enter.

Joan soon joined them in the aisle, "mysterious one, that doctor is," she said.

"Who's that?" Bonnie asked.

"I don't know,—it's his eyes, I think,—like he's looking through my soul or something and then he says to me, 'did you say your prayers today?'"

"Yeah, he said that to me yesterday," Mick added.

"Maybe she's in a more serious condition than we thought," Bonnie said.

"I don't think that's it," Mick said. "But you can get your prayer cards in the chapel downstairs."

"Yeah, we'll do that," Joan said. "And by the way, we have to work a cruise to Alaska. We'll be gone for a week."

"OK, I'll be here or at home when you get back. I have no other plans."

THE MICK AND MARIE STORY

"Great," Bonnie said, "You'll be able to visit Marie every day then?"

"You bet," Mick said.

They all waited for the doctor in the hallway to finish his exam, then the girls peppered him with questions of concern. Starting with, "What are all those tubes for?"

"Right now she's being fed with liquids. It's called a percutaneous endoscopic gastronomy tube. She may have to relearn how to swallow when she awakens. You see," the doctor said, "she has what we call a Coup/Contrecoup injury. Her brain had some bleeding and swelling which has subsided."

Then it was, "with a brain injury you are reborn, she may or may not be the same person she was before the accident."

Mick quietly soaked the information in, as the doctor went through a series of explanations. His next answer was, "physical therapy may be necessary, first she'll have to open her eyes, then sit up before she stands, and stand before she walks." He went on explaining, answering questions before they were asked, "vicariance, in which uninjured neurons take over for the injured ones. Diastases, in which the brains resiliency enables the brain to heel over time. It may take a lifetime of diagnosis, or, better yet, when she wakes up she may be fine. If you'll excuse me now, I have other patients to visit. Remember, talk to her about things she knows and say your prayers." With that he walked on down the hall.

"Thanks doc," Mick called after him. Then going back into Marie's room, the girls gathered up their things and said their good-byes to her.

Mick sat down in a chair gathered her hand in his and started to tell her about his fish story again. He only repeated it twice in monotone before he became bored with himself. "Did I ever tell you someone once told me that I was paranoidingly ill? The reason she said that I figure is because I no longer trust the government. It doesn't always show I know, but after your forced to deal with all their lies over a lifetime one tends to get a little cynical." With no response he felt free to ramble on. Then he asked in vain, "did you hear the news today?"

Talking to one's self, or the wall, tends to disenfranchise emotion. But this subject naturally gave Mick verve. "The Constitution is being attacked again," he started. "We might as well have the Ayatollah Komainie as president. The radical religious right wants to write discrimination into the

Constitution. Just because some states want to legalize gay marriage is their excuse. The Feds are going to try to ban it by Constitutional Amendment. So now the 10 Amendment and states' rights are being sacrificed. The Equal Rights Amendment, which is kind of redundant anyway, because of the Constitution its self will be meaningless. I mean, after all, men and women are already equal under the law. Then there's the 14th. Amendment, guaranteeing equal protection and due process. Why hell, if this new Amendment passes we might as well junk the whole thing because we won't be on the slippery slope of self-destruction anymore, we'll be deluged under an avalanche of personal right removing Amendments. Freedom will be eliminated as we know it, there won't be anything like self-determination. The thing is, the Constitution is supposed to protect us from excessive government. The spirit of Constitutional Amendments has always been to expand, rather than restrict individual rights. To use the Constitution to discriminate is not only divisive, shameful, and un-American, it's flat out evil. I mean, I could care less if gays want to marry, there are more important things to worry about in this world than that. I care about unconstitutional laws and the lack of personal freedom. What kind of priorities does this country have anyway?"

Mick paused. He was talking to Marie but looking at the wall above her head, he was just riled by the events of the day. He sighed, then gave Marie's hand a comforting squeeze before continuing. He talked about Constitutional issues, basically just to himself, for several more hours.

Talking to an answerless space was making Mick say things he would have never considered saying before without feedback. Keeping a comforting, familiar voice in her ear was the important thing, not the content of babbling speech, he honestly thought.

He paused again to regain his mental. He got the feeling he got side tracked somehow. Looking longingly into her face, and then back to the blank spot on the wall. Then he said, "Yeah, I started out talking about marriage. You have to wake up, so we can go to Hawaii and get married."

Then an applause broke out, a group of nurses had gathered behind Mick while he was orating. He was startled and flush to say the least and while he was blushing at the nurses, Marie slightly twitched her approval while a lone tear escaped from the corner of her eye.

"Sorry sir," one of the smiling nurses announced, "visiting hours are over."

CHAPTER 36

Paul Dupree was elated, the indictments came through for the CalCon Health executives. The FBI's Financial Forensic Team named Terrance DeVour and Lawrence Marsi in 20 securities fraud counts, plus various counts of wire fraud and insider trading.

The complex accounting gimmicks, misleading public statements and false paperwork filed with securities regulators all added up to artificially inflated profits to balloon Cal-Con Health's stock price. Specialized FBI analyst unraveled a myriad of financial machinations, oversea corporations that were set up to hide debt, inflate profits, and shield the companies growing debts. The complicated conspiracy enriched the CEO and the Chief Accounting Officer.

Possible penalties ranged from 100 million in fines, forfeitures, and up to 200 years in prison. Paul knew the penalties were exaggerated, but now he was aware of a bonanza of new charges. The EPA had discovered an illegal septic tank that was contaminating the ground water with pollutants. Not that that would be enough to satisfy his drooling palate either. All the gold lay in a mass grave just inside the National Forest boundaries. Being located on federal property, he was now in charge of the biggest mass murder case in his district. Spotlights of the stars were shining on him now, he relished in his glory.

His bonus was, the listening devices he planted in Marie's house paid off big time. When Mick called in his fish story to the AP editor, Paul now had the knowledge that one Mickey Swift was in Eagle Lake at the time of the murders. Revenge was the motive, Paul figured. Why else would he drive all the way to Eagle Lake? Certainly not for a fish story, a fish alibi is more like it. He had already sent a team of criminal forensic investigators to find out the how's and why's for killing all those employees—then, he figured, he's got his man. Then he could keep Mick away from Marie for a lifetime.

★ ★ ★

The Holy Hunter literally was suffering from a painful emotional crisis. He wanted to escape conscious contact from reality. He had plenty to worry about as it was, but when he found out about the shot out and all the dead bodies in the Exotic Wildlife Sanctuary warehouse. Panic took root. It was his decision to remove the dead men from the semitrailer and bury them in the forest. What else could he do with every kind of lawman hovering around the Cal-Con Health building.

Four trailer tires were flat and that would take a day to replace. By that time the bodies would be stank. Besides, what would happen if some State Trooper pulled the rig over on the highway? Or took a look inside at a weigh station? Rightly so, worry and paranoia gobbled him up.

At no other time in his life did he have so many heart palpitations. His body was having a difficult time breathing. His twanging nerves were being played like a hillbillies fiddle. A real heart attack would be welcome.

He just wanted to escape. That, he and his men did, but there's no escape from panic. They had left Eagle Lake first thing the next morning. They left without the trailer of Comfitine. At this point in time he wanted nothing to do with it. Let the Flat Hats move it, he thought. He just wanted to escape.

Tired, exhausted, dizzy, he didn't want to make any more decisions. The hallucinations were all too real. Each diabolical fiber of his nature quivered with the metallic slam of jailhouse doors.

He couldn't even find comfort in his own office. He was wearing his best black suit but felt naked. Even his bodyguards felt the heat, cashed in their chips and took off for Mexico. The walls were closing in like a garbage compactor. He paced back and forth with big rat speed, going nowhere fast. He was trapped like a tiger in a cage. He wanted to roar but was afraid to make any noise. He wanted to go outside but was afraid too. He wanted his ol' lying con-artist self to return, because for the first time in his life he contemplated committing suicide, but was afraid to do that too.

'Go to the doctors. Get yourself committed to a health retreat,' he told himself. 'Start making excuses now before the curtain falls,' he further theorized. Knowledge can benefit or destroy, depending on what kind it is. The reality was he didn't even get his indictments served yet; he was just expecting them as a matter of due course.

All the while the Great White Hunter was oblivious to the goings on. He was in the middle of the Panama Canal cruising to the port in San Diego.

CHAPTER 37

Airs about Marie's room were feminine that next day. Flowers of all sorts were sent by her editor and friends. Lily of the Valley bells were stand out white amongst the purple Lilacs. Mick added a "St. Michael—Dragon Slayer" prayer card to the shrine-shaped arrangements. Floral fragrance snubbed out the mundane smell of medicine.

He took his seat and announced his presence with a, "how are you today?" A gentle squeeze of her hand made him feel better. The oration he went through the other day left him exasperated with a sense of hopelessness. 'There must be better things to talk about,' he thought. And he found his answer and solace in reading the poems Marie had written on her laptop.

So he opened the file and started reading MB 1 to her. By the time he got to MB 5, his thirst needed quenching and he took a swig of spring water. During his pause, he also noticed Marie's lips looked parched from the lack of lipstick or dry air. So he poured some of his spring water on a napkin and dabbed her lips with the moisture.

Settling back in his chair he continued his reading until he finished poem MB 8. Then he took another drink of spring water and wet Marie's lips again. He made a mental note to ask the nurse to apply some Chap Stick or Vaseline to prevent her lips from chaffing. Then he continued to read, "this is MB poem #9," he told her.

Love expressions Hanging in thin air

Gentle as breeze combed hair

Kindness makes lasting impressions

How prophetic

Soon they would marry

To Hawaii they will ferry

Caring was the tactic

The isle of romance

Gardens of plenty

The fruits are many

Sway to the islands dance

She was the intellectual

Her mental was glee

Her spirit free

He made her feel sensual

Now lovers

See the light

The stars are bright

Even under covers

No need for improvisations

This love will survive

As long as we're alive

Love expressions

Mick had to choke back a tear with the swipe of his hand before he continued.

"This is MB poem #10."
The best is already there

Not feasible to ameliorate

Absorb with all your stare

Jealousy, bestowal to their hate

Love, honor your first

Like a babe in arms and all the rest

With these truths, no need to thirst

Time honored traditions, passed the test

To all a birth right
Freedom of speech
Changes bring plight
To all the children teach
Privacy when we pray
Let us assemble
Doesn't matter what we say
Can't make us tremble
Freedom of press
Hear our grievances

A choice to redress Let us freelance
The best is already there
Not feasible to ameliorate
Absorb with all your stare
It is documented, dare to debate

Mick had read the last poem with a positive masculine verve. He knew what she was talking about. It was as if she pre-approved yesterday's oration. That made him feel better, but he didn't know why she didn't have any titles for her poems. So out of curiosity he asked, "what does the MB stand for?" "Memory Bank," she whispered.

"Memory bank—of course!" He said blandly as if he was still talking to himself. Not expecting an answer, Mick was caught off guard for a nanosecond until her answer suck in. "What did you say?" he asked with an excited tone. "Memory bank," her eyes were open now and she saw the shocked expression on Mick's face. Then she said, "I'm thirsty."

Mick handed her the sport bottle with spring water and she took several sips before asking, "Where are we?"

"In the hospital," he replied.

Before she asked "what are we doing here?" Mick hit the nurse call button. Then she tried to wiggle herself into a sitting position but grimaced in pain.

"Don't move, honey," Mick instructed. "I've signaled for the nurses."

"My chest hurts," she complained.

"You've some fractured ribs," Mick explained.

"Oh yeah, from the crash," she slid back down, and started to feel her bandages. Privately Mick felt sad that she was in pain but glad she had her feelings back. He knew it was a good sign.

Then the nurses entered with the doctor in pursuit. Mick took cue, closed the laptop lid and made his exit. This time his aisle exile was filled with jittery joy. Her fragrant room lingered in the valley of his heart. Hopelessness vanquished, no longer did he sulk while he waited. His smile was as radiant as a new dawning day.

"Hello," he said to a passing patient. "Beautiful day," he said to the nurse pushing his wheelchair.

"Hello" and "Yes, it is a beautiful day," were returned to him as his contagious good spirits multiplied.

On feathery feet, Mick seemed to float as he paced the aisle. Optimism was his fuel, and the doctor confirmed Marie would be fine but cautioned, "she still needs time to recuperate and would remain hospitalized for further observations."

Then he said, "she's been asking for you. Better go on in and talk to her."

"Thanks, doc, and I did say my prayers."

The doctor just smiled and said, "I know you did," before he went about his appointed rounds.

CHAPTER 38

The Flag ship had left Panama after refueling. Terrance DeVour was at the helm. Light rain multiplied the spray from the bow. Wipers swashed back and forth hypnotically on the windshield. He had been expecting a report back from his men concerning a Comfitine shipment. Dalliance of duty always riled the Great White Hunter. His concern was turning into anger.

While he was steering his vessel he missed the CNN broadcast. The FBI and Paul Dupree had arrested Lawrence Marsi. Head bowed in embarrassment, he was led through a midst of a photo frenzy of reporters, in handcuffs, out of the Cal-Con Health Headquarters to an unmarked squad car. Then rushed to the Federal Building for his arraignment.

His planned escape to a Health Resort was foiled by minutes. The spectacle was arranged by Paul to defuse public opinion and criticism about his department not doing enough to corral corporate scandals.

At the Federal building Lawrence Marsi was briefly grilled as to the whereabouts of one Terrance DeVour, Paul's missing link. Stating, "I don't know." Then, "in Africa I guess."

Paul then, in a threatening tone asked, "are you going to take the fall for destroying this company all by yourself?"

At which time Marsi's attorney interjected, because he knew any miss statement considered a lie told to the Feds would result in jail time, "he's innocent, and we were trying to cooperate with your investigation. But at this time I must insist that my client refuse to answer any more of your questions by invoking his 5 Amendment rights."

It was too early for the FBI to offer any plea bargain deals for complete cooperation. So he was brought before a Federal Magistrate and read the charges against him. As it played out, shifting the blame to the two now deceased financial officers was going to be the defense's strategy. To wit:

Lawrence Marsi had to put up the title of his Texas ranch to cover a 5 million dollar bond.

Not considered a flight risk, prosecutors failed to get a passport forfeiture. But that was exactly one of the options the Holy Hunter was considering. No matter how his attorney put on a happy acquittal face. He didn't believe the propaganda. And he didn't like his chances of staying out of jail considering the hostile climate of all the investment swindles he was personally responsible for. Then again, the only thing he had left of value was cash on hand and the formula for Comfitine. Which could be worth a small fortune in its self.

The miraculous story of Marie's recovery ran the next day. Mick had sold his first AP story and the editor was more than happy to run it. An exceptional story indeed, complete with proposal and engagement. Marriage and honeymoon was to take place in Maui. No date was set, but the couple wanted to go as soon as arrangements could be made.

Bonnie and Joan were in the middle of their cruise liner duties when they received the news. Marie was still in the hospital under observation but she had cell phone in hand and was back in charge of communications.

She was inundated with more congratulations from people she has never met before. There were free airline offers, free hotel accommodations, even a free cruise proposal. So much so fast, Marie was wary with options. She did her best to explain it all to her friends.

"Don't you dare go to Hawaii without us," the girls demanded. Marie assured them she wouldn't.

CHAPTER 39

Scratching at his scalp, Paul Dupree had his chalkboard full of eraser marks. Trying to figure out the time line of the crimes plus the how's and why's isn't necessarily an exact science.

Five dead LA Flat Hats, two men in suits with body armor, none of which could be traced to employment at Cal-Con Health. Ballistics proved four different guns were used to murder the victims. By the time he procured a search warrant for the Exotic Pet Facility it was empty.

Lab techs found blood samples soaked into the concrete. Despite attempts to wash away blood evidence with a garden hose. Shell casings were swept up but found in a nearby garbage can. There were multiple foot print samples and the crime scene investigators calculated there were four murderers.

Paul was perplexed about the findings and disappointed that he wasn't going to be able to pin the murders on Mick. 'Did he actually go up there to go fishing,' he asked himself. He had to assume the murders were carried out by a rival LA street gang or organized criminals, but didn't know why. Further some agents deduced the murders were committed before the explosion. The exact time of death was impossible to pinpoint because of the cold damp conditions of the shallow grave the bodies were buried in.

But by all accounts, Lawrence Marsi and his men were sleeping in the Eagle Lake Resort the night of the explosion. That left the Flat Hat security guards and or any number of the housed laborers that have been evacuated and dispersed to who knows where.

Paul was scratching at his head again, added some questions to the board and erased others. He pounded out Mick's name with the eraser. No matter how he tried to fit Mick into the mix, he still found himself drawing on a preordained theory that the Cal-Con building was deliberately destroyed for insurance money as the corporation was in deep financial troubles of its own doings.

The arsonists were murdered Al Capone style after the explosion is the theory he was going to work with. But how did all those people get by the sheriff, the EPA, and the ATF. Where they also busy that the murderers slipped right by them without being noticed was a good question. Proving who was responsible in a court of law would be another matter.

Much worse than that, he thought Marie was going to remain in a vegetable state for the rest of her life. Gauging from what the doctors told him that first day he brought her in. The prognosis was that bad. That's why he never bothered to visit. Then he had to read the story of Marie's complete recovery and now, 'that Mick,' and Marie are engaged. OH how he hates Mick, he just moved right in with his woman. He slammed the eraser into the spot where his name used to be.

He was still looking for an angle to dispose of his rival and he had better do it IRS quick. He's been too busy with his own job of late. But he'll just have to find a way to take some time off for, "Marie's my girl, Marie's my girl," he thought to distraction, titch, titch, titch.

CHAPTER 40

Marie was in full bloom after a little R&R. Mick, Marie, Bonnie, and Joan gathered at the Hitching Post for dinner. The girls had long forgiven Mick, after all they were embarrassed by their own misconceptions. Especially after privately quizzing Marie mercilessly about, "are you sure you know what you're doing?" For the millionth time, her answer was still, "yes I do." The girls succumbed to fate.

All arrangements had been arranged and confirmed. Gaiety was premium, laughing, drinking, anxious to set sail for Hawaii in the morning. The girls would have preferred to fly, being faster, but when Marie explained that she was being offered a chance to sign a book deal she could author. Then there was a movie contract with industry moguls and they had a chance to star in the movie, made the difference. The girls were on personal leave from their cruise duties, but wouldn't have missed this cruise to Hawaii for anything.

Seated at their favorite table in front of the picture window, they all stopped chatting as the oranges and yellows prism the sunset dipping behind the mountains. The colors danced in their eyes, oblivious to the waitress clearing the dinner plates from the table. Minds peace reassured by the glory of nature's spectacle.

The trance was broken by Marie's comment, "I can't wait to see the sunset in Hawaii."

"Yeah," they all snapped to in unison.

"How about I play some tunes on the juke box," Mick offered. "Play C4," Bonnie guided.

"B9," "G3," Marie and Joan added.

On the way to the jukebox Mick paused, a silent shiver went down his spine. There it was again, on the bar just like before, curses of a bad dream. All alone it stood out like a white ghost in the middle of the night, an empty glass of milk.

He shook it off and carried on, 'no one was going to spook his marriage plans,' he promised himself.

Bonnie was singing Karaoke style with, 'Love Me Tender," upon Mick's return. Marie was feeling song induced romantic. An urgent, immediate physical need came to her. Her heart picked up speed, her nipples hardened. Her breasts felt heavy under her brassiere. She wanted Mick's paws to massage them.

They both had refrained from intimacy while she was healing. But now her breasts hurt for lack of attention. Her chest heaved as she longingly looked into Mick's eyes. He recognized the look immediately. He was in need too.

Mick picked up the check and suggested, "we'd better get going, we've a busy day tomorrow."

The girls, "awed," like why so soon, but realized he was probably right. Then Bonnie said, "ok, we'll meet you at the house in the morning and drive down together."

"Perfect," Marie said. "See you in the morning." And with that they were off.

As soon as they were in the Jeep, Marie lunged for Mick's lips. He kissed her back falling into the same hot-glittery rush. Hardly waiting while kissing, her hand fell to his thigh to caress. The kiss was broken but not the heat. Mick put the Jeep in drive as Marie undid his belt and zipper. Mick was driving while distracted as his excitement got intense with encouragement. Yanked out, exposed to the cool evening air was one thing, then engulfed with the heat of her lips was another. He was dizzy and driving. But not that distracted not to realize where he was going.

Pulling into the driveway, right next to the RV, the passion was carried over into the RV's bedroom, at Marie's insistence, the bed was closer. There was nobody around to disturb their love rocking this night.

Early the next morning, Marie's smile reflected the beaming dawn sun. The aroma of cinnamon toast and fresh brewed coffee permeated the senses to a grand new day. Mick filled several sport bottles with spring water while Marie finished packing for the trip.

The Jeep was loaded when Bonnie and Joan pulled up behind the RV. Their suitcases were added in the back of the Jeep. They climbed in the rear seats. Marie elected Mick to drive so she would be free to chat with her friends, and they were off.

CHAPTER 41

Mick jumped on Route 15. The ride lasted an hour, but it seemed to go by quicker. The girls sang along with every song on the radio and gossiped during commercials. Mick was quietly impressed with the panoramic scenery: especially when he pulled into San Diego proper.

The girls ooh'd and ah'd at the sights of the mansions and the lush floral grounds in the Mission Hills district. A walk down the paths in Balboa Park was suggested, and just as quickly ex-nayed. Marie didn't want to be late.

The Spanish-Moorish buildings that lined the Gas Lamp Quarter with cafés and galleries looked inviting too. Promises were made to stop and shop on the return trip. For no everyone agreed to save their money and appetites for the expected appetizers aboard the yacht moored at Embarcadero Marina Park.

Parking was convenient and they could see the American Flag ship was within walking distance. Grabbing their suitcases, they joyfully strolled dockside. It was an awesome looking yacht, bigger than most. It had red and blue stripes, running fore-and-aft, on a white hull with five stars stenciled on the bow.

"I believe you're expecting us. We're the Swift-Sweet party," Marie said. "Yes, yes indeed. Welcome aboard. I'm Captain Hunter, but just call me

Terry. This is my brother Larry."

The captain took Marie's suitcases so she could easily ascend the boarding ramp. Mick carried his own while two stewards hustled over to assist Bonnie and Joan with theirs. Terry was wearing a white shirt with authentic looking captain stripes on his shoulders with a matching hat and navy blue trousers. The most striking thing about him was his albino pure white hair that protruded around the caps brim. His piercing black beady eyes were unnatural. Larry had a toothy welcome grin, but seemed out of place wearing a black suit.

The guests, in casual attire, were led past an expansive living area and galley, downstairs to their quarters by the stewards. A ghostly chill swirled the stairwell bottom. Mick noticed ceiling air conditioning vents, and the sleepy hum of motors idling behind rear engine room doors. The cabin suites resembled those reserved for first class. King-size beds, not bunks, individual heads with full baths.

Goose bumps spooked Mick's arm hairs to attention. Cold as a morgue in here, he thought. Or was it realization, he was on a floating mansion with moneyed men. Oddly, he felt puny. Out of his element. He set the suitcases down and shivered slightly.

One of the stewards blandly announced, "Appetizers will be served when you're ready."

The stewards appeared bored, malcontent bored. One was a big muscular man. He didn't seem to fit the server position or the stewards uniform, Mick thought.

Unpacked in a jiffy, all joined up on deck in the massive living area. Terry and Larry were conversing by the bar and on the coffee table by the wrap around Italian Leather sofa was an iced down silver platter of peeled shrimp. They were encircled in rows like synchronized swimmers, ready to be dipped into the luscious red cocktail sauce in the center pool. Pineapple, papaya, and orange slices garnered the perimeter. Mick was the first to dive in, the girls followed.

Captain Hunter came over to inquire, "Is everything all right?"

"Very nice," Marie said.

"Nice boat you got, cap'," Mick added.

Terrance DeVour didn't like the tone of the compliment and thought it an indignant remark. "It's a ship," he tersely snapped back. He could never get used to casual, well-meaning jibing. He commanded respect and would not accept contempt. But he caught himself, and his tone changed to bravado. "This is the most sophisticated sailing vessel of its size, Mr. Swift. Completely computerized, it practically sails itself. I'm sure you will find all the comforts of home here."

Then Marie politely broke the tension with, "Pretty patriotic ship you have, Captain Hunter."

"Yes, I'm a retired five-star admiral. My brother is the movie mogul."

THE MICK AND MARIE STORY

"Tell me about the book and movie proposal again." She also wanted her friends to hear for themselves.

"Not now," the captain said. "We'll have plenty of time for that later."

That's when Mick noticed Larry's snide grin again. He was standing next to the captain. But that grin bothered Mick. It was a "consensus bullshit" grin. Pure bullshit, sales job; but why would they lie? Or was he reading the body language wrong? Mick started to wonder.

"We'll be shoving off soon," the captain continued. "Make yourselves at home." The Hunter brothers turned to climb the stairway to the bridge. Then the stewards brought champagne with stem glasses on a serving cart. Clumsily opening the bottles like amateurs, then walking off without pouring again aroused Mick's suspicions. Marie noticed the slight too, but said nothing. Mick did the pouring honors.

"I for one would like to lose this classical elevator music," Bonnie complained. She found the stereo system and stopped the tape. Changing the system to CD player, and putting on Harry Connick, Jr. She loved that sweet soul horn blowing, New Orleans style. Then she found some New Age jazz, and put them in the auto-changer. Soothing acoustics will have to do. There wasn't an overabundance of choices.

Up on the bridge Lawrence Marsi was getting the third degree about the goings on at the company and what happened to his men and the Comfitine. The FBI closed down everything and the men took off for Mexico, he lied. "And what are your plans to do with your guests," he asked deliberately changing the subject.

"They'll be disposed of at sea," Terrance replied, "just like the James Gang."

Lawrence Marsi had joined the cruise at the last moment. He had received DeVour's phone call days earlier and was surprised to find he was back in San Diego. He had serious decisions to make. One of them was to flee the country and set up a Comfitine shop in Africa with the Great White Hunter, or else.

Mick and Marie had moseyed out past the patio style glass doors, to the rear deck. The stewards were casting off the mooring lines. When something else caught Marie's eye.

"What's that guy's problem?" She wondered aloud. "Who?" Mick asked.

"The guy in the parking lot."

He looked in the direction Marie was pointing and saw a man waving his arms frantically overhead like a flagman on an aircraft carrier. While they were looking; some dark suits popped out of nowhere and wrested the crazy acting man into submission. Just beyond that scene, Mick noticed a black sawed-off Brink's truck; a Humvee.

"Looks like he's getting arrested," Marie said.

They were a full 100 yards away from the action and walked further aft to where the dinghy was secured, for a better view. Marie thought she recognized one of the men but the distance was such; she couldn't be positive. While Mick stood between the rear bench seats, holding the chrome gate rail that led to the dinghy and lower stern launch platform, a call came from behind him by one of the stewards. "Hey, don't go by the lifeboat."

Mick turned and replied, "I wasn't going to."

"Then get away from there," the steward snarled.

Mick knew he was perfectly safe where he was, but moved over and knelt on the cushioned bench seat to console the concerned. Still the steward persisted.

"I don't want nobody falling overboard. Now get away from there."

"What's your problem, man?" Mick retorted with a hint of anger. "Just stay away from the lifeboat" was his final warning.

Mick turned his back on him instead of telling him to "fuck off," which he felt like doing.

Marie had joined him. Sitting properly on the bench seat as Mick peered back to the parking lot and saw the man being led away.

"What was that all about?" Mick wondered silently after Marie asked.

He was in perfect position to eye the dinghy. It had a small main sail neatly wrapped and folded down the center. There was a 20-hp motor with fuel line leading to gas fuel container located next to a tackle box. Everything looked to be in order with the exception of visible floating devices. But he figured there must be life vests tucked somewhere on board. Probably under the very seat he was sitting on.

The roar of the twin turbo props were now spewing a wake as the American Flag Ship pulled away from the dock. They could see the heads of the captain and his brother chatting with each other at the helms wheel on the bridge.

"They don't look like brothers" was Marie's comment.

"Yeah, you're right." Mick's mind started spinning as fast as a blank computer disk. Nothing in particular computed or registered as fishy dangerous; however, there was that unconscious cutting edge of suspicion gnawing at his guts.

"Maybe I can rustle up a few beers. Do you want one?" Mick asked. "Not now," Marie replied.

"Be right back," Mick went fishing. He felt a beer would ease his already queasy stomach. Marie tilted her head back and let her golden hair flutter in the slight breeze while her face soaked up the warming sun's rays.

Mick found the stewards talking with Bonnie and Joan at the bar. The big safety expert was behind the bar. The smaller steward was sitting next to Joan; obviously staring at her cleavage.

"Can I have a beer?" Mick interrupted.

"We don't have any beer aboard," the steward snapped back. "What? What kind of cruise is this?" Mick disbelievingly inquired.

"We have wine, tequila, gin, vodka, and whiskey—no beer," the steward replied with a smirk.

The thought of asking the captain to turn around to get some entertained Mick before he asked, "Do you have any scotch?"

Settling into the barstool next to Bonnie expecting service. Only to be informed. "It's in the rack, I told you." Was Mick's rude awakening. Bonnie and Joan were a bit surprised by the ignorance too. After all, they had made them a pitcher of Margaritas, but since have been hanging on to their every move like a pack of horny sailor dogs.

They were feeling the uncomfortable tension and weren't shocked when Mick huffed, "Never mind," and walked off. He really didn't feel like hitting the hard stuff before noon anyway. He plodded off to his room and grabbed a sport container of his spring water and rejoined Marie who had moved to a lounge chair.

"Something weird is going on here," disrupting her tranquility. "Why do you say that?" She dreamily asked.

"Well, for one thing, there's no beer aboard, and the service sucks."

"What do you expect for free?"

"Nothing, I guess. Maybe that's the point. Nobody ever gets nothing for nothing." He took a pull from his water container, then asked, "Want some spring water?"

"Sure," she said. At first, she quenched her thirst daintily.

The American Flag Ship was well away from port and cruising the Pacific when Mick thought he heard some raised voices arguing on the bridge. Instinctively, if for no other reason, he climbed the stairs to inspect. The voices stopped on cue at his presence. The Hunter brothers were still at the helm, but none at the wheel.

"What can I do for you?" The captain asked.

"Can you stop at the nearest liquor store and pick up a case of beer?" Mick asked with obvious sarcasm.

'Smart ass,' The Great White Hunter thought while wearing his conning smile. "Sorry, I don't drink beer—peasant piss. If I would have known you wanted beer. I surely would have ordered some with the provisions. Come sit in the captain's chair. You could steer the ship awhile if you like," He politely offered.

"OK."

Mick had to step up to sit. The seat was taller than a barstool. And once there he could see why. The additional height afforded a complete view of the bow.

Then the captain explained, "the controls are in automatic pilot now. The system is run off a GPS satellite. If you turn the wheel, it will override the system. But when you let go, it will automatically reset the coordinates I programmed into the chart plotter."

"Got ya," Mick said.

'Insular fuck,' the captain thought. Then the natural pirate in him thought he really would enjoy 'keel hulling' this indignant. His thought was interrupted by Marie's "Hi."

"Hello there, Ms. Sweet," the Hunter brothers chimed.

"That reminds me," the captain said. "I've got a surprise for you." Then he turned to Mick and said, "See this compass?"

"Yeah."

"Keep the heading due west. Do you think you can handle that while

I'm gone?"

"You bet, cap'."

This time Terrance DeVour ignored the arrogance. He had become smitten with Marie's beauty. He felt he needed a ruse to lure her into his stateroom. He still planned on killing her but he's been without a prostitute since he left Greece. Not that he thought this pompous bitch of a reporter could be bought, but he sure enough wanted to fuck her before he killed her. He figured the only way he would be able to accomplish that was to dope her up with enough Comfitine and date rape her. He had more than enough pills in storage to pull off that trick. Fact was, he had enough pills ground into a powder to knock out an army. Drug them at dinner and when they pass out load them into the dinghy, easy enough. But he would do Marie before they are cast off and blown to smithereens. 'Shark bait all': not a single drop of blood spilt on his precious ship. He so really wanted to fuck the bitch that fucked up his Pet Rescue Facility and Comfitine operation. After she pays her contrition; he accomplishes his mission. Then back to the safety of Africa.

The stateroom was large and took up the whole forward bow. Port hole windows lined the suite. The décor was impeccable. Marie was immediately turned off, nonetheless, by the lion skin on the floor. Polite manners silenced her disdain.

Captain Hunter retrieved a valise. Upon opening she saw an array of diamonds. There were trays, right and left, front and back; in the center was a large diamond with a crystal clear blue hue. It was positioned on black velvet; not yet mounted, but obviously too big for a ring.

"This will be yours on completion of our deal," the captain said.

Marie didn't know what to say. Her stare was transfixed. Part of her wanted to pick up the diamond for a closer inspection: another part was afraid to touch it.

The president of Nigeria gave it to me," the captain bragged. Before he closed the case and removed the glitter from her eyes. Momentarily impressed, mixed with a dose of reality, and a dash of bitters whirled around her brain like a mixed drink.

'Get out, get out,' she heard from the prone lion skin roar. Flashing lights pulsed through her brain. They were bright blood red warning lights. Fast as lightning they circulated until she took a deep breath. Her hand held her pounding heart. Her feet took a step backwards.

"Thank you," she politely said. Taking another step backwards toward the door. She no longer trusted the black eyes that were staring at her. She could see something else in the reflecting irises. Perhaps she was seeing a hallucination, she no longer cared; they reflected evil.

"Can I make you a drink?" He asked while pointing to his personal bar. It was off to the side, not far from his bed.

"No, thanks. I've got to get going."

"Where do you think you're going? We're at sea."

"I know, but I need some fresh air. I might be getting sea sick." She wasn't far off either. She glanced again at the lion skin and her stomach did a flip- flop. Then she turned and went through the door at a quick pace.

"I have some Dramamine," he called out to deaf ears. She didn't need any seasick pills; she needed Mick's strength. Making a crooked beeline to the bridge where Mick was idle-braining about the ocean's expanse.

"Beautiful," he said upon seeing her. "You and the ocean."

"Thank you," she smiled. Grabbing his free hand, made her feel better instantly.

The captain who had followed her said, "I'll take the wheel now."

"You bet, cap'," Mick replied while climbing down.

"Are you feeling better Ms. Sweet?" The captain acted concerned. "Yes, yes indeed. Come on Mick." She tugged at his hand.

"See ya later, cap'," Mick said.

'Ignorant fuck,' Terrance DeVour thought.

Mick and Marie settled on the lounge chairs and Bonnie and Joan joined them on the rear deck. They had changed into their bathing suits, primetime sunbathing attire. Bonnie was wearing a yellow and white sunflower bikini. Every pedal amplified her curves and cleavage. Joan had a pansy purple, floral over honeycomb design. Two of the pansy's had a perfect 3D, paint on depth. Her slopes looked slippery even when not wet.

The admiring stewards quickly followed with, "Can we get you ladies anything? Another pitcher of Margaritas, perhaps?"

"Not now," Bonnie answered.

THE MICK AND MARIE STORY

When the men retreated, Joan said, "those guys can't give their eyes a rest."

"No kidding." Bonnie replied.

"I've noticed that, too," Marie added. And that gave her an idea. "Mick, I want to talk to you. Follow me." She got up with Mick and led him to their room.

While she changed into her more modest 2Pc swimsuit, it had all the colors of the sun from sunrise, to sunset, in an authentic Indian print. The suit was an eye-popper, his ears opened too when she said, "I think there's something funny going on here. I will take the girls forward on the bow to distract the stewards. I want you to snoop around if you can, but don't get caught. I think our lives are in danger and the captain has an arsenal in his stateroom. It just came to me, there's no such thing as a five-star admiral, and that was Paul in the parking lot. I recognized his gait. I'll have to call for help if you find anything. And do you have any more of that spring water? I drank all that was in the bottle. You're right, that's good stuff, even at room temperature. It has a flavor that comes alive."

"Yeah, I've got more."

What they didn't realize was the spring water had been contaminated with chemicals from Comfitine at the Cal Con Health operation. Marie had a mental buzz going. Actually she could think faster and clearer than ever before.

Mick gave her another bottle. Then she said, "give me five minutes." She kissed him quickly and added, "Good luck." He stayed behind while she gathered up the girls and headed for the bow. Just as she suspected, the stewards followed.

Marie had previously whispered to Bonnie and Joan, "Engage the men in conversation, no matter how much they disgust you. I'll explain latter."

Re-emerging, Mick went to the vacated bar and made himself a scotch on the rocks for a ready excuse, and as he contemplated his next move. He knew Marie wanted him to snoop around. 'But for what?' He asked himself. Liquid crutch in hand to ease his apprehension, he nonchalantly peered through the forward window. Spotting the stewards busy with the girls, he felt it was safe to prowl. He didn't know how long the girls could keep the men distracted, but he knew there was something wrong with the pair. He set his drink back down on the bar.

The little boyish curiosity in him thought to investigate the forbidden fruit first. 'There must have been a reason why he was told to stay away from the life boat,' rang his bell like a foghorn. He moseyed over by the aft railing and upon seeing the backs of the Hunter brother's heads upon the bridge he flipped over the railing and landed in a crouch position on the platform next to the lifeboat.

The tackle box was practically staring him in the face. Normally he would have opened it anyway, just to see the type of lures were in there. This box was an oddity of sorts—not that it was out of place—it was because there were no poles to accompany it. He reached in and flicked the latch. It had no lures at all, but in the center tray, he saw what looked like white putty wrapped in cellophane with wires sticking in it. There was also a telecommunications device on the other side of the wires.

'This can't be good,' he recognized the explosive situation they were in. He removed the tray and components, upon closing the tackle box. 'What now?' He quizzed himself over and over in nanoseconds.

Peeking between the railing, on the bridge he saw the two Hunter brothers were still looking forward. He slinked through the gateway with stealth. Flashed past the bar, down the stairs and discretely selected a spot in the bowels of the engine room to stash his tray. Figuring Marie would call her FBI friend, and there would be evidence that something was amiss.

His mind was a flutter with other things as well. How was he going to politely explain to the captain that they would like to turn around now? Thanks for the ride, he could say. But I don't want to get married anymore, is one. We're out of beer is another lame excuse. Not a likely scenario. Or sneak off in the dead of night, a hazardous prospect indeed. Make a secret mayday distress call was most likely to work but first he felt he had to disarm his adversaries.

He quickly ran back up the stairs to make sure the stewards were still busy. He had a nip of scotch while he was at it. Back down the stairs he prowled. He had to guess which rooms were where the stewards berthed but it didn't matter. There were no locks on the doors—only deadbolts for absolute privacy were operable from the inside only. And he found what he suspected in the first closet he looked in. Suits, five pairs of tailored black suits, white shirts and one bulletproof vest greeted his eyes. These guys are phonies. They're bodyguards; they drive black Humvees. The complete picture developed faster than a Polaroid.

On the shelf under a Stetson hat he found a holster and a 9mm automatic. He stuck the gun in his waistband. Across the aisle he found the same set up. This time however, he removed the clip, emptied the chamber, and took all the bullets from the clip before returning the gun to its holster. Bolting to his room to stash his finds, he selected Marie's handbag for the gun in exchange of her cell phone and the excess bullets were going overboard. He didn't like the dead weight clicking in his pockets.

Heart racing, he reached for his drink back at the bar. 'Compose yourself,' he thought. He sucked in a soothing fresh breath. Looking out the forward window, he could see the stewards were still busy with the girls. Bonnie looked to be singing, and everyone laughing. This gave him more confidence. Dare he raid the captain's quarters?

CHAPTER 42

"Look at those boobs bounce," Terrance DeVour said to the Holy Hunter. "When they get seasick, I've got Comfitine in the Dramamine jar for them. After we dope them up, we can have our way with the bitches." He was deliberately steering into the ocean swells for maximum effects of a roller- coaster ride.

"Yeah that's fine and dandy, but what are we going to do about our Comfitine business and this other venture you've got me into in Africa? As you know, Cal-Con Health is going down the tubes," Larry bemoaned. "The Feds got the company under lock and key."

"Is that all you can think about, business? I told you a hundred times already, the fix is in. You're all set. You've nothing to worry about. And quit bugging me about business. I want to watch the show," the captain scowled.

"They don't look seasick to me," Larry flatly stated. "But I feel a bit queasy.

Where do you keep the real Dramamine?"

"In my room."

"And while you're fucking the broads, what are you going to do with that Mickey Swift guy?"

"Damn you and your questions. He'll be doped up too, either before or during dinner. I've got enough Comfitine ground up to knock out a herd of horses. Where is that ignorant fuck anyway?"

"I don't know."

"Well go find him and keep an eye on him." The captain was tired of answering the Holy Hunter's nosy questions, and he was pissing him off. Getting the 'pain in the ass' Lawrence Marsi to take a walk was the least of his problems. As he switched back into auto navigate, he noticed his computerized compass spinning oddly. No longer were they headed west.

"Shit," the captain cried.

Mick was sitting at the bar sipping his scotch when the Holy Hunter found him. "Where have you been?" he asked.

"Right here. Why?" Mick innocently acted.

The Holy Hunter didn't reply. He just looked around suspiciously, like he was investigating something but didn't know what he was looking for. Then he went into the radio control room and silently pretended he knew what the functions of all the electronic equipment was for.

"All hands on deck," the captain was screaming from the bridge. His stewards came in a trot and hustled up to the bridge. The girls heard the captain's cries and sauntered their way back to the main cabin and bellied up to the bar with Mick. With a wry smile and a, 'every things been taken care,' wink at Marie he moved behind the bar. "What are you ladies having?" he asked.

"Water," Bonnie said. "That spring water that Marie gave us was so good."

"Sorry, it's below deck. And I can't go now." Then he leaned over and whispered, "the show is about to start. But why don't you go below and get dressed. We'll be abandoning ship." Looking directly at Marie, he said, "don't forget your purse."

Then the captain and the muscular steward entered and made a beeline for the radio control room. The captain had ordered the other steward to man the helm after he cut the throttle to idle. The ship had dual controls; the upper bridge was the Great White Hunter's favorite. The height gave him airs of superiority. The lower wheelhouse was forward in the main cabin, just to the right of his stateroom door. He didn't know much about the computer system in his ship. Sure, he knew how to enter the longitude and latitude coordinates—he had a complete destination chart to help him with that. Switching the Global Positioning System on automatic was simple too. But in reality, he wouldn't know a sextant or how to use one if it hit him in the head. His own ignorance of how to navigate his ship without the computer's help left him embarrassed.

Green lights lit up the control room, not a red warning light in sight. The captain couldn't find anything wrong with his system. But according to the compass, the ship was going around in circles.

"Where was that Swift fellow when you found him?" he asked the Holy

Hunter.

"Sitting at the bar. Where he is now."

He spied at him with an evil stare from across the room. Mick wasn't all that oblivious to it even from the distance. Dagger stares can be felt in one's back by the perceptive. He didn't have to look directly at them as their refection on the mirrored bar background spoke volumes. Ignoring the penetrating gaze with his nonchalance, he still felt like the butler in a murder mystery. The captain suspected, but couldn't prove a thing. This made him partially satisfied, and now his goal was to get everyone off the ship.

Marie had her purse when she returned with the girls. Bonnie and Joan had brought their overnight bags too. This even looked suspicious to Mick. Terrance DeVour was all over it. He and his men vacated the control room and headed full steam toward the group.

"Where do you think you're going?" The Great White Hunter aimed his question at the girls.

"Going? We, we aren't going anywhere," Bonnie stammered nervously. "What's the problem cap'?" Mick blurted out. He didn't want the girls to answer any more questions.

The captain turned his stare back at Mick. Oh, how he hated his guts. His face was glowing with frustration. He turned and ordered his steward to check the rudder in the steerage motor room. Mick became concerned he might stumble upon the tray he hid.

"We're sinking!" he exclaimed, looking at Marie with a feigned fearful face. "We're sinking?" She quizzed before she caught on. "We're sinking!" She stated with more fervor.

"Where are the life preservers?" Mick carried on.

"We're not sinking," the captain shouted, trying to calm the idiots.

Then Bonnie and Joan joined in the panic. "Oh my god, we're sinking! Call the Coast Guard!"

"We're not sinking, we're just a little off course is all." the captain stated. "Where are the life preservers?" Mick asked again.

The captain wasn't about to give them any lifejackets. He had other plans for his shark bait. But he had to find out what was wrong with his ship. So he turned away and repeated over his shoulder, "I told you, we're not sinking."

He headed back to the main controls with the Holy Hunter on his heals. "What are we going to do? Call the Coast Guard?"

"No, you fool." The captain wasn't about to do that either. Terrance DeVour was so flustered he couldn't think straight around a corner.

Mick saw his opening to take advantage of the distractions. "Come on," he said in a calm whisper. It was now or never as far as he was concerned. For sure he didn't want to hang around to find out if the steward had found the tray he placed in the motor room. He led the group outside to the lifeboat.

At the controls, the captain switched out of the auto-sail mode. The ship had been floundering in the ocean swells in idle throttle. Then he checked his computerized coordinates. He was sure the problems started when he switched back into auto-sail.

While Mick had the girls in the dinghy and was removing the last of the nylon harnesses, the steward on the bridge spotted them abandoning ship. He called the captain on the intercom. He had just discovered the computer coordinates had been changed and the steering, switched back into manual, worked fine.

"Son-of-a-bitches!" echoed out of the main cabin as Mick slid the dinghy into the ocean. He wasn't mad that they pirated his lifeboat; he was pissed because his planned sexual exploits were foiled. The other steward reemerged from the engine room and reported he couldn't find anything wrong with the rudder.

"Get my rifle," the Great White Hunter ordered. "Never mind. Take the wheel. I'll get it myself." He wanted to use his new rifle, not the ones in the rack.

Mick had started the outboard motor and the girls had unfurled the sail and hoisted the sail. They were making headway to distance themselves. Mick had given Marie back her cell phone to call a mayday to the Coast Guard. She hit the emergency numbers. "It's not ringing," she said. The text message claimed she was out of range and her battery power was low. "Damn, double damn," rand through her head.

The Great White Hunter was laughing now, he had power in his hand. So much power, he climbed back on the bridge to scope down on his victims. The source of his power came in the form of an Anschutz bolt-action rifle, complete with scope. He unzipped the case.

He loved this gun, even though he had only fired it on the testing range. He had it custom made in Monte Carlo. The rifle stock had a rollover cheek piece and a Rosewood grip-cap with diamond inserts. But most of all he loved hunting and this time he was going human hunting. Excitement was going to make this a true pleasure cruise. Mick was in his crosshairs.

The lifeboat was only 100 yards from the American Flag Ship when the first shot rang out. The thunder roll from the rifle got everyone's attention.

"I thought you through all the bullets overboard?" Marie asked.

"Obviously not all of them," Mick apologetically replied. Indeed he missed a whole closet full and more.

The captain ejected a shell and inserted another bullet. Oh, how he treasured the metallic clicks and manly thrusts of the breech-block bolt. For him, the smell of spent shells worked like nitro jump-starting a heart.

This time the Great White Hunter had Marie scoped, because she had a phone in her hand. The bullet hit the tackle on the main mast before they heard the thunder of the shot.

"Ha, you missed—me," Bonnie yelled out in a mocking tone of false bravado. Actually she was frightened beyond reality. Her automatic wise cracking mouth fired before her thought process rationalized the danger they were all in.

She also realized it wasn't a smart idea to antagonize the enemy, as they were still in rifle range but the distance between the boats was growing.

That's exactly why the captain ordered his steward to steer directly at the lifeboat; "ram em if you have too" he said. Besides, he wanted to see the fear on their faces when he keelhauls those pirates. Changing his mind faster than he could change the grin on his face, he realized he couldn't ram the lifeboat; it still had the plastic explosives hidden in the tackle box. Besides, he really didn't want to scratch his mighty American Flag ship. He reloaded.

Mick and company were none too happy about seeing the ship headed straight for them.

"What do we do now?" Bonnie bemoaned.

"Yeah, we can't outrun them in this tub," Joan said in a state of panic. "When will the Coast Guard get here?" Bonnie wanted to know. "Better hand me your purse, Marie," Mick said.

"Why did we have to get off the yacht again?" Joan cried. "They were planning on killing us." Marie tried to soothe.

A bullet streaked through the sail. The report from the rifle was getting louder and louder.

"Keep your heads down," Mick demanded.

The Flagship was bearing down on them when seemingly the yacht halted. Mick could clearly see white hair sticking out from behind the rifle. The Great White Hunter was posed to take another shot. A bullet streaked a foot through the ocean before penetrating the lifeboat. Like a faucet, seawater sprouted through the hole.

"Oh my God! What do we do now?" Joan's panic was in full bloom.

Mick was trying to steady his aim on the bridge with the 9mm automatic. The constant motion of the ocean swells made aiming and accuracy extremely difficult. Then inexplicably the white headed fiend was no longer in sight on the bridge.

"Put the rifle down," the Holy Hunter ordered the captain. He had a 9mm pointed at his head.

"What are you doing? Are you fucking nuts?" The captain protested.

"Not nuts enough to go to Africa with you. You fucked me for the last time. I had to flip on you for my freedom. The Feds were going to hunt you down anyway. It's a small world with no place to hide for men like you and me. Not even in Africa." Larry Marsi rationalized correctly.

"They're lying to you, Larry. Look, we're safe. The government doesn't have any jurisdiction out here. We're in international waters. We can cruise the Mediterranean forever. We can be partners again. Run the granite pit in Africa and smuggle diamonds on the side. I've taken care of everything. Fuck the Feds. They've got nothing on us. We can just blame the accountants. They're the ones that signed off on the books." Although Terrance DeVour had set his rifle aside, he was planning on making a play for it the first chance he got. Then he was going to blast the traitor. Meanwhile he'll just have to talk down his guard.

Actually the Holy Hunter could care less if Terrance DeVour killed the reporter and friends. He was only out to save his own skin and since the FBI was kind enough to outfit him with the wire he was wearing, now he has everything on tape and more than enough to get him off the hook. What ingenious listening devices the FBI has, he thought.

Promises of dropping all charges against him for his cooperation was what sold him on the turncoat idea, besides he knew Terrance DeVour for what he really was: just another lying, thieving, murdering CEO. He doubted that he would ever be his partner again. No matter what he promised. Fact being, it takes a con artist to recognize a con. The Great White Hunter was probably planning on burying him at sea after the show was over anyway. Then he would be rid of all the witnesses against himself.

Maybe he should just pull the trigger now he thought; then he could be the hero. He could always claim self-defense. A life and death situation, he made me shoot him, he could explain. Of course, he would have to kill the steward at the helm too, to get rid of the witness. Who's to be the wiser? While the Holy Hunter was in contemplation, he failed to notice the steward-turned- helmsman switched the intercom back on to warn his partner of the mutiny.

As it was, the other steward had listened. He went to get his gun.

The captain continued trying to talk some sense into the Holy Hunter with promises of wealth beyond imagination. But all his lies were falling on disbelieving ears.

Lawrence Marsi had already signaled for the Coast Guard via the emergency transponder in the radio room and had called the FBI on a special cell phone they provided. He also positioned himself so he could keep an eye on the captain and the ladder rungs that led to the bridge. He was all too aware of the missing bodyguard that posed as a steward. His simple plan was to keep him at bay or get the drop on him too. The rest of the plan was to wait on the Coast Guard.

Larry Marsi's nerves were already on death-defying edge, stomach queasy, sea legs on strike. He neglected to take a Dramamine tablet earlier. The ocean was calm but the waves continued to pitch and wallow in a gentle cycle. Up and down the flagship floundered. Up and down with a side roll his stomach made like a washing machine tumble. The Holy Hunter hadn't planned on a physical debilitating upheaval. The almighty hurl.

The captain had noticed the green gill ill face that was panicking. He sensed his chance was near. They had been staring at each other, but now the Holy Hunter followed the captain's eyes to the rifle. That's when he raised his 9mm, pointed it at the captains head and said, "Don't even think about it." But his guts said, 'fuck it.' He pulled the trigger.

The captain grimaced at the movement. The Holy Hunter grimaced himself because his gun didn't fire. A different shot rang out. Lawrence Marsi flinched as he felt a thump in his vest. A sickening feeling overcame him as he stared blankly at his gun. Terrance DeVour grabbed his rifle. The Holy Hunter pulled the trigger again and again. He didn't understand why his gun didn't fire. Another shot rang out. A burning pain ripped through his buttocks. He felt his bone shatter. Falling to his knees he hurled his sickness.

The other bodyguard had made his way and waited patiently on the port- side railing for his opening. He fired twice more, striking the Holy Hunter in his rear quarters. His face now lay in his own vomit. There would be no getting up for him. The captain had retrieved his rifle.

A spent shell was ejected, one inserted with a click and a slam of the bolt. The Holy Hunter was bleeding on his knees, face on the floor, arms outstretched as if he was pleading for mercy with Allah. That didn't matter to the Great White Hunter though. "Damn you to all hell," he shouted at him before shooting him in the back. The vest he was wearing didn't stop this bullet, not this caliber, not at this range. The Holy Hunter expired.

Mick and company had distanced themselves as best they could and were puzzled by the rumblings coming from the American Flag ship. But they were rather shocked to see a body tossed into the ocean from the bridge.

The captain had reloaded his rifle and ordered his helmsman to resume the hunt. He had fresh blood on his hands and wanted more. Actually, he never felt better in his life. His gleaming white teeth and smile told all.

"There's a ship on the horizon," the helmsman reported. He had spotted a Coast Guard Cutter.

"I found the emergency transponder on in the radio room, but I turned it off," the other bodyguard stated.

Too late to continue the hunt, the captain realized. He correctly presumed it was the Coast Guard barreling down. But he wasn't about to let his quarry escape unscathed. "We'll have to resort to the original plan then," he retorted. Calling off the hunt disappointed him, but he was perfectly happy to send the pirates' splatterings sailing like chum. One thing he had to prevent was a rescue of any kind. 'No witnesses,' was his motto. Reaching in his pocket for his own frequency transmitter, he punched in a code.

The explosion that followed was horrific. A fireball, resembling the sun, erupted as the ship's fuel tanks ruptured. Plumes of smoke rose off the ocean. Debris rained like hail.

The plastic explosives had sent the motor works to the bottom. The aft deck was in splinters. The muscular bodyguard was impaled with fiberglass. The bridge and bow were afloat yet as the licks of fire climbed the banner and flagpole.

Mick's crew were long-jawed and awed at the sight of the destruction.

Mick cracked the tension with, "Don't they know, they can go to jail for burning an American Flag?"

CHAPTER 43

Bonnie had ingeniously plugged the lifeboat's bullet hole with a tampon. They were no longer afraid of sinking. "I swear, these things will plug anything," she quipped.

"That was meant for us?" Joan asked. "Afraid so," Marie answered.

"But why?" Bonnie wondered aloud. "Greed—pure greed," Mick figured.

Bonnie suggested they go to the debris field to look for survivors. Mick gave pause to inform her, "they wouldn't do it for us, you know."

"Doesn't matter. It's the right thing to do. And the Coast Guard will be here soon enough." Bonnie defended her position.

They had noticed the cutter headed their way too.

"It's every boat's duty to search for survivors," Joan added. "Let's go, Mick," Marie encouraged.

Against his better judgment, Mick turned the outboard and aimed for the burning debris. Bonnie and Joan took the sail back down as they headed back into the wind. The mast was only 6' tall and everything folded neatly.

Patches of fuel burned right atop the water as Mick slowly zigzagged through. The fire field was downwind of the bow and broken up by the current. They could see the air-locked bow of the ship clearly. Two of the five stars were above the water line. Bits of furniture and floating cushions littered the water resembling a flooded junkyard.

The sputter of the outboard motor was the only sound to break the eerie silence. Nobody was speaking, everybody listening, not even the squawk of seagulls was present. They were looking for dead bodies, not a very pleasant chore. Nobody could have survived the explosion was the consensus. The solemn sea air hung heavy in the lifeboat like an impenetrable fog.

The Pacific was as smooth as pond water; inexplicably calm, some smoke clung to the water; some roiled skyward. Ocean litter was clunking against the boat, no matter how carefully Mick steered. "Look! A life vest!" Marie shouted.

Mick maneuvered so Joan, who was farthest portside, could pluck it from the ocean. She put it on directly. Cold saltwater penetrated her cotton top. That made her shiver, but she was warmly comforted by the extra security. "This is like a scavenger hunt," she said adventurously.

Everyone felt secure in the knowledge that the ship on the horizon was getting visually bigger and that they would soon be rescued. Marie was sure it was a Coast Guard cutter, as the last time she called, she was told one had already been dispatched to her area.

They could also see the destroyed American Flagship better. The helm was detached from the bow. Both were air-locked and miraculously still afloat. The helm's mast and radar dish were still burning; flags and banners totally disintegrated.

"Mick! Oh! Oh! Do you see that silver case?" Marie asked while pointing. "Yeah." He steered alongside so she could reach it. She knew what it was. She recognized the case; it was the one with the diamonds. Her heart was in overdrive as she reached out to grab the handle. But before she could open and admire her find; a shot rang out.

It was no ordinary shot. The reverberation was ear piercing. Close range deafening. They all heard that sound before from a distance, but this rifle shot made Mick groan, "ahh-ooh." The bullet hit him with such force, it knocked from his sitting position and he lost control of the tiller.

Joan screamed out of fear. She was the first to spot a white hairy head sticking out of a red life preserver. He had a rifle in his hand and the click clack of reloading could be heard.

While everyone was focused on the aluminum brief case, the Great White Hunter lurked in the debris on the other side. He was lucky to survive the explosion but he wasn't unscathed. Splinters of fiberglass had penetrated his legs and buttocks like sharp darts. He was able to put on a handy life preserver before the bridge listed: effectively dumping him into the ocean.

Murder was on his mind now. Sweet revenge. He was going to kill everyone in the boat, then climb aboard. No more hunting, his prey was right before him.

Marie pulled the 9mm automatic back out of her purse. Mick had returned it thinking it was no longer needed. Then she shifted her body to Mick's seat; shielding him from further harm and shouted, "You dirty bastard. We were trying to save you!" Then she fired and Terrance DeVour fired. Both missed their targets.

She fired again before the Great White Hunter could reload. Marie had never fired a gun before and her shots were reactive. She also made an instantaneous mental note to go to a firing range and take advantage of her 2 Amendment rights as soon as she could.

Joan and Bonnie had huddled as low as they could in the boat. Marie sat up proud and defiant as she could be. She tried to get the best angle possible and missed another shot. She was madder than a queen hornet in a disturbed nest. Terrance DeVour was surprised he missed her too, and that she had a gun.

He thought; he was bumped by floating debris and that's why he missed her with his last shot. It's a tricky thing to reload a rifle while thrashing about in a life vest while ducking bullets, but he managed sufficiently. This time though, he had, 'that fuckin bitch reporter,' in his sights, and something else had him in its sight.

The Great White Hunter was bitten by another great white hunter. But this bite severed his whole leg in one crunch. The tug sent his head underwater momentarily. The life preserver's buoyancy brought him right back to the surface.

Marie didn't know what to think. Her target resembled a fishing bobber with a white top and a red body. She saw he still had his rifle in his hands but was no longer facing her. He was also farther away. She was better off not seeing his face, which was blank with shock.

Then the bobber went under the water again. His other leg was surgically removed by rows and rows of serrated teeth. There was no color in his blood-drained body now. He frantically squirmed about like a water bug with his arms momentarily. He had dropped his rifle, but, with his black beady eyes, he still managed a Manson style revenge glare until they closed.

Marie turned her attention back to Mick and told her friends, "It's safe now."

The thing about explosions and blood in the water is a major attraction for the most proficient hunters of all time—the shark. In this case, the Great White Hunter's own blood and thrashing about was like getting an invitation to the Oscars. Only this time, the Great White Sharks did the feasting.

CHAPTER 44

The Coast Guard cutter was upon them and in position for their rescue operation. None too soon for the girls as the lifeboat was slowly taking on water. They had busied themselves bailing, slow but steady, handfuls at a time.

The girls weren't the only ones happy to see the rescuers. Never in the annals of this vessel were there so many men literally salivating over the rails in anticipation of participating in rescuing these buxom waving beauties.

Mick had smacked his head and cricked his neck on the side of the lifeboat when the bullet knocked him off his seat. He parked his head in a happier time and place; wasn't sure if he was seeing stars or diamonds, everything was so surreal. One minute he was sitting in a flowing spring in a valley of Hummingbirds; the next, he was being stirred with a gentle shake and an "are you all right?—Come on, get up, the boat's sinking." He had subconsciously clamped his good hand around his wound, sufficiently plugging the bloody holes. His mind was fluttering like the blades of the rescue helicopter that launched from its aft helipad.

A pair of surf rescue boats was set afloat by the ship's boom. They sped and surrounded the imperiled lifeboat.

"Glad to see you handsome men," Bonnie quipped upon being transferred to safer environs.

"I love you guys," followed from Joan.

Marie was glad to see them too, almost to the point of laughter but she didn't dare. The rescuers were all decked out in bright orange floatation suits with matching helmets. It wasn't the helmets that struck her funny— she didn't feel they were out of place at all—it was the helmet story Mick had predicted would come true. One of his obvious larks, or was it? He looks so serious sometimes when he spins his yarns. It was the one about the flying Asian Carp; a fish she never even heard of before, that was going to overtake the Mississippi River and spread upstream into every tributary and the Great Lakes.

Is the one she remembered and how the government is going to conspire to sell helmets for favored manufacturers, by requiring all fishermen with licenses to wear safety helmets; because one never knows when some fish will fly out of the water, hit you in the head, knock you out, or the boat and drown you. But now he's sitting in a pool of water on the bottom of the lifeboat holding his arm with a grimace or half smile on his face; she wasn't sure which, not that it mattered, but she was worried about him and realized she loved his stories and him too.

The rescuers propped him up, had the copter lower a transport basket and despite his feeble, "I can make it," protests, he was put into a safety basket and hoisted up to the hovering helicopter. On his way up, Marie hollered in vain over the copter noise, "be careful with him." She instantly felt lonely. Then prodded her rescuers to hurry back to the ship. So near, but far away, all's she wanted now was to be by her man.

Mick was told to relax and enjoy the ride when he was strapped into the safety basket and he did just that. Finding that happy place in Hummingbird Valley, his comfort zone took over his mind. He was sure he saw diamonds; then he imagined a team of sparkling neurologists lined up like marching cartoon characters, all with funny names, equipped with picks and axes, pulsing in unison down the caverns of his veins. They sang a happy going to work song as they distributed serum; while hiking through his nerves. Repairs were needed.

Marie had just entered the infirmary when she saw the medic thumb the piston to remove air from a syringe. A stream of fluid ejected from the needle tip as he posed to inject Mick with morphine. The stream Marie saw reflected a blue green prism and a premonition came to her as clear as the pearly gates themselves.

"Stop!" she cried. "Don't give him any barbiturates!"

"But we have to ease his pain. It's a long way back to port." the medic explained.

"No! You don't understand,—can't you see he's already in la-la land?"

"No morphine," Mick managed to confirm. He knew he didn't need any mental blocking painkiller. He had his own way of blocking pain with positive mental visions. A concentration trick that redirected Beta-endorphins; (a natural painkiller), to the proper places. Unbeknowest to him, he also had a boost from his spring water that he liked so dearly. In the watered down form of Comfitine was a natural opiate that effects emotions and neurotransmitters. So naturally, he was more upset about his concentration being interrupted. The comfortable knowledge of Marie looking out over him allowed him to get back to his garden dream. He smiled at Marie when she squeezed his hand. Then he closed his eyes and was gone.

Thunderbolts of lightning were lighting the darkness. Poisons were fleeing his body. Mick was quietly naming his endorphins. There were millions of them, but he tried to name them all anyway. There was Neuro the lightning- fast leader lighting the way, Micro, the only one inspecting things with a scope, Specks, for his enlarged magnifying minds-eye iris, and then there was Ohm, the yoga expert, who could wiggle out of any situation.

Marie was sitting in a chair next to his bed, clutching her valise like it was an autographed football in a stadium of rabid fans. Actually she was in her own state of stupor. Deep in concentration of how she was duped. She questioned herself over and over again about how she was fooled and what had transpired. How lucky they all are and how grateful she is that they all survived.

FBI agents interrupted her thoughts when they entered the infirmary. Pompously, they flashed their badges. Marie was all too savvy to their ways

—obnoxious ways—that demonstrate their authority. She didn't always feel that way, but she knew it was highly irregular for FBI agents to be on a Coast Guard cutter and instantly recognized their presence as Paul's meddling again.

The agents were only following orders. They were assigned to track and record conversations between Lawrence Marsi and Terrance DeVour. All communications had ceased with the explosion of the American Flag ship. They weren't exactly sure of the demise of their informant. Some of the later recordings were garbled, and they aimed to find out why.

Their original plans were to arrest Terrance DeVour, for securities fraud, and—since Paul felt he had to stop the wedding—Mickey Swift, for failing to file income taxes, in Hawaii, as that was thought to be their destination.

Then according to the GPS system, they were drifting off course and the FBI had to adjust their intercept point. The fact that they were in international waters wouldn't save the Cal-Con executives either, as piracy and kidnapping charges were already planned as an alternative if their destination, Hawaii, was altered. But the explosion changed everything once again. Paul didn't plan on that.

Paul was still calling the shots from his L.A. office. He had arrested the sole survivor from the James Gang episode on San Diego's dock that morning. He claimed he was only trying to warn the passengers as he thought they might be in danger because he recognized Terrance DeVour as the one who chartered his captain's boat. Paul thought the opposite was true at the time. He thought the kid had recognized the observing FBI agents and was trying to warn Terrance DeVour that a sting operation was on. The kid had to unfold a newspaper story that he had kept in his wallet to prove he wasn't lying. After confirming the kid's story, he was cut loose.

Paul was determined to find out exactly what happened. That was now his agenda and his agents' top priority. So far, all he knew was the ship they were following exploded and his informant was missing along with the target. But that wasn't what he was sulking in his office about. He was worried about getting another promotion and getting that "fucking dickwad" that was with his girl. *Marie's my girl, Marie's my girl*, skipped over and over though his scratched, one-track mind.

Now it was time for the agents to interview Mick and Marie who were resting comfortably in the infirmary. Marie was ready for them though. They started out introducing themselves and asking mundane questions. Mick was aware that they were there also, but pretended to be sleeping. In Marie he trusted to do the right thing.

He felt a pain in his arm when he heard the agents ask Marie what was in the briefcase. She replied, "My laptop." Mick quietly sighed in relief.

Mick's arm had been bandaged and put into a temp-cast. He was also given penicillin orally but, again feeling more disturbed, he quickly set his Iris back in minds-eye. Mick had split his Neuro legions at Red River. Cerebro sent reinforcements. Iris reported seeing a disaster area, a real battlefield. He was still naming all his friends: Hallu was repairing a wall of bone, Cino was paying unexpected HMO "you're too healthy taxes," and Gen and Ic were mending soft felt draperies.

Marie handled the naturally inquisitive FBI agents like the pro she is.

She had reported almost everything exactly as it happened. It was more like she was interviewing them.

The agents were suspicious about the way Marie clasped onto the briefcase. Besides, it didn't look like a laptop case. It was aluminum, completely out of black leather, laptop style. The agents still tried to get her to open her case with trick questions like, "What brand of laptop do you use?" then "What do you use it for?" and finally, "What kind of stories do you write?" But she never let the agents see her laptop like they wanted. She danced around the prying questions on her tippy toes like a cliff dancer, but her refusal answered their questions anyway. Now they knew she was hiding something.

The agents broke off the interview when they got word that the redeployed rescue team found "a live one." The helicopter crew spotted a man clinging to a polished teakwood rail that was floating along with the air-trapped bow. Along the way, the surfboat rescue team also found the remains of Terrance DeVour. Using a gaff hook, they snagged the life preserver and pulled in half a man.

While Mick was in sickbay, the FBI agents were interrogating the lone surviving bodyguard, who told them that the captain shot Mick for stealing the lifeboat. Then one agent asked, "Why would anyone want to steal a lifeboat?" After an "I don't know" shoulder shrug, he then asked, "What's in the briefcase?"

"I don't know," he replied, but now he did know. Mick and Marie had the briefcase of diamonds; and, more importantly, the formula for Comfitine—which was more valuable than the diamonds—was hidden under the foam that lined the case. Then he swore that he "didn't know anything about nothing," claiming he was just an employee. From then on out, he refused to answer any more questions until he had an attorney present. Even when the agents suggested immunity from prosecution, he said he didn't know anything. He felt he could beat any trumped up kidnapping charges that they threatened him with anyway; but the main thing was, he now knew Marie had the briefcase. With his boss dead, he now had a new set of priorities: get the briefcase—no matter who he had to kill to get it.

Bonnie and Joan had refreshed themselves and were sporting some official Coast Guard jackets, generously donated by their fans. And when they joined their friends in the infirmary, Marie had sworn them into secrecy. They could split up the diamonds *only if* the FBI didn't find out about them, reasoning that, if they did find out, the gems would only be confiscated. And to keep their stories straight, they'd best keep it simple, as they were just an innocent wedding party. The deal was cut and cast; and they all agreed to protect Mick. No one was sure how he did what he did or if he did anything at all, except save their lives.

Paul was still sitting in his L.A. office when his agents reported to him about the lack of cooperation from all parties concerned. His orders were to arrest the bodyguard anyway to fingerprint him and find out if he was who he said he was, and check for outstanding warrants. Then cut the wedding party loose. He didn't care if Marie was acting suspiciously about a briefcase. He already had his spy gear wheels spinning in overdrive and was sure to find about whatever it was she was acting suspiciously about. Paul didn't know about any formula and never heard of Comfitine.

What he really needed to know was what happened to the billions of dollars that Cal-Con Health executives absconded with. Paul was buried in reports from his financial forensic agents and was prepared to bring indictments against Terrance DeVour and now he couldn't even do that. After all his work, after all the hours he'd put in, this left him disgusted and drained. *How was he going to get his "saved the day" promotion now?* He obsessed, 'she's my girl, she's my girl.'

The sun was setting and, with the unlikelihood of other survivors, the Coast Guard's orders were to return to port. But first, a well-placed cannon shot was fired into the bow of the American Flag ship to clear the shipping lanes of dangerous debris.

CHAPTER 45

Mick was on the mend with a brand-new cast. After the Coast Guard cutter docked in San Diego, he and the girls went to the local community hospital. A bank was conveniently located across the street and while Mick was waiting to be attended to, because he didn't have his insurance card with him, with time to kill, he suggested they get a safety deposit box. So Marie and the girls ran across the street to tend to business.

Something happens to a woman's eyes when she sees diamonds; they sparkle and glisten more so than the diamonds themselves. Marie's eyes mirrored the Blue Nile Diamond perfectly and as she stared into the top facet her wide eyes crystallized in a kaleidoscope of different visions. One in particular was reflecting a bluish green tint that reminded her of the fresh clear spring water, the very spring that she saw in the National Forest behind Cal-Con Health. She didn't know what it meant, but she suddenly longed to be with Mick. The vision made her hauntingly lonely.

It really pained the women to tuck their treasure in a cold steel box inside a bank vault, but they all agreed it would be safer this way. Besides, they had no clue as to the value or where to sell them, especially the Blue Nile Diamond.

Paul had traced Mick's license plate number from his RV long ago and he had his friend at the IRS track his returns. They were modest except for the fact that for the last two years weren't filed at all. Automatically he felt Mick was a crook like he suspected from day one, no visible means of support is one clue and most people were according to him. He has used tax scare tactics to send Marie's previous men friends to flight quite successfully, but with all that has been going on, he hadn't had time to get Mick alone or arrested yet. But this was one thing he was sure of: he'd be leaving soon.

Nobody takes advantage of *his girl*.

Upon arriving at Marie's house, the girls sat in her office further discussing what they might do with the diamonds.

Bonnie quipped, "What if that one was Cleopatra's? I mean, it came from the Nile!"

"We don't know that for sure. That's just what the Captain told me. Could be all BS, that guy was sooo full of it." Marie hooted.

Joan added to the running joke, "What if it has a mummy's curse? After all, it didn't bring those guys any luck."

Then the big question became, "is this a treasure find? Like deep-sea stuff?

Or is this income and how do we claim our find to the IRS?"

That's when Mick hollered out "Fuck the IRS!" from his resting spot on the couch.

He was joining in the ribbing of course. He really thought the girls were worried over nothing that couldn't be settled latter. Marie wasn't so much interested in what to do about the diamonds, she wanted to cancel all her wedding reservations and make new ones. She wasn't about to let the recent events ruin her plans to marry Mick.

In LA, a voice activated emitter beeped in Paul's office. He had heard it all and he had it on tape. 'Diamonds,' he mulled over with, 'fuck the IRS,' I've got the bastard now he figured gleefully. Then he heard Marie making more marriage plans, and it was, 'damn that stupid woman,' became the curse for the moment. He was getting stuck in his one-track mind and boiling tired of getting scorched by Mick. He cursed and cursed, once again he knew he had to stop her. Stop him; stop her—it didn't really matter how to him anymore. Stop him. Stop her. Got to stop him!

Frozen pizza was the consensus for dinner, Bonnie and Joan left soon after. They opted to get back to their apartment for some much needed rest. Mick had grabbed a beer out of the fridge. He thought it was flat, tasting like stale starch.

He drank it anyway but decided to get some spring water out of his RV for a wash. Marie wanted some too and had made a fire in the hearth. The logs crackled and orange plumes danced. It was good for them to just curl up together on the couch. Bodies interlocked in silent solace. The fire cast a warming glow—their souls melded in body heat.

Mick fixated on the mesmerizing pottery glaze. The trance opened Mind's doors but made weary Eyelids heavy with closure. Déjà Vu prowled like a tiger. A big tiger was circling the vase. Masculine muscles rippled under the stripes. He was being followed by a beautiful, feminine feline. The fire crackled; plumes flew up the chimney. His gaze was fixed, his mind wandered. The tigers were smaller now and more of them. They were chasing a tail. His good arm curled around Marie and hugged her comfortably closer. His eyes closed but he could still see. In solace, he exhaled a sigh.

A bright light penetrated his eyelids. He dismissed the glare and turned his head.

"OK, assholes. Get up!"

He couldn't dismiss that disturbing sound. It didn't belong in Marie's house.

She was rousted by it too.

A flashlight bounced from Mick's face to Marie's and back. There was a dark shadow of a figure blocking the firelight, and protruding from that figure was an arm with a gun. Of that Mick was sure; he was no longer dreaming.

"Get up, bitch, and lay on the floor!"

Mick was sure he heard that voice before but he still couldn't make out the stranger. The shadowy face was covered by a black ski mask and protruding from the figure was a gun. One thing he was sure of, though; they were in big trouble.

"What's going on?" A dazed Marie asked the intruder. "Shut up and get on the floor!"

Marie didn't know what to do. She sent a surrendering glance Mick's way. He didn't know what to do either. The surprise attack was like a bad storm on the horizon. They were caught with their shutters open. Marie as usual didn't lock the doors after Bonnie and Joan left. The raining thoughts of how could this be happening to us were flooding their survival emotions with torrents of water.

"Do as you're told or I'll shoot you both."

"Don't shoot us!" Marie cried out. "We'll do as you want. Please don't hurt us." She held out her hands in a stop sign as she rolled off the couch and laid face down on the carpet.

"Crawl over here by me."

The intruder wanted complete control and he wanted to handcuff Marie away from Mick. He had learned his lessons years ago as a new police recruit. "Separate and control" was his specialty. He never liked the regimented life but he loved the police powers part, and he planned on cashing in on the power trip. He wanted those diamonds and the formula for Comfitine.

When Marie was in position, he dropped his knee to the small of her back. Pointing his gun at her head, which froze Mick with fear, resulting in desired effects. Then setting the flashlight aside momentarily to free up a hand, he fastened a set of handcuffs behind her back.

"What do you want with us?" Marie pleaded. "Shut up!" was his answer.

"Don't hurt her," Mick said, hoping to distract him into making a mistake. "You shut up too, or I'll kill her!"

Mick figured he could roll off the couch and make a tackling leap at him, but he couldn't take that chance with the gun pointed at Marie. This situation called for a different tactic.

The intruder was playing love against love. Neither one could do anything to save themselves without chancing losing the other. Not that they had much of a chance of surviving anyway. He got off Marie and tossed Mick another set of handcuffs. "Put those on," he demanded.

Mick didn't like the idea at all but he had no choice. He couldn't do it behind his back because of his cast, so he snapped on the cuffs as loosely as he dared, making fists to show they were on but hiding the facts like a magician. He figured he could maybe club the intruder with his cast or jump him from behind and choke him with his own handcuffs as soon as the guy turns his back but he was still too far away to make any attempt, yet.

The intruder was sure he was in complete control. He backed further away and flipped on a light switch illuminating the ceiling fan. Then he said, "All right, where is the briefcase?"

Mick and Marie both recognized him now but he didn't care. He was planning on killing them both after he got what he wanted. The latex gloves and ski mask were more for not leaving fingerprints or hairs that could be analyzed for DNA.

She was in the most uncomfortable position of her life, physically and mentally. Rolling to her side she managed to speak, "The diamonds are in a safety deposit box."

She was glad to get that information out, figuring the intruder couldn't kill them now if getting the diamonds wash is plan.

Then she felt an instantaneous telepathic message. It burned through her brain. She wasn't even looking at Mick but felt he was saying, *trip him*, or was it, *trip him up?* She curled her legs up into the fetal position, just in case she needed to strike. Frank Wayne was the surviving steward. He was also Terrance DeVour's favorite bodyguard. He was in on the majority of the Great White Hunter's murder plots. The smallest one of the group, he was also the meanest. His size meant he had more to prove. The FBI had arrested him, only to let him go "He was only an employee," they decided.

He became enraged at the news. "I'll kill your boyfriend right now if you don't tell me where that briefcase is!"

He meant to scare her into confessing immediately. Not believing her story for a minute led him to bellow, "I don't believe you! Ya can't get a briefcase in one of those safety boxes! *Now where the fuck is it?*" He finally screamed like the mad man he was.

"I already told you. The diamonds are in a safety deposit box. The key and the receipt are in my purse on the kitchen table." Marie tried to explain the best she could because he would need her signature to get in the vault and, when necessary, she would lie and tell him that Mick's signature would be needed also.

"I want the briefcase and the diamonds, bitch! If I don't get them right now you're gonna be dead!"

She had infuriated him with a new set of problems to overcome. He was used to working in a pack, under bosses' orders. Now what was he going to do? The prospects confused him.

He fired a shot in the floor to scare her more, feeling he had to do something. "Where's the key? What bank? Where's the bank? Where's my fucking briefcase?"

"The key is in my purse in the kitchen. I'll help you get your briefcase. You don't have to shoot us!"

Marie was at wits end. The guy didn't seem to listen. Actually she had the briefcase in her office closet. But didn't know why he wanted it so bad. She wasn't about to give it to him though, thinking their only chance to get away from him was at the bank. Security guards would be there to help them.

A sharp pain rifled through Mick's broken arm, the most severe to date because of the gunfire. Eyes, eyes—Iris eyes. He was seeing things. He knew he heard something too. *Wanting to find his comfort zone again, wanting Halo to finish the bone repairs, Cino already told the health taxman to go to hell. Gen and Ic were already through repairing the drapery, but now he was getting mad. Some intruding germ was making his life miserable; Marie's too. That won't stand.*

"Hey you, Mickey! Get your ass off the couch and get that purse." Mick slowly got up and lethargically walked past Marie.

"Don't even think about trying to be a hero. I've got the gun and I'll be right behind you."

Frank Wayne backed away some and ordered Marie not to move. His gun was now trained on Mick's back.

Mick had crossed the archway and entered the kitchen. That's when he saw it. Another gun was pointed at him by a figure by the back door. Mick instinctively froze like a deer in headlights. That mistake was costly as he was grabbed from behind and the hard barrel of a gun was pressed into his ear.

"Drop your gun," Frank Wayne shouted from behind Mick. He saw that figure, too. It was the telltale white shirt and tie that spelled FBI. The new intruder had let himself in the back door. The lighting wasn't the best from his vantage point. What little there was came reflected in from the living room. Shadows covered his targets faces, but he could see well enough to recognize a gun pointed at Mick's head and a man hiding behind him.

Long hours of training had instilled within him the practical urge never to give up his weapon, so that wasn't even a consideration.

"Drop your gun or I'll blow this guy's brains out!" Wayne shouted again.

Paul privately thought, *So what if he catches a stray bullet. He'll drop like the dead weight he is and then I'll have a clear shot at the man with the gun.* Paul didn't even know who the robber was, but he had a good idea he was after the diamonds. So Paul said exactly what he was thinking, "Go ahead and shoot him. That'll save me the trouble."

Frank Wayne was thinking, *This guy is FBI and there's got to be more outside.*

Wayne had been cut loose that morning when the Cal-Con Health lawyer showed up to bail him out. A tail followed him all the way up to L.A., but he gave them the slip out of the underground garage after picking up some firearms and a spare set of keys for a company car.

But now he just wanted to forget about the diamonds and the Comfitine formula. He wanted to escape. One hostage ought to do the trick, and he could beat a trail to Mexico. It wasn't that far away. So he tried once more, "I said drop that gun!"

Mick was thinking, *I have two too many guns pointed at my head.*

Frank had one arm wrapped around his neck in a chokehold, and a gun in his ear. Paul's gun looked like it was aimed between his eyes, and mere seconds seemed like a lifetime.

Paul had made up his mind to shoot and ask questions later. The FBI is trained to come up with excuses. *So what if Mick winds up as collateral damage? Since I've got the opportunity and a fully loaded .45 automatic.*

Bam! Bam! Bam! Marie screamed.

There were two distinct thumps that hit the kitchen floor.

Marie was up and standing under the archway of her kitchen. The gun smoke left Paul in a cloud. He moved to turn on the kitchen lights.

When Marie saw Paul, she didn't know what he was doing in her house. Then she saw Mick on the kitchen floor. She screamed, "Mick, Oh my God. Why did you shoot him?" There was blood all over and she feared Mick was dead. Then she saw something move, she screamed again, "Mick! *Mick!*"

Frank Wayne was partially lying on top. Part of the scull was missing. The first bullet entered the top of the head, exploding with such force that the ski mask flew off. The second bullet hit him in the back. The third went flying through the front room window. Lucky for Marie, she stayed low on the carpet.

She went up to Paul and demanded he take off the handcuffs. She wanted to help Mick. He was struggling to get his knees under his body. His ears were still ringing from the reverberation of the shots and he was pinned under a body.

Mick had seen Paul's finger twitch as he ducked. In doing so, he grabbed on to the arm that was around his neck with sufficient speed that rivaled an expert judo move. Frank was already on Mick's back when the bullet passed through his skull. Mick's cast hit the floor first; his head second. His lung air was knocked out of him when Frank landed on top. He could have sworn he saw diamonds or stars again. He really didn't care as long as he saw something.

Paul took off Marie's handcuffs.

Frank's blood had splattered Mick good. His head slammed on the floor right next to him. Marie screamed again at the ungodly sight.

Then Mick just bucked Frank's body off himself and stood up.

"Are you OK?" she asked, wanting to hug him but stopped short. His face was bloodied and bruised.

"Yeah."

"Are you sure you're all right?"

His face was a fright. "Yeah, I'm sure."

"Paul, take off his handcuffs," she demanded, and then, "Call your people and get this body out of my kitchen!"

Blood was pooling under the head and Marie's stomach was doing flipflops. All she wanted was some serenity and relaxation, wired and fried nerves, is what she got. Being rung through the terror mill was making her blood boil like molten lava waiting to explode. Torn from being grateful that Paul showed up when he did but still annoyed enough to ask, "and what are you doing here anyway?"

Taken off guard, Paul stammered, "ah,—ah, I'm here for the diamonds."

"What diamonds?"

"The ones Mick stole from Terrance DeVour." "Mick didn't steal any diamonds and where the hell are you getting your information from?"

Marie had him painted into a corner and Paul was stammering to get out.

He couldn't tell her he had planted listening devices in her home. "I would think you'd be glad I saved your ass's?"

But Marie was wise to Paul's treacherous ways. "This guy was arrested by your agent's this morning. Did you let him go so he could come over here and kill us? Is that why you're here to clean up the slaughter?"

"No, no,—no, that's not it at all. His lawyer got him out a d I put a tail on him."

"Then where's the tail?"

"Ah,—I don't know,—excuse me a second." Paul didn't want to debate with her any more. He got on his cell phone and called in.

Mick had put his face over the sink to wash the gooey blood from his face while he soaked up all the conversation. Then he took a drink of spring water from the sports bottle he stashed in the fridge. Marie took a drink too, as her lips were parched and her nose full of gun-smoke aroma. Her lips weren't the only things soothed. She almost immediately felt relief. Animosity drained from her soul, a new awareness warmed her like 40-year-old Scotch Whisky. Recognizing the same feeling she felt at the National Forest spring behind Cal-Con Health made her mind wonder. Feeling warm all over, yet realizing the spring water was cool. Still, she couldn't help noticing her mind was alive with colors and a serene melody of nature. She caught her fainting balance on the kitchen counter and focused on her wonderment.

Paul was still yacking on the phone, ordering a coroner and forensic team. When Marie came over to him and kissed him on his cheek. "Thanks for saving us," she said with a wide smile. Mick was somewhat surprised by the developments but didn't say anything.

"Now," Marie said, "what about those diamonds?"

Paul was disarmed. She hadn't kissed him in a long time; now he was face- flush-red and at attention. Thoughts rambled to *her finally loves me again!* Then he said, "Those diamonds that, ah, ah, Mick stole…I need the evidence. Cal-Con Health is in bankruptcy court."

"And what makes you think Mick stole some diamonds?" she asked with a melting smile.

"Because he's a crook and didn't file his income taxes. Besides that, he already had the diamonds when he stole the life boat, then he tricked you

THE MICK AND MARIE STORY

women into following him," he added with an indignant tone.

"Paul, Paul, my dear Paul, don't you know it's not nice to spy on people?" she asked in a mild-mannered tisk-tisk tone.

"But I have to protect you."

"No you don't, Paul. As a matter of fact, I'm going to have my house swept for listening devices. So you may as well get your bugs out of my home after your people clean up this mess on my floor!"

Marie knew Paul better than he realized. She just made a reasonable calculated guess that he had her home bugged, and his facial contortions confirmed her theory.

"And *then* I never want to see you again. Am I making myself perfectly clear?"

Paul was such a lousy liar. Marie read him like a comic book. He didn't know how to respond so he blurted out his authoritarian demand. "This is a crime scene. Don't touch anything.—You'll all have to come down to headquarters for questioning." Her rebuff only made him mad. He was determined to bust Mick for something; everybody's guilty of something, he reasoned. Get him out of the way and then Marie would see the light. Then she'll see, 'she's my girl, she's my girl'

The thing was, the IRS didn't want Mick arrested for not filing, "He's chump change, not worth enough to bother with, we can't go around arresting everyone who doesn't file. The country would go broke if we did and that's not the way we work," Paul was told.

"But he's a jewel thief," he rebutted. "Then you arrest him," was the last thing he listened to before hanging up.

Mick refused to cooperate with the FBI in any way, shape, or form; he proudly stood up for his Constitutional Rights. Marie did the same, only in a different form. She interrogated, the interrogators. Her wits were all about her, dancing around questions with questions of her own. Her silver tongue was slicing whip cream, twirling the flavors around her taste buds with a gourmet's flare. She also had them rolling in the isles with her insidious jokes. Imitations of Paul, their supervisor, added to the hilarity. She learned the art from Bonnie over the years.

Paul sulked in his office upon their release. She didn't even have to call her lawyer, she called her editor instead; one thing the FBI is allergic to more than anything is bad press. Once her editor was alerted to the story Marie was going to submit, they couldn't kick them out of the Federal building fast enough. Besides, the FBI had nothing to hold them on.

"Catch him cashing on the diamonds," he was told by his advisors, "then we might have something." Pouting and sulking, he played the, inadmissible in court, tape over and over again. And he was no longer mental skipping to the beat of, 'she's my girl.' Now it was, 'I'll fuck you, fuck the IRS. I'll fuck you, fuck the IRS.'

They stayed overnight in a LA hotel while her home was being cleaned; the local Real Estate Agent, and friend of hers, took care of that business.

Understandably she didn't want any remnants of the FBI or any other grotesque thing left behind.

Once they returned home Marie pulled out the briefcase from her closet.

Silently waving for Mick to follow her; she led him out to his RV.

"I've got to find out why the steward was so interested in this briefcase." Mick opened his RV door. "You're acting a little clandestine. You think Paul still has bugs in your house?"

"No,—but I'm not taking any chances."

Opening the case on the table; then removing the foam lining, she found a glossy folder. Removing that exposed a false bottom and what appeared to be a junkie's kit. An assortment of silver spoons, a hand held scale, syringes, jewelers packets with what looked like heroin or something. Picking one packet up and giving it a closer examination, she could see some bluish or green flakes mixed amongst the white powder. Pill containers were there too. Opening one and spilling some tablets out on the table, they resembled a breath mint, white with blue and green speckles.

"This stuff looks like candy!—Could be dangerous for kids if they found this stuff. I'm going to have this stuff analyzed."

Picking up the folder again; she read the word, 'Comfitine.' Leafing through the technical manual reminded her of an Algebra or Quark class; all was quantum leap jargon to her.

"What do you think it is?" Mick asked.

"I don't know, but I think it's in your spring water."

"What?"

"Wait a minute, I have an idea. I'll be right back."

She ran back in her house and grabbed two crystal glasses, filled one with her tap water and went back to the RV and told Mick to fill the other glass with his spring water. Dropping a pill in hers, they waited for it to dissolve, but it didn't completely. Taking a silver spoon, she stirred. The tiny blue green flakes whirled around in the wake. Holding both glasses to the sunlight, both observed a fancy prism.

"Looks tasty enough to drink," Mick said.

"Don't you dare!—It doesn't dissolve completely;—must be some kind of synthetic material. I'm going to have it analyzed first."

"But I like it."

"No buts, you don't know what's in there. It might have some weird side effects."

"But you drank it too. How did it make you feel?"

"I felt great. I feel great."

"I gave you some spring water before you woke from your coma."

"You did?"

"Yeah,—maybe it has some healing qualities like stem cells."

"You think it cured my coma?"

"I don't know.—Maybe it will cure a coma and Alzheimer's disease."

"You know, maybe you're right. That's why that guy wanted it so bad."

She took a good look at both glasses again and just like the forbidden fruit, her curiosity got the best of her. Temptation led to justification; it's all watered down, was one, in pursuit of pure science, was another. A new story behind discovery sold her; she took a measured drink. It quenched her thirst just like before and it tasted good. She paused and waited awhile as if something magical or disastrous would happen. She felt better and more courageous without realizing it. She took another swig and Mick followed her lead.

"That wasn't so bad. Nothing to this watered down stuff," she said.

Then she took a good guzzle and felt warm all over. Setting the half full glass down and taking a longing look at Mick while he finished it. Her head was suddenly swirling with sensuous ideas. Itching for some action, she laid a kiss on him, a long sensuous kiss. Now she was hot; physically and mentally, she removed her blouse and undid the button to her jeans. Suddenly hungry, hungry for more than love, he looked good enough to eat.

Mick picked up on her mood and he felt the same way. They were both completely naked with the exception of one, 'ain't gunna stop me now,' cast. Laughingly they skipped to the bedroom of the RV. Marie started doing daring things she never dreamed of doing before; acting out the frolicking fancy colors like butterflies suckling flowers, intertwined with natures melody of hummingbird wings. They were in Mick and Marie's garden now. Bonded souls sizzled like eggs in a buttery pan. The heat of love they generated radiated enough photosynthesis to grow their own National Forest.

Every touch, every caress, every tingling nerve felt like magic. Coming together was never so natural, energy so well spent. Marie wouldn't let it end though, she got off the bed and said, "I have to write a new poem.— Come on." Naked as you please, they both pranced like cupids nymphs, out of the RV, through the yard, romping in all of nature's freedom, organs flopping in the musical breeze, circling her water fountain twice for a laugh, through the patio door and into her office.

Still au naturel, she booted up her computer and started to type. Mick caught an extra breath, while still admiring her beauty and studying her graceful fingers dance across the keyboard when a thought came to him. "I'm sorry you lost the poems that were on your laptop that went down with the American Flag ship."

"Oh—don't be silly honey, once a poem is written with feelings, the author will never forget it.—Listen:

The best is already there

Not feasible to ameliorate

Absorb with all your stare

Jealousy, bestowal to their hate

Love, honor your first

Like a babe in arms and all the rest

With these truths, no need to thirst

Time honored traditions, passed the test

To all a birth right
Freedom of speech
Changes bring plight
To all the children teach

Privacy when we pray
Let us assemble
Doesn't matter what we say
Can't make us tremble

Freedom of press
Hear our grievances
A choice to redress
Let us freelance
The best is already there
Not feasible to ameliorate
Absorb with all your stare
It is documented, dare to debate

"See?"

Would you like to see your manuscript become a book?

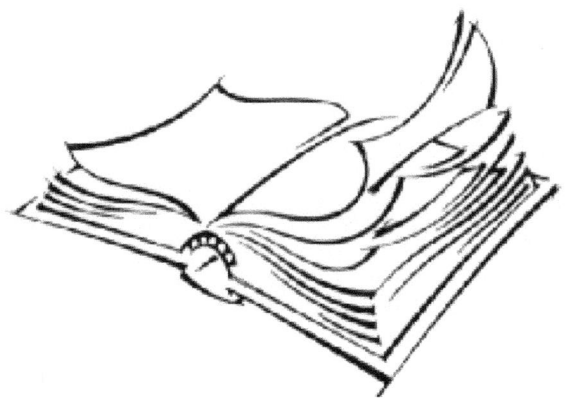

If you are interested in becoming a
PublishAmerica author, please submit your
manuscript for possible publication to us at:

mybook@publishamerica.com

You may also mail in your manuscript to:
PublishAmerica
PO Box 151
Frederick, MD 21705

www.publishamerica.com
P HA A

www.ingramcontent.com/pod-product-compliance
Lightning Source LLC
Chambersburg PA
CBHW071428070526
44578CB00001B/34